KU-182-932

MANAGING ENVIRONMENTAL ISSUES: A CASEBOOK

Rogene A. Buchholz
College of Business Administration
Loyola University of New Orleans

Alfred A. Marcus
Curtis L. Carlson School of Management
University of Minnestoa

James E. Post
School of Management
Boston University

WITHDRAWN

PRENTICE HALL, *Englewood Cliffs, New Jersey 07632*

NAPIER UNIVERSITY LIS
3 3042 00774 7684

CRL
658.408 BUC+

Library of Congress Cataloging-in-Publication Data

Buchholz, Rogene A.
    Managing environmental issues : a casebook / Rogene A. Buchholz,
Alfred A. Marcus, James E. Post.
        p.   cm.
    Includes bibliographical references.
    ISBN 0-13-563891-7
    1. Environmental policy--Case studies. 2. Industry--Social
aspects--Case studies. 3. Industry--Environmental aspects--Case
studies.   I. Marcus, Alfred Allen   II. Post, James E.
III. Title.
HC79.E5B82 1992
658.4'09--dc20   91-20646
                                                           CIP

Acquisition Editor: Alison Reeves
Editorial/Production Supervision
    & Interior Design: Beth McMacken
Layout & Production: Andrea Greitzer,
    Tania Liepmann, PageWorks, Cambridge, MA
Copy Editor: Diana Gibney
Cover Designer: Ben Santora
Prepress Buyer: Trudy Pisciotti
Manufacturing Buyer: Bob Anderson
Supplements Editor: David Scholder

Cover Art: Vincent van Gogh, *The Starry Night*. (1889) Oil on canvas, 29 x 36 ¼".
    Collection, The Museum of Modern Art, New York. Acquired through the
    Lillie P. Bliss Bequest. Photograph © 1992 The Museum of Modern Art, New York.

© 1992 by Prentice-Hall, Inc.
A Simon & Schuster Company
Englewood Cliffs, New Jersey 07632

All rights reserved. No part of this book may be
reproduced, in any form or by any means,
without permission in writing from the publisher.

Printed in the United States of America
10 9 8 7 6 5 4 3 2 1

ISBN 0-13-563891-7

Prentice-Hall International (UK) Limited, *London*
Prentice-Hall of Australia Pty. Limited, *Sydney*
Prentice-Hall Canada Inc., *Toronto*
Prentice-Hall Hispanoamericana, S.A., *Mexico*
Prentice-Hall of India Private Limited, *New Delhi*
Prentice-Hall of Japan, Inc., *Tokyo*
Simon & Schuster Asia Pte. Ltd., *Singapore*
Editoria Prentice-Hall do Brasil, Ltda., *Rio de Janeiro*

CONTENTS

Preface   vii

Introduction   ix

Part I   Changing Perspectives on the Environment   1

    1-1   The Amazon Rain Forest   8

    1-2   Delta Environmental and the Advance of the
           Greens   26

    1-3   The Big Spill: Oil and Water Still Don't Mix   43

    1-4   Save the Turtles   61

Part II Public Policy, Economics, and the Environment   71

    2-1   The Auto Emissions Debate: The Role of Scientific
           Knowledge   80

    2-2   The 1990 Clean Air Act and Du Pont   94

    2-3   Groundwater Contamination: A City with Problems   106

    2-4   Ocean Spray Cranberries, Inc.   121

    2-5   The Forgotten Dumps   130

    2-6   The Politics of Recycling in Rhode Island   141

Part III Business and the "New Environmentalism"   157

    3-1   Oakdale: A Success Story   170

    3-2   Marine Shale Processors, Inc.   176

    3-3   Polaroid's Toxic Use and Waste Reduction Program   193

    3-4   Dow Chemical: Environmental Policy and Practice   211

    3-5   ARCO Solar, Inc.   230

    3-6   Ashland Oil Tank Collapse   247

    3-7   DuPont Freon® Products Division   261

ACKNOWLEDGEMENTS

The authors gratefully acknowledge the following organizations for the generous financial support which has made the curriculum program and this casebook possible:

ARCO
Ciba-Geigy Corporation
Dow Chemical, U.S.A.
Duke Power Company
E.I. Du Pont de Nemours and Co., Inc.
IMC Fertilizer, Inc.
Johnson & Johnson
3M Company
Miller Brewing Company
Monsanto Company
Shell Oil Company
USX Corporation
Waste Management, Inc.
Weyerhaeuser Company

Members of the National Wildlife Federation
Corporate Conservation Council

Asea Brown Boveri, Inc.
AT&T
Browning-Ferris Industries
Ciba-Geigy Corporation
Dow Chemical, U.S.A.
Duke Power Company
E.I. Du Pont de Nemours & Co., Inc.
General Motors Company
Johnson & Johnson
3M Company
Monsanto Company
Pacific Gas & Electric Company
The Procter & Gamble Company
Shell Oil Company
USX Corporation
Waste Management, Inc.
Weyerhaeuser Company

PREFACE

We are pleased to present this book of case studies addressing an area of growing concern to companies everywhere: corporate management of environmental issues. Much has been said about heightened environmental awareness in society and the "greening" of the corporation. But little has been done to really explore the complex nature of the relationship between corporate decision making and environmental protection. That is the purpose of this casebook. The program that led to the development of the casebook tells a story of how productive a unique collaborative effort between corporations and a major environmental group can be.

This book is the result of a three-year effort conducted through the sponsorship of the National Wildlife Federation's Corporate Conservation Council. Established in 1982, the Corporate Conservation Council was created so that senior executives from industry could engage in frank discussions on environmental issues with the leadership of the nation's largest conservation education organization. Comprised of executives from seventeen major corporations, the council was built on the recognition of a fundamental interdependency between environmental protection and economic growth. The council believes that programs based on common interests can help meet the environmental and economic challenges we face now and in the future.

The genesis of the council's effort in environmental education stemmed from years of discussion on the impacts environmental issues have on corporate operations. The theme was that environmental issues are woven into the entire fabric of business operations, and improved environmental understanding and sensitivity needs to become an integral part of management education. A survey of faculty confirmed that little was being done in schools of business and management to train future professionals in this area. Therefore, the council began to develop plans to fill what it considered to be a major educational gap.

In 1987 the council enlisted the help of three management scholars: James E. Post, Boston University School of Management; Rogene A. Buchholz, College of Business Administration, Loyola, New Orleans; and Alfred Marcus, Curtis L. Carlson School of Management, University of Minnesota. Their mission was to assist the council in identifying issues concerning the physical environment that could be articulated, developed, and introduced into business school study. Working with the council, the faculty consortium developed new curriculum materials, formed conceptual teaching approaches, and offered pilot courses in their universities. The response from the business and academic communities has been enthusiastic, and the council is deeply appreciative to Professors Post, Buchholz, and Marcus for their foresight, dedication, and commitment to the project. The success of this effort and the attention it has generated could not have been accomplished without their help.

This book is a compilation of the teaching materials created through this curriculum development program. These case studies examine a wide variety of environmental issues and corporate responses to them. While the opinions expressed do not represent those of the National Wildlife Federation or the Corporate Conservation Council, the studies reflect an accurate portrayal of circumstances faced by organizations. For this we thank the participating council companies and other corporations which generously contributed their staff time, resources, and information.

Our experience with the program suggests that the work has only just begun. An important lesson learned from this project is that many different disciplines of study have much to contribute to the area of corporate environmental management. New types of collaborative efforts, institutional linkages, and development strategies must be pursued. The council is proud to have served as the catalyst in initiating this field of study. It is the hope of all involved in this effort that other organizations and institutions of learning will join the council and endeavor to expand upon this process.

Jay D. Hair
President, National Wildlife Federation

Robert P. Bringer
Staff Vice President Environmental Engineering and Pollution Control, 3M Company
Chairman, Corporate Conservation Council

INTRODUCTION

Preserving the natural environment has become one of the foremost public issues of the late twentieth century. What was once treated by business as frivolous concerns for "birds and bunnies" is now widely understood to be a real problem of planetary and human survival. The cumulative effect of human activity is threatening the ecological systems upon which we all depend. Many political leaders, including Mikhail Gorbachev of the Soviet Union, Francois Mitterand of France, Margaret Thatcher of Great Britain, and George Bush of the United States, have called for higher levels and new forms of international cooperation to ensure global environmental security. Environmental catastrophes such as Iraq's destruction of Kuwaiti oil wells and the deliberate pumping of oil into the Persian Gulf are now openly denounced as environmental terrorism that threatens global security.

Environmental concerns have affected the political relationships among nations. The United States and Canada bargained for years over acceptable methods to deal with acid rain. The U.S. and Mexico have found environmental concerns a greater stumbling block than most economic issues in the development of a free-trade agreement in the early 1990s. The European Economic Community's evolution toward integration in 1992 has been affected by intense negotiations among members as to proper environmental standards. As the twentieth century closes, it is unmistakable that environmental concerns are not far from the top of any political leader's agenda. Political concern mirrors public concern.

BUSINESS AND THE ENVIRONMENT

Environmental issues have been rising on the agenda of critical issues for business leaders as well. Virtually no industry in the United States, and probably in the world, is immune from environmental problems. Whether the problem involves the extraction or use of natural resources, processing operations, manufacture of final products, or the packaging and sale of consumer and industrial goods, business activities cannot be conducted without attention to the environmental dimension.

There can be no doubt that environmental issues have a profound impact on business management. All aspects of the production and sale of goods—from the extraction of resources to their transport, conversion into useful products, consumption, and eventual disposal—have serious environmental repercussions. Ironically, environmental education for business managers, and for public officials who routinely interact with business managers, is seriously deficient.

EDUCATIONAL GAPS

Since the first wave of modern environmental legislation in the 1970s, law schools have trained attorneys in the practice of environmental law. Medical schools and schools of public health have offered courses on the effects of environmental problems on human health. A field of environmental science has arisen, drawing heavily on chemistry, geology, and biology and such applied sciences as epidemiology and toxicology. Despite the progress made in these fields, two conspicuous gaps have persisted.

First, students in business schools have been exposed to little or no teaching in the environmental field.[1] This permits them to leave universities ill-informed about factors that *really* shape modern business decisions. The concerns that led the National Wildlife Federation's Corporate Conservation Council members to initiate the curriculum development program on which this book is based were very basic: the undergraduate and graduate students these firms were hiring from business schools were ignorant of the profound effects environmental issues were having on their business operations and finances. We took the Council members' interest to be a concern shared by a large portion of the business community. If myths are taught in universities, neither students, their future employers, nor society are well-served. The curriculum program that the council sponsored has been designed to begin the process of correcting the mythology that "business as usual" can be conducted without attention to environmental performance.

A second gap has been the relative lack of information on effective organizational responses to environmental issues.[2] Lawyers study laws and regulations; physicians and scientists study processes of disease and natural adaptation to environmental harms. Virtually no scholars have systematically studied the processes that businesses go through in responding to environmental laws, regulations, and concerns. Too often, scholars in other fields have assumed that companies would "just do it" when standards or knowledge changed. Nothing could be further from the truth. No organization will change its behavior without the conscious hand of management guiding the process. The desire to see companies protect natural habitat, minimize toxic risks to workers and communities, and clean up dangerous operations or dump sites does not happen without committed managers inside the organization. This book includes case studies of managers and companies whose actions have made a difference in dealing with environmental problems. The research that has produced these cases makes clear the complex challenges that well-intentioned people in business and government face in trying to improve their organization's environmental performance.

THE CASE APPROACH

The cases we have presented are meant to achieve a number of purposes:

- increase readers' appreciation for the magnitude of environmental problems;
- provide a working knowledge of government environmental policy, laws, and regulations; and
- stimulate thinking on how to get companies to consider the environmental impact of corporate decisions and respond effectively.

The case studies are meant for discussion. Students should consider them in terms of the dilemma posed, the managerial implications, and the options for alternative courses of action. This realism is meant to complement other works on the environment which are rooted in the natural or physical sciences. This book is anchored in the social science of organizational and human behavior; it is about the efforts of people and institutions to manage environmental issues.

ISSUES THAT CRY OUT FOR SOLUTIONS

These cases demonstrate that local, regional, national, and global environmental problems cry out for feasible, implementable solutions. An increasing number of environmentalists and scientists are suggesting that the window of opportunity for addressing these problems is relatively short. Actions are called for now, not in the distant future. Yet, the obstacles to immediate change in lifestyle, government and corporate policy, and institutional arrangements are numerous. They include:

- the failure of markets to reflect the full social and environmental costs, including the cost to future generations, of goods or services;
- the difficulties of establishing risks, costs, and benefits with certainty;
- the general unwillingness of individuals and organizations to make investments with long-term, uncertain paybacks;

- the widespread desire and need (whether innate or socially instilled) to preserve or maximize individual and corporate self-interest;

- the difficulty of gathering, understanding, and comparing information about environmental impacts of individual or organizational actions and their alternatives; and

- the difficulty of clearly assessing the nature and extent of trade-offs which environmentally sound alternatives may offer for other socially desired ends (economic growth, employment, social justice, women's rights).

The 1990s will introduce new realities into business management that will play an increasingly important role in the world economy in the twenty-first century. A 1989 communique of the major democratic industrial nations (G-7) put the political spotlight on building support in all nations for environmental action. Events such as the wreck of the Exxon Valdez in Prince William Sound, Alaska, demonstrate the central role management systems and corporate policies play in dealing with environmental issues. Trash, toxic waste, global warming, ozone depletion, and acid rain are but a few of the many examples of environmental issues challenging managers in the public and private sectors as the world closes the last decade of this century. The EPA estimates that business is spending more than $100 billion each year on environmental responses. Solid waste disposal is a $150 billion business. Environmental issues are now among the most powerful influences on business profitability and performance. Corporations worldwide battle to get environmental expenses under control, avoid environmental catastrophes, and maintain credibility with the public.

Examples of companies acting to show their concern are numerous. Here are just a few: IBM has cut the use of CFCs by over 30 percent and has made climate study the theme of its Bergen, Norway, research center. General Electric is assessing all new products with respect to their environmental implications and is investing more than $200 million per year on environmental projects. McDonald's has announced it will replace its foam containers with paper packaging, and is considering composting and other recycling options. Kodak has announced that it will recycle its disposable cameras, and that it will spend $100 million to upgrade or replace its chemical storage tanks and $46 million to reduce methylene chloride emissions 70 percent by 1995. Monsanto will reduce toxic air emissions 90 percent in four years from 1988 levels and spend over $600 million on the environment in 1990 and 1991. Du Pont has committed itself to reducing air pollution 60 percent by 1993 and toxic wastes 35 percent by the start of the next century. Its phase-out of CFCs and development of alternatives is the subject of the last case study in this book.

The environment, then, is a growth industry, with opportunities for profit making. In the competitive world of business, it is easy to understand why private sector managers need to know this. But, it is also important to realize that public sector managers need to know how to harness private sector needs to serve public ends. Public sector managers who combine the "stick" of traditional "command and control" regulation with the "carrot" of profitable business opportunities offered by environmental protection will be better able to carry out their jobs.

The technical and managerial challenges provided by environmental issues are of a high order. The companies and governments that are best able to meet these challenges will likely be the ones to survive and prosper in the twenty-first-century economy.

KEY AREAS OF STUDY

Students may find it useful to use a checklist of important questions and considerations to guide their reading of these cases. There are three broad areas that should be considered for each of the cases in this book: (1) What types of business activities are affected by the environmental problem(s) described in the case? (2) What public policy and economic dimensions exist and what ramifications do these have for business and government? (3) How are the businesses and government agencies organized to cope with the environmental issues raised in the case? Each of these areas can be discussed at great length and instructors may choose to emphasize one or another of these areas in discussing a specific case. It has been our experience, in both teaching and researching these cases, that all three dimensions are inevitably involved in the search for solutions to the environmental problems of our time.

Types of Business Activities Affected by Environmental Problems

- Extraction of raw materials (e.g., offshore oil, strip mining)
- Manufacturing (e.g., smokestack emissions, hazardous solvents)
- Product use (e.g., vehicle emissions, pesticides, CFCs)
- Product disposal (e.g., solid and chemical wastes and recycling)
- Facility siting (e.g., manufacturing and power plants and disposal sites)

- Distribution (e.g., energy use in transportation, communication medium impacts)
- Institutional infrastructure (e.g., office energy use, recycling programs, workforce community)
- Global dimensions of the impacts
  - global competitiveness (e.g., comparative pollution control policies)
  - economic development (e.g., Bhopal, alternative power production in Africa)
  - international agreements (e.g., Montreal CFC protocol, Law of the Sea)

This first set of topics shows how environmental issues impinge on every stage of the production process. The topics also reveal the international dimensions of environmental problems.

Public Policy and Economic Ramifications

- Legal liability
- Governmental sanctions
- Consumer reactions
- Employee and career-related issues
- Environmental performance and economic performance
- New product introductions
- New manufacturing processes
- Business strategy decisions (e.g., mergers and acquisitions)
- Solution approaches
  - market forces (profit-making opportunities and making companies pay for the damages caused by environmental degradation)
  - scientific and technical solutions (from disciplines such as ecology, toxicology, the environmental sciences, and engineering)
  - reliance on environmental ethics and the environmental movement and the voluntary assumption of corporate responsibility
  - government approaches (the legal and regulatory systems)
  - alternatives to command and control regulation (taxes and other mechanisms for ascribing the full social cost to a good)
  - environmental mediation and negotiation

Environmental impacts on the firm extend beyond legal liability and government sanctions. For example, there are marketing questions (e.g., the extent to which it helps to advertise products as "green"), issues of employee training and well-being, and strategic issues. Moreover, solutions to environmental problems come not only from government. The market plays a role in motivating environmental problem solving. Voluntary assumption of corporate responsibility also plays a role.

A third area concerns what individual managers and organizations can do today to address these problems. It is easier to see the big picture, the long-term directions in which a society must move to resolve issues, than it is the near-term steps that individual managers can take. There is a need to focus on the level of managerial action, on how managers in individual companies are organized to cope with environmental issues.

How Companies Are Organized to Cope with Environmental Issues

- Internal functional specialists
  - the environmental management function
  - meeting regulations (finance, MIS, operations)
  - product and process design (R&D, engineering, marketing)
  - environmental opportunities (R&D, marketing, finance, planning)
  - improving environmental responsiveness (human resources, MIS, accounting)
- Stakeholder management and external relations
  - legal issues (law)
  - public opinion (public affairs, marketing)
  - community relations and politics (public affairs, lobbying)
  - international
- Environmental oversight
  - planning and forecasting (environmental management, public affairs, planning)
  - leadership (CEO, Board of Directors)
  - control (board, accounting, environmental auditing)

Environmental concerns impinge on the duties and responsibilities of persons working at all levels in the organization. Figure 1 illustrates a simple framework that may help organize these ideas for readers as they proceed through the book.

Figure 1

Planning Grid: Policy Issues and Major Factors to Consider

	Multiple Stakeholder Interests	Complex Costs–Benefits	Risk—Reward	Policy Formulation (Public–Corporate)	Policy Implementation (Public–Corporate)	. . . (Etc.)
1. Air pollution (Clean Air Act)						
2. Water pollution–ocean dumping						
3. Solid waste						
4. Toxic dump site cleanup						
5. Toxics in the workplace						
6. Wetlands						
7. Naturally occurring environmental problem (e.g., radon)						
8. Indoor pollution						

HOW THIS BOOK IS ORGANIZED

This book has three sections corresponding to the three areas of study outlined earlier. Each section begins with a briefing note, followed by several case studies. Part I deals with the impacts of business activities on the global environment and the resulting perceptions of environmentalists. An ecological point of view based on the biological sciences is in many respects antithetical to a business manager's approach based on accounting and economics. Ecological principles and the ecological way of viewing problems are introduced in this section, emphasizing the global reach of environmental issues. Cases include ones on the Amazon rain forest, the European Greens, the Exxon oil spill, and endangered species. These cases are preceded by a briefing note on the implications of environmental philosophy for business management, and demonstrate how the costs of environmental issues affect many more people in society and throughout the world than just those involved in particular marketplace transactions.

Part II addresses the legal and economic implications of impacts on the business environment, presenting more fully the financial, social, political, and institutional costs of environmental protection. Students should be able to make comparisons between the costs of environmental protection and the benefits of environmental improvement. How society makes the trade-offs between economic growth and environmental protection is considered, as well as how society manages the troublesome products and technologies. Risk communication plays as much a role here as does risk assessment. The cases include ones on the auto emissions debate during the Ford administration, the 1990 Clean Air Act and du Pont, groundwater contamination in Los Angeles, the Ocean Spray Cranberry litigation, hazardous waste dumps, and the politics of recycling. The role of business as a partner with public officials in managing risks is emphasized. The cases are preceded by a briefing note on public policy and economic approaches to environmental issues.

Part III examines specific business responses to environmental problems, showing how some corporations respond proactively to environmental challenges. By managing their environmental risks, these corporations seek to reduce their liabilities, regulatory compliance costs, and negative publicity. Managerial practices (e.g., environmental auditing) that are being implemented to manage and minimize environmental risks are featured. Programs of special relevance to functional areas (finance, accounting, marketing, and operations) are included. The cases include Polaroid's toxic use and waste reduction program, Dow's management of environmental issues, and the Du Pont Freon® Division. The briefing note that precedes the cases presents numerous specifics about how managers can improve their companies' environmental management. The specifics cover all the functional areas from finance to marketing to accounting.

CONTRIBUTORS

The authors are grateful to the members and staff of the Corporate Conservation Council. Barbara Haas, Executive Director, and Mark Haveman of the Council staff have provided encouragement and invaluable support throughout this process. Thomas W. Peters and Gordon Rands have been important contributors to the development of briefing notes and case studies. A number of research associates and graduate students have made vital contributions to the research and drafting of these cases. They are named at the beginning of each case to which they have contributed. We are grateful to each of them.

This introduction would be woefully incomplete without recognizing the important contributions of the students who have participated in the pilot courses at our respective universities. Without your enthusiasm this project would have never been possible.

Rogene A. Buchholz
Alfred A. Marcus
James E. Post

NOTES

1. James E. Post, "The Greening of Management," *Issues in Science and Technology*, Summer 1990, pp. 64–72.
2. See W. Michael Hoffman, Robert Frederick, and Edward S. Petry, Jr., *The Corporation, Ethics, and The Environment*, (Westport, CT: Quorum Books, 1990).

─────PART I─────

CHANGING PERSPECTIVES
ON THE ENVIRONMENT

This background note was written by Alfred A. Marcus and Gordon P. Rands, of the Curtis L. Carlson School of Management, University of Minnesota.

Public perception of the environment has been changing over the past two decades. In this first section of the book we consider the "new environmentalism," its impact on human activities, and its implications for business management. The cases show how difficult it can be for businesses to manage environmental problems and develop effective responses. Debate often revolves around the nature of the problems and the priorities that should be established. Case 1-1 tells the story of the Amazon rain forest, its usage for economic development, and its role in the larger ecological context. Differences have yet to be resolved, and much destruction of human, animal, and plant life continues. The next case illustrates the strength of the environmental movement in Europe and its impact on one U.S. company, Delta Environmental. Case 1-3, about the Exxon Valdez oil spill, demonstrates the relationship between industrial development and environmental preservation, and the enormous impact a single accident can have on public awareness. The last case in this section discusses different perceptions on the importance of preserving endangered species. After reading and discussing these cases, students should have some idea of how complex environmental issues can be, as well as the different perceptions that make resolution so difficult for the public and private sectors, the focus of Parts II and III.

The 1990s have been called the "Earth decade" (Kirkpatrick 1990), an era that reportedly will spawn a "new environmentalism" different from that of the 1970s. What are some of its features? First, the movement is now worldwide and showing new sources of strength and vitality. Second, it provides a political alternative to the recently discredited traditional ideologies. Third, environmental consciousness appears to be on the rise. In 1981, according to a *New York Times*–CBS poll, only 4 percent of Americans agreed that "environmental improvements must be made regardless of cost." In 1989, 79 percent thought so.

Today, environmentalists and institutional investor groups are united in their request that companies subscribe to the Valdez principles in reducing waste, using resources prudently, making safe products, and taking responsibility for past harm. This new philosophy has evolved out of the writings of some prominent thinkers in the environmental movement.

CONSERVATION VERSUS ENVIRONMENTALISM

The philosophy of the environmental movement is a blend of diverse sources and ideas which do not easily harmonize with the views and practices of business managers. One strand that is *not* at odds with business management is conservation. Conservation generally adheres to the tenets of good scientific management—the avoidance of waste, the rational and efficient use of nature's riches, and the maximization of long-term yields, especially of renewable resources.

In contrast, thinkers who provide some of the inspiration for the "new environmentalism" have made a broader attack on society and its dominant values. Following the lead of George Perkins Marsh (1801–1882), they argue that the unintended negative effects of human economic activities are often greater than the positive ones. For example, links between forest cutting and soil erosion, and between the draining of marshes and lakes and the decline of surrounding wildlife, are predominantly negative. Drawing on the writings of John Muir (1838–1914) and Aldo Leopold (1886–1948), they further argue that humans are not above nature but a part of it. Nature is to be revered for the spiritual experience it provides and should be preserved, not simply for economic use, but for its own sake; it is not for humans to subdue.

This form of environmentalism stresses technological limitations. Humans should neither control nor dictate to nature. Thinking politically as well as ideologically, environmentalists question the logic of private investment decisions on production, expansion, and economic growth, and would replace this logic with a strong asceticism which is at odds with a mass consumer society.

SCIENCE, THE ENVIRONMENT, AND PUBLIC POLICY

Rachel Carson, in her best-selling book *Silent Spring* (1960), linked science, the environment, and public policy. She warned of the dangers in unrestricted use of pesticides, and brought together, in a form politicians and the general public could understand, findings from toxicology, ecology, and epidemiology. Weaving together scientific, moral, and political arguments, she combined scientific knowledge about the environment with the need for political action.

Barry Commoner's *Science and Survival* (1970) continued in this vein. He expanded the scope of ecology to include not only the physical, chemical, and biological, but also the social, political, economic, and philosophical worlds. All fit together and must be understood as a whole. The symptoms of environmental problems may be in the biological world, but their source is in socioeconomic organizations, and the solutions are ultimately political.

This blend of science and politics has been turbulent. Many in the scientific community oppose it, and many in the environmental community are equally hostile to what science has to offer. Scientists generally feel they must improve material conditions; environmentalists question whether additional material progress is necessary. Their ecological perspective teaches that nature establishes immutable limits to human progress. Furthermore, within the scientific community, physical scientists (e.g., in engineering) and life scientists (e.g., in biology) differ. Those in the physical sciences tend to have greater faith in technology; those in the life sciences are more sensitive to technological limitations. They criticize the linear, nonintegrated character of the physical sciences as being responsible for many environmental problems. This narrowness, they argue, may mean that environmental costs and consequences are not being considered when humans interfere with natural processes.

ENVIRONMENTALISM AND ECONOMIC GROWTH

Conventional economics emphasizing economic growth and efficiency has been criticized. For example, in discussing economic expansion in affluent societies, environmentalists warn that resource abundance is followed by population increases of such magnitudes as to threaten the carrying capacity of the resource base. They claim that economists fail to consider the unintended side effects of mechanization. In modern industrial societies growth is promoted for many reasons—to restore the balance of payments and to create jobs for example—and the public is encouraged to focus on the statistics of productivity and ignore the obvious costs. Not all growth, however, involves material goods. Some can directly reduce harm to the environment, or at least have very little environmental impact. The goal of many environmentalists is a steady state economy where population and per capita resource consumption stabilize. People and artifacts are maintained at a low level by the smallest possible flow of matter and energy (see Paehlke 1989, p. 130). Environmentalists imagine that the economy of the future will be based on products that last longer because they have been better designed. These products should be lighter, stronger, and easier to repair. They also should consume less energy. They will be traded again and again.

Human services do not require much energy or material, yet they too contribute to economic growth. Environmental remediation and energy conservation also contribute to economic growth while having a positive effect on the environment. Growth can continue, according to environmentalists, but only if the forms of growth are carefully chosen. As Paehlke writes (1989, p. 136), "What is manufactured will be less of an object than an idea, or proportionately less an object and more an idea." Additional leisure time (i.e., a shorter work week) would have to be part of an environmentally acceptable future economy. Once removed from potentially harmful production, people can participate in alternative production processes: organic gardening, recycling, public transportation, and home and appliance maintenance for the purposes of energy conservation. These would be needed if the emphasis on conventional economic growth were reduced.

Critics of these views hold that there are serious problems with reduced economic growth. Less growth would heighten class tensions. Rising output satisfies the demands of the poor and middle class for better living conditions without threatening the privileges of the wealthy. Without economic expansion, the struggle for income might increase and the social order might be threatened. Environmentalists respond that a requirement of an environmentally acceptable economy is that people learn to live with fewer material possessions. Labeled the "new frugality," environmentalists also have called this requirement "joyous austerity," "voluntary simplicity," and, poking fun at Thorstein Veblen, "conspicuous frugality."

Thus, the values of the new environmentalists are not in complete accord with traditional economic values, which are secondary to environmental ends. When a trade-off has to be made between clean air, water, and wilderness on the one hand, and jobs, profits, efficiency, and cheap goods and services on the other, environmentalists favor the former to the detriment of the latter.

ENERGY AND THE ENVIRONMENT

Following the energy price shocks of 1973 and 1979, environmental values were reformulated by Amory Lovins, a physicist whose books were highly influential in the 1970s. Environmentalists opposed offshore oil drilling and favored auto emissions reductions, increasing U.S. vulnerability to OPEC. Lovins countered by proposing policies for an alternative energy future based on renewable resources and energy efficiency. His program promised to reduce pollution while increasing economic growth.

Lovins argued that human beings were at a crossroads. They could choose the hard energy path (HEP) of the past or the soft energy path (SEP) of the future. HEP involved nonrenewable energy sources which were capital-intensive and threatened the environment. In contrast, SEP was based on the efficient use of energy as well as obtaining increasing amounts of energy from renewable sources such as geothermal, wind, waves, tides, biomass, alcohol, and solar photovoltaics. Lovins struggled against the presumption that the more energy people used, the better off they were. Another part of his argument was that there were diseconomies of scale in distributing energy from central sites to dispersed consumers. SEP meant a decentralized society in energy consumption and distribution.

Lovins was also a major critic of nuclear power, which he opposed because of potential malfunctions, the magnitude of potential accidents, and problems associated with reprocessing, terrorism, sabotage, and theft. Safety in the nuclear industry required rigorous standards and control mechanisms to prevent accidents. Lovins therefore believed that nuclear power could only succeed in planned economies like the Soviet Union and France where personal control over individuals was greater and where bureaucratic power could override economic limitations.

Ultimately, it was the economic weaknesses of nuclear power that Lovins stressed. Nuclear power simply was not competitive in the free marketplace. His basic premise was that conservation and renewable resources would win in the marketplace if the full social and environmental costs of a technology were included in the price consumers paid for energy. Utilities would have to charge what new energy sources cost without averaging them together with the already-paid-for energy sources. Lovins advocated what many economists had proposed for the electric utilities, that is, marginal cost pricing, which would charge users the full cost of new supplies. He also advocated flat or inverted rate structures, which meant that large users would have to pay as much or more per unit of energy as small users.

The basic approach was in harmony with economic values. Price signals emanating from the marketplace would provide people with the incentives they needed to adapt and conserve. Environmentally benign alternatives to fossil fuel would be introduced in the context of a free market. The role of the government was to remove economic and political barriers and allow individuals to find creative solutions. Lovins's non-interventionist approach was in contrast to earlier environmentalists, and more in line with the theory of business management where the market—not government—makes critical choices in society.

With OPEC and SEP, environmentalists could free themselves from an almost knee-jerk opposition to all forms of economic and technological advances. SEP provided an impetus to accept new technologies and emerging industries (telecommunications, computers, information industries) that appeared to be environmentally benign. It freed environmentalists from confrontation with the many opposing organized political forces of contemporary society. Lovins also provided managers with a major challenge: Implementing SEP meant replacing or substantially modifying the whole capital stock of society—appliances, autos, housing, and the design of cities.

Not all environmentalists were happy with Lovins's approach. Some pointed out that under SEP fuel and food industries would compete for biomass. Even if the entire corn crop in the United States were converted to alcohol it would provide less than 10 percent of the nation's need for motor fuel and only a little more than one percent of the nation's total energy needs. The country's coastlines and mountaintops would be cluttered with windmills, and endless acres of land would be devoted to biomass-derived fuels. Some even believed nuclear power would be necessary, because it produces large amounts of energy on relatively small amounts of land.

THE "END OF NATURE"

The issues of atmospheric pollution—ozone depletion and carbon dioxide buildup—provide environmentalists with new opportunities to develop their views. The popularity of Bill McKibben's book *The End of Nature* (1988) follows other environmental works in addressing the key issues of the time. McKibben's reverence for nature and his resentment of intrusions on nature from human technologies are classic "new environmentalism" views. He is concerned that nature will be "crowded out" by human interference and opposes the idea that humans should exercise their dominion over nature for the sake of material progress. What is surprising is the radicalism of his ideas, his willingness to sympathize with the notion that "individual suffering—animal or human—might be less important than the suffering of species, ecosystems, the planet" (as quoted by Kevies 1989, p. 35). For much of history, most humans have experienced nature not as kind and gentle but as harsh and dangerous and have therefore felt compelled to subordinate nature in order to protect themselves. McKibben's radicalism is partially a consequence of his desperation: "The greenhouse effect is the first environmental problem we can't escape by moving to the woods. There are no personal solutions" (as quoted by Kevies 1989, p. 36). Because solutions entail infringements on individual rights they are far different from the market-based solutions to the energy crisis proposed by Lovins. They put environmentalism even more in conflict with the tenets of business management and end the partial accommodation that was achieved by Lovins.

In conclusion, the new environmental philosophy does not necessarily blend easily with the tenets of business management. Environmentalists point out that nearly every economic benefit has an environmental cost and that the sum total of costs in an affluent society often exceeds the benefits. With few exceptions, they are defenders of limitation and accept growth only when it does not involve expanding the use of materials and energy.

REFERENCES

Kevies, Daniel, "Paradise Lost," *New York Review of Books,* December 21, 1989, pp. 32–38.

Kirkpatrick, David, "Environmentalism: The New Crusade," *Fortune,* February 12, 1990, pp. 44–55.

Paehlke, Robert, *Environmentalism and the Future of Progressive Politics* (New Haven, CT: Yale University Press, 1989), pp. 13–41, 76–143.

1-1

THE AMAZON RAIN FOREST

This case was written by Thomas W. Peters under the editorial guidance of James E. Post, Professor of Management Policy, Boston University School of Management.

HISTORICAL BACKGROUND: BR–364

The destruction of the Brazilian Amazon rain forest has been a lengthy and complicated process. Since 1980, the pace of deforestation has accelerated: it is estimated that over 80 percent of Amazon deforestation has taken place since 1980.[1] Destruction is so rampant that experts believe there will be no forest to protect by the year 2050.[2]

Traditionally, indigenous populations develop the rain forest. A small patch of forest is cleared through slash-and-burn techniques. After approximately two years of cultivation, the group abandons the patch and moves to another area for clearing. Early abandonment of the land allows the forest to regenerate as abutting flora disperse seeds over the cleared area. After seven to fifteen years the forest has reclaimed the clearing through a pioneer growth phase; after 150 to 400 years the clearing is restored to its mature phase.[3] Also, indigenous populations harvest fruits, nuts, game, fibers, plants, and other sustenance items, and destruction of the forest is unnecessary.

For the past century rubber tappers have used the forest to secure latex from wild rubber trees. Cyclical cutting of the trees drains the natural latex; no harm is done to the tree and the land remains intact. Unlike Brazil's 200-plus Indian populations, rubber tappers have no historical or legal claim to the forest.[4]

The Amazon rain forest occupies approximately 40 percent of Brazilian territory. The forest abuts Peru, Colombia, Venezuela, Bolivia, Suriname, French Guiana, and Guyana. In 1964 when Brazil's military took political leadership the concept of developing the forest burgeoned. The government was initially interested in securing its national borders and eventually eradicating insurgents and drug traffickers from the area. Favoritism toward the elite was exercised in the form of forest land grants.

8

To expedite development, the military government borrowed from the World Bank and private lending institutions. The acquisition of loans from industrialized countries was simplified during the latter half of the 1970s and the first half of the 1980s. The World Bank aggressively made industrialization loans to lesser developed countries. Government lending programs as well as private lending institutions eagerly recycled petrodollars. In their lending decisions, banks did not assess nations as credit risks.[5] Brazilian political leadership viewed this lending program as a means of becoming industrialized. Plans for highways, hydroelectric facilities, cattle ranches, mining operations, and timber industries were underway. The government attitude at that time was that Brazil had the right to do what it pleased with its land—the rest of the world be damned.[6]

The explosive development of the rain forest can be traced to development of the trans-Amazonian highway, a World Bank project. This highway, known as BR–364, connects the Amazonian state of Rondonia with the densely populated eastern part of the country. BR–364 is a portion of a $1.5 billion industrialization scheme to develop the northwest section of the rain forest.[7] Known as Polonoroeste, this scheme involves opening up 160,000 square miles of forest.[8]

BR–364 was originally a 900-mile dirt road. Traveling time through the Amazon was reduced from several months to several days. Because construction was crude, the road often washed out during the rain season. In addition to military usage, the road allowed for minimal timber extractions, but not the masses that would follow with the asphalt capping of this road.

The capping of BR–364 in 1982 required a $432 million loan from the World Bank.[9] As part of the loan agreement, the Brazilian government would create Indian reserves to protect the indigenous populations. However, upon completion in 1984, BR–364 unleashed a flood of impoverished people into a vast and unprotected wilderness. The government supported this migration by giving Brazilian nationals 100-acre plots of land. For them, Amazonian development was an economic necessity, and they saw it as their manifest destiny.[10] Environmental measures were not enforced to protect the forest, or its indigenous inhabitants, from rampant destruction.

Land grants to Brazilian nationals were made without soil analysis. Water rights, crop evaluations, infrastructures, and health and educational facilities were never planned. Brazil, in essence, was transferring its fermenting social problems to a distant and rural area.[11] Some observers believe that Brazil has enough nonforested agricultural land on which most of its population can settle.[12] To do so, however, would entail revamping the current land distribution system, thereby evoking political dissension.

The poor were given land that could not sustain agricultural productivity beyond two or three years. Crops grow well in the first year of clearing because the slash-and-burn technique creates a bed of nutrient-rich ash. The ash, however, is quickly depleted or washed away in the rainy season. When land fails to yield, the farmer is forced to clear another patch. The forest has developed a unique ecosystem where nutrients are found not in the soil but in living or rotting material.[13] Continual burning to rid the soil of weeds and new growth irreparably compacts and damages the soil, reducing the dispersion of seeds to open areas. Rubber trees, passion fruit, cacao, and Brazil nuts do not grow well in mono-plantations, where unknown tropical diseases and fungi annihilate closely compacted crops. It is estimated that only 17 percent of the land in Polonoroeste will sustain agricultural development.[14]

Conceptually, the rain forest is a natural utility.[15] Trees and plants absorb carbon dioxide from the atmosphere and recycle it as oxygen. Burning the forest emits environmentally destructive gases, concurrently destroying the mechanism by which the gases are reduced. In the summer of 1988 flights were canceled due to excessive smoke.[16] The forest's burning releases carbon dioxide—a major source of greenhouse gas—into the earth's atmosphere.

The ramifications of the BR–364 migration are complex. By 1989 the population of Rondonia swelled to 1.5 million from 115,000 in 1970 due to the paving of BR–364.[17] Crude roads are built further into the forest. This random development leads migrating farmers into conflict with indigenous populations. Epidemics of smallpox, influenza, and other diseases have taken a significant toll on Indians and many have been kidnapped or murdered by farmers and elites interested in timbering, mining, and farming claims. Conversely, the farmer is attacked by the Indian and murdered for intrusion on Indian land. On either side, laws are difficult to enforce and justice rarely prevails.

Other consequences of the migration include the transformation of forests to cattle ranches. Although the average pasture is sustainable for only about two to seven years, thousands of acres are slashed and burned annually.[18] Timber and mining interests are also at stake. The industrialized countries of the north need lumber, iron, tin, bauxite, gold, and other limited resources. The Amazon contains these resources in quantity. Brazil possesses the world's largest deposit of iron ore—an estimated 18 billion tons.[19] Brazil is also the world's fifth largest gold producer.

Scientists know little about tropical timber. Hard woods such as mahogany are highly valued, but most lumber is unspecified and their properties unknown. To remove the valued timber, swatches of land are systematically leveled. The remaining trees are left to rot or are burned to make way for cattle ranching. Contributing to this dilemma are corrupt authorities who allow illegal deforestation for personal gain.[20] In most developing countries firewood is the main energy source, and often tropical woods are used to make charcoal. In either case, there are no efforts to reforest afflicted areas.

INTERESTS IN THE RAIN FOREST

The destruction of the rain forest has alarmed many international groups. Protecting unknown plant and animal species which depend on the rain forest's unique ecosystem for survival is one of their concerns. Tropical forests cover approximately 7 percent of the earth's land mass, but they house 50 to 80 percent of the planet's species.[21] Brazil contains 30 percent of the world's tropical forests.[22] Some argue that by eliminating the forest and its diversity potential cures of current and future diseases are lost. Approximately 25 percent of U.S. pharmaceuticals contain ingredients derived from wild plants.[23] The forest also contains plants that could be developed into foodstuffs for large-scale agricultural production (the potato, for example, was discovered in the rain forest). Others argue that destruction of the forest interferes with the evolution of plants and animals and that altering evolution's selective process will adversely affect future life forms.

Still other groups are alarmed over the global warming trend. The elimination of rain forests is linked to the rise in global temperatures and the alteration of climate patterns. Should the global temperature continue to escalate, the polar ice caps will eventually melt, elevating sea levels. Flooding of coastal cities will follow, and the earth's land mass will shrink due to water encroachment. More people on less land will create famine, disease, and other hellish scenarios.[24]

Still others focus on the rights of indigenous populations. They believe forest development inevitably denies indigenous populations the moral right to adjust to the modern world at a rate they deem appropriate. Also, these tribal populations understand forest plant and animal species, and are thus a rare and unique source of medicinal and agricultural scientific knowledge for future generations and the planet's survival.

Additional interest pivots around the economics of timber and mining exploitation. Some say the current form of exploitation benefits only the industrialized nations, since they are the ones that acquire, process, and consume the resources. Raw resources are sold for less than their ultimate value.

The destruction of the forest has numerous consequences for Brazil. In the short term, Brazil is able to service its debt—$121 billion, primarily owed to private lending institutions—through exportation of resources.[25] Delays in loan servicing only increase interest payments and jeopardize future possibilities for foreign assistance. In the long term, unsustainable development strips the forest of its plant life, soil, watersheds, and other natural benefits. Eventually, the land becomes decimated, and the Brazilian population slips further into poverty and dependence.

U.S. interests in preserving the rain forest include discovering agricultural and pharmaceutical products as well as creating a sustainable resource base for future production. Climate changes induced by rain forest destruction and the impact on U.S. agricultural production are of U.S. domestic policy interest. Conversely, U.S. foreign policy interests include assisting Brazil with its development. A benefit of this assistance is an increase in economic markets for U.S. goods, thereby increasing U.S. prosperity.[26] A developed Brazil could also lead to political stability, thereby contributing to U.S. security.[27]

Due to international attention on the Amazon rain forest, the planet's greatest oxygen-producing environment, Brazil has hardened its position on forest exploitation and rejected international monitoring of protection efforts.[28] The scrutiny of forest development has led one Brazilian official to state, "This is the greatest international pressure Brazil has experienced in its history."[29] The pressure comes principally from industrialized nations, the major source of global pollution, and Brazilian officials fear that this interference is an attempt to internationalize the rain forest, rather than address problems of atmospheric pollution.[30] This hypothesis has led Brazil's foreign minister to state, "Brazil isn't going to become the ecological reserve for the rest of the world. Our biggest commitment is with economic development."[31]

PRESERVATION STRATEGIES AND IMPLEMENTATION

The major players involved in preserving the Amazon rain forest are (1) the indigenous populations and settlers, (2) the sovereign government and Brazilian environmental groups, (3) lending institutions, and (4) industrialized governments and their nongovernment-organization communities.[32] This section outlines how the nongovernment-organization community in the United States targets, interacts with, and influences these four major players.

1. Indigenous Populations and Settlers

Among the groups that address the issue of indigenous people's rights and survival are Cultural Survival and Ashoka. Often, indigenous peoples are forced into the modern world in a brutal manner. Cultural Survival, founded in 1972, assists indigenous populations to adjust to change in a dignified and culturally appropriate way.[33] All choices for integration are left to the affected people, and Cultural Survival garners resources to support and implement their decisions.

Rain forest populations need to claim land rights, demarcate the land, and engage in litigation to enforce claims. Cultural Survival provides legal counsel, funding, letter-writing campaigns to Brazilian authorities, and procurement of programs such as health and educational facilities or microenterprise activities.

At the international level, Cultural Survival, through its publications, seeks to educate and inform individuals who have the power to affect policy. Articles are written to influence US AID, the World Bank, Congress, and other entities that make policy decisions. These publications also aim to mobilize the general public.

Cultural Survival has had some success in devising policy. A Tribal People Policy has been developed by World Bank-Africa and is being adapted to meet regional needs. In Peru, Cultural Survival revised a World Bank infrastructure project which required population relocation. As revised, the project was relocated and no recolonization procedure was necessary.

A disadvantage is that Cultural Survival has only a limited, on-site impact on indigenous peoples in the Amazon. For example, while tribal groups try to protect their land, protection actually rests with the Brazilian authorities. Law enforcement is maintained through the local police force, the Bureau of Indian Affairs, and other authorized bodies. Often there is disregard for the law. Ambushes, raids, and massacres work toward the elimination of tribal peoples. Laws are poorly enforced.

Another nongovernment organization working with global populations is Ashoka. Ashoka provides fellowships in education reform, slum development, agriculture, and human rights in developing countries.[34] In Brazil, Ashoka has supported Chico Mendes and Marie Allegretti. These individuals are "public service entrepreneurs." They address the problems and solutions of forest destruction and preservation.

Chico Mendes was a rubber tapper in the Amazon rain forest. Few rubber tappers possess land titles. Their economic survival rests on the land and trees of others. As land owners transform the forest for cattle ranching, mining, and timber, rubber tappers are jeopardized. Mendes believed that rubber tappers could unite to slow the destruction of the forest and the consequent destruction of their lifestyle. He promulgated the formation of the Rural Workers Union, a 30,000-member organization which represents 70,000 rubber tappers.[35] His efforts gained international attention. The rubber tappers, he proclaimed, had devised a way to sustain forest development. The forest provides infinite opportunities for economic prosperity, and its destruction was unnecessary. Mendes said, "Our struggle is to alert international banks to the dangers of financing new roads in the Amazon. We're not against development, but we don't want destruction."[36]

In 1986 Mendes fought the Inter-American Development Bank's (IDB) financing for the asphalt capping of a 600-km extension road off BR–364 through the forest state of Acre. Consequently, in 1987 the IDB suspended its $77 million loan to the Brazilian government until it incorporated environmental protection measures into the project. The Brazilian government responded by creating forest reserves in Acre, two of which are for the protection of rubber tappers.[37]

In 1988 Mendes was assassinated at his home, by the sons of a cattle rancher. It is suggested that had not Mendes enjoyed international acclaim, his death would have gone unnoticed in an area where approximately 250 murders per year are related to land disputes.[38]

Like Chico Mendes, Marie Allegretti is dedicated to rain forest preservation. Allegretti's belief is that indigenous populations are a vital part of the rain forest environment. The loss of these people would ensure the complete destruction of the rain forest. Allegretti's vision has led her to create extractive reserves, expanses of forest for rubber tappers and Indians to harvest latex, gather nuts and berries, and conduct small-scale agricultural production.[39] Future sustainable development may include the harvesting of medicinal and agricultural plant and animal species.

To promote her idea, Allegretti has organized groups of rubber tappers. Her attempts to make them politically visible have focused Brazilian media attention on their plight, and their link with the survival of the rain forest. Consequently, the National Council of Rubber Tappers now represents their interests within the Brazilian government.[40] This council later forged an alliance with the Union of Indigenous Peoples to keep the interests of these groups before the national press.[41]

Allegretti has gained an international following for her concepts of extractive reserves and sustainable development. In November 1988 she attended the meeting of the International Tropical Timber Organization (ITTO) in Yokohama, Japan. ITTO has made a $1.2 million grant to create an extractive reserve in the state of Acre, Brazil. The reserve will utilize 100,000 hectares of forest to create a sustainable forest development project.[42]

Ashoka has supported Mendes's and Allegretti's efforts through its fellowship program. Fellowships consist of a stipend which allows fellows to pursue the promotion of their idea. Grants are made by the chapters of Ashoka members, which select fellows through a nomination process and commit themselves to supporting them for from one to four years. To draw nominations, Ashoka engages in a network of international private volunteer organizations, government organizations, and nongovernment organizations. In turn, the network submits nominations. Once a fellow is selected by an Ashoka chapter, the network assists the fellow with contacts, technical resources, and other assistance. Ultimately, through this network, individuals such as Mendes and Allegretti persuade leaders to pursue alternative forms of development.

2. International Environmental Groups

In a September 17, 1986, speech commemorating the World Wildlife Fund's (WWF) twenty-fifth anniversary, then-president William Reilly announced that the WWF and other environmental groups must pursue a new strategy for conservation abroad. This new approach combines conservation with the economic need to develop the environment.

Historically, the WWF promoted conservation through financial grants to groups working in the field. While this approach has had some successes, sustainable conservation must also incorporate sovereign governments and populations. Rather than simply opposing industrialization schemes, conservationists must work with institutions in implementing development programs that benefit both the economy and the environment. Long-term conservation comes through a combination of solving the economics leading to deforestation and embedding a cultural conservation ethic.

While parks and sanctuaries continue to be important to conservation, the WWF believes that ecological promotion must go beyond these reserves. As populations increase and productive land becomes scarce, escalating pressure is put on the environment outside the designated reserve. Eventually the population invades the reserve in pursuit of land for economic survival.[43] Moreover, while reserves act as wildlife sanctuaries, few animals actually live there.[44] Reserves account for approximately one percent of the earth's land mass.[45] As such, most species exist in areas of agricultural, lumber, and mining development.[46]

Reilly outlined six areas of development in the WWF's new conservation strategy.[47]

1. *Institutional self-sufficiency,* so that government units and non-governmental organizations can devote themselves to designing and implementing alternative conservation activities.

2. *A cadre of local conservationists,* who will be responsible for educating the public and implementing, monitoring, and maintaining environmental projects. These conservationists must first be trained.

3. *A conservation ethic* compatible with local culture.

4. *An ecological information base* to assist and support environmental decisions.

5. *A system of parks and protected areas,* so that the biodiversity of the area can be preserved.

6. *A development program* that promotes sustainable economic prosperity through the managed use of the environment, not through its destruction.

The WWF's creation of a cadre of conservationists has been successful. In collaboration with various Latin American governments, the WWF conducts in-country conservation training and educational programming for government employees. Moreover, the WWF has sponsored Latin American students at U.S. universities in areas of forest and wildlife management, biology, and other relevant fields.[48]

The creation of a conservation ethic is ongoing. In 1981 the WWF assisted the Costa Rican government in developing an environmental lesson plan for teachers of elementary school students.[49] It is envisioned that by educating children to the importance of the environment, an awareness of conservation will eventually take national priority. Said Gerald Lieberman of the WWF, "Conservation education is not an end product. But it is a necessary part of wildlife conservation. People have to learn why they should care about wildlife and national parks before they will preserve them."[50]

The WWF has also created "centers of excellence" within various Latin American universities. Through the creation of these centers, expert knowledge can be easily accessed. Students may study, for example, wildlife biology, land use, or parks management.[51] These centers have the potential to serve as an information data base on ecological issues.

Current WWF endeavors include the Tropical Forestry Program. This program creates sustainable development projects which support the economic needs of local populations while maintaining the forest's integrity.[52] Aware of the link between environmental health and economic prosperity, major donors and lending institutions have indicated interest in funding sustainable development programs, including forest tourism, cultivation of a high-revenue timber stock, and methods for increasing revenues on fuel wood, palm oil, nuts, and rubber.[53]

The WWF plays several roles in rain forest preservation. However, in order to involve sovereign governments, nongovernment organizations, and affected populations in conservation, it interacts with the second group of rain forest players, the nongovernment-organization community, which targets the remaining rain forest players. While many of these groups attempt to influence lending priorities, much of the permanent lending change comes from congressional legislation. Thus, these groups often seek to alter lending practices through legislative regulation.

3. Lending Institutions

Three types of financial institutions are involved with international development programs: multilateral lending institutions, private lending institutions, and industrialized government grant agencies. The World Bank is a consortium of industrialized governments lending money to third-world countries for development programs. Loans are approved for hydroelectric facilities, highway construction, recolonization projects, mining and timber projects, and other development schemes. Loans come from taxes paid by citizens of the industrialized countries and accrue interest which must be repaid. Private lending institutions loan money to help developing nations industrialize. This money is privately controlled through shareholders of individual banks. These loans accrue interest and must be repaid. Finally, grants are given by individual governments to specific developing countries for purposes of economic, social, health, and educational development. Funds come from taxes paid by citizens of the granting country and are not repaid.

The destruction of the rain forest has led to the scrutiny of the lending practices and priorities of financial institutions. Until recently neither the economic institutions nor the requesting governments have given environmental impact studies serious consideration. For example, the World Bank approved a series of loans for hydroelectric facilities in the Amazon rain forest. Indigenous populations, whose ancestral lands have been flooded, were never consulted. Moreover, questions of silt buildup, water contamination, waterborne disease breeding grounds, annihilation of wildlife, and other environmentally relevant concerns failed to be addressed.

Because the World Bank is a consortium, it is often necessary to influence bank policy through its member governments. Most industrialized countries are pluralistic and democratic, thus ensuring a style of participatory government. As such, the U.S. legislative branch has been a target of nongovernment organizations to regulate World Bank procedures. The United States has considerable power within the World Bank, due in part to the proportion of U.S. funds supporting World Bank loans.[54] By providing directives for loan approval and project implementation, Congress has international impact on World Bank policy. An example of this impact is the standards imposed upon the International Bank for Reconstruction and Development (U.S. World Bank representative) relating to rain forest development projects. These standards were enacted by the Tropical Forest Protection Act of 1987.

The National Wildlife Federation's International Affairs Division believes international environmental issues are affected by economic development institutions.[55] To promote ecological protection, the division focuses on influencing lending institutions to modify their perception of the environment. Rather than viewing the environment as a short-term exploitable resource, lending institutions must learn to perceive the environment as the key to a strong economic base for long-term, sustainable development.

An example of how nongovernment organizations influence World Bank policy is the bank's internal reorganization to create an Environment Department.[56] This top-level department formulates bank policy as it relates to environmental issues, initiates environmental planning and research, and implements environmental components in the bank's regional offices.[57] Moreover, the World Bank has doubled its funding for environmentally sound forestry projects and has increased funding for other environmental projects.[58]

Despite these changes, the World Bank maintains it cannot enforce policing of environmental projects, and that ultimate responsibility rests with borrower nations. Critics, on the other hand, maintain that the World Bank must withdraw funds once the environmental agreement has been violated. The withdrawal of funding before project completion may have separate economic ramifications. For example, revenue from the proposed project may never materialize. As such, the World Bank may not recoup its investment. Moreover, the debtor nation could slip further into financial jeopardy. Diplomatic relations between developing countries and World Bank countries may become strained.

With World Bank policy changes taking effect, Brazil may be forced into altering its methods of developing the forest. Continued forest destruction is preventing Brazil from securing additional development loans.[59] To alter its domestic policy on forest development, Brazil may be forced into altering its social values. Ultimately, the social issue of land distribution may have to be addressed. In Brazil, approximately 70 percent of rural families hold no land titles.[60] To achieve long-term sustainable development, Brazil must revamp centuries of social and political tradition.

Nongovernment organizations also address the hardships loan obligations impose on developing nations, forcing the rapid and exploitive development of the natural resource base. But forest destruction is more than economically motivated. It is politically, socially, and culturally embedded. The belief that forest preservation can be obtained solely through economic incentives is false. On the other hand, altering Brazil's cultural, social, and political identity is construed as intrusive and unwelcome. Yet, movement in this direction has begun. Legislation imposing specific loan conditions on foreign governmental structures is supported by various organizations. For example, the borrowing government must make changes in its agricultural system, its land tenure system, or its land use laws.[61] Proponents claim this approach will provide the incentive for long-term forest preservation.

4. Industrialized Governments

Because the political ideologies of industrialized nations encourage participatory government, nongovernment organizations often build and mobilize constituent groups to support and rally their causes. These groups in turn influence their congressional leaders for action. The Rainforest Action Network (RAN), for example, built broad-based support for tropical forest preservation. The RAN seeks to inform, educate, and involve all levels of society in the rain forest issue. Also, the RAN has conducted boycotts against corporations that purchase raw materials from rain forest countries, leading to forest destruction. The RAN sponsored a boycott against Burger King for buying beef from rain forest cattle ranches, thereby sending a message to the entire industry. The theme was acknowledgment of corporate responsibility to the environment.[62] In 1988 Burger King supplied conclusive evidence that it no longer purchased rain forest beef.

Another target for nongovernment organizations is the International Tropical Timber Organization (ITTO). Under the auspices of the United

Nations' International Tropical Timber Agreement, the ITTO promotes sustainable forestry development, forest management research, industrial timber reforestation projects, and fuller utilization of timber products; it also encourages nations to develop and implement policies on forest preservation.[63] The ITTO represents the interests of forty-two member exporting and importing timber countries. These member countries account for 95 percent of the world's tropical timber commerce.[64]

Friends of the Earth (FOE), an international nongovernment organization, believes the ITTO should adopt a code of conduct. This code would eliminate international trade in hard woods that are not harvested from sustainable plantations. FOE also suggests that the ITTO create a rain forest preservation fund. This fund would assist tropical timber–producing countries to create and manage reserves for endangered species and indigenous populations. Finally, FOE seeks to inform the industrialized nations that they are equally responsible for rain forest destruction through their demand for timber, ores, beef, and other resources.[65] The demand for raw resources by the industrialized nations far exceeds demand from developing countries. Between 1950 and 1980 Japan's consumption of tropical wood grew from 1.5 to 35 million cubic meters; the U.S. consumption increased from 0.8 to 10 million in the same time period.[66]

Specific examples of how nongovernment organizations influence the U.S. government include the Tropical Forest Protection Act of 1987 and the National Energy Policy Act of 1989. The Tropical Forest Protection Act of 1987 was sponsored by Congressmen John Porter and David Obey. It gained over ninety cosponsors within the House of Representatives and the support of a wide range of local, national, and international nongovernment organizations. The act is rooted in the debt-for-nature-swap concept. The first debt-for–nature swap occurred in Bolivia on July 13, 1987. Conservation International, a nonprofit organization, purchased $650,000 of Bolivia's $4 billion debt at an 85 percent discount. In exchange, the Bolivian government agreed[67]

1. to set aside nearly four million acres of habitat to protect 13 of Bolivia's endangered species;
2. to make laws to protect the land;
3. to devise a management plan for this reserve (sustainable development projects and reserves are to be conducted); and
4. to set up an endowment totaling $250,000 of Bolivian currency for management.

The Tropical Forest Protection Act links World Bank loans to preserving tropical forests. The bill mandates the U.S. Treasury to conduct two studies on global forest destruction and one study on the inclusion of the International Monetary Fund into the forest preservation process. The act also calls for two experimental programs that link bank loans with environment preservation.

The first Treasury study is to assess current forest destruction and the ability of the host government to rectify the damage on its own. The second study assesses foreign government self-ability to manage and maintain forest protection. The two World Bank pilot programs which the act mandates are intended to create long-term sustainable development projects. The first program allows debt restructuring to alleviate the short-term environment exploitation needed to meet debt servicing. This program enables foreign countries to receive funding to create sustainable forest development programs such as nut gathering and rubber tapping.[68] The second pilot program entails creating environment reserves in exchange for World Bank debt service forgiveness.

The National Energy Policy Act of 1989, sponsored by Senator Timothy Wirth, relates to rain forest preservation. The bulk of the act addresses the greenhouse effect and creates measures to reduce the genesis of carbon dioxide. A portion of the bill mandates U.S. Agency for International Development (US AID) and the Secretaries of Agriculture, Treasury, and Interior to develop a report on the planet's tropical forests. The report is to include conservation plans for each tropical forest country. Moreover, the bill requires US AID and other development agencies to direct resource incentives toward afforestation and disincentives on deforestation.[69] Wirth has also sought the creation of a 25-million-acre rain forest reserve to be managed under Brazilian authority.[70]

The increasing involvement of the U.S. Congress in rain forest preservation has led the executive branch to act upon the issue. The U.S. Department of State has been working with the Brazilian Foreign Ministry to arrange a meeting between the two countries' presidents.[71] The meeting is intended to discuss linking Brazil's foreign debt to Amazon preservation. In addition, in January 1989 Secretary of State James Baker addressed the issues of global warming and tropical deforestation at an international environmental conference. Baker stressed the need for international cooperation in solving the globe's air, water, and resource crises. Analysts foresee environmental cooperation becoming a focus of diplomacy in the 1990s.[72]

Discussion Questions

1. Who are the stakeholders? What are their interests? Which matter most? Why?

2. Who has the responsibility to act? Who has the capacity to act?

3. How can a "true value" be established for the rain forest? What factors should be included in calculating its "true value"?

4. Is the rain forest a global resource which requires global management or a local resource which simply happens to have value to non-Brazilians? Compare the rain forest to other global resources like oil, the ozone layer of the earth's atmosphere, and oceans. In what ways is the rain forest similar? In what ways is it unique?

5. One expert has noted that "good science has made it possible for bad politics to destroy the world." How does such a point of view apply to the science and politics of the rain forest?

Notes

1. "Reprieve for the Rain forest?" *World-Watch*, January–February 1989, p. 35.

2. Rainforest Action Network, letter of membership inquiry.

3. Nicholas Guppy, "Tropical Deforestation: A Global View," *Foreign Affairs*, Spring 1984, p. 936.

4. Jason W. Clay, "Editorial: Indians in Brazil," *Cultural Survival Quarterly*, vol. 12, 1988, p. 1.

5. *Foreign Service Careers, U.S. Department of State, U.S. Information Agency, and U.S. Department of Commerce*, May 1988, p. 30.

6. William S. Ellis, "Brazil's Imperiled Rain Forest," *National Geographic*, December 1988, p. 786.

7. Ibid., p. 780.

8. Ibid., p. 786

9. Ibid., p. 778.
10. "Reprieve for the Rain Forest?" p. 35.
11. Guppy, "Tropical Deforestation," p. 939.
12. Robert C. Stowe, "United States Foreign Policy and Conservation of Natural Resources: The Case of Tropical Deforestation," *Natural Resources Journal,* Winter 1987, p. 63.
13. Guppy, "Tropical Deforestation," p. 934.
14. Ellis, "Brazil's Imperiled Rain Forest," p. 787.
15. Henry R. Breck, "Rain Forests for Rent?" *Newsweek,* December 5, 1988, p. 12.
16. "Reprieve for the Rain Forest?" p. 35.
17. Roger Cohen, "Amazon Tug-of-War Reaches Fever Pitch," *Wall Street Journal,* April 7, 1989, p. A–12.
18. Guppy, "Tropical Deforestation," p. 941.
19. Philip Bennett, "Industry and Peril in Brazil," *Boston Globe,* December 20, 1988, p. 1.
20. Linda Greenbaum, "Plundering the Timber on Brazilian Indian Reservations," *Cultural Survival Quarterly,* vol. 13, 1989, p. 23.
21. Ibid., p. 32.
22. "Debt-for-Nature Swaps: A New Conservation Tool," *World Wildlife Fund Letter,* No. 1, 1988.
23. Eugene Linden, "Biodiversity: The Death of Birth," *Time,* January 2, 1989, p. 33.
24. Guppy, "Tropical Deforestation," p. 931.
25. Bennett, "Industry and Peril in Brazil," p. 1.
26. Stowe, "United States Foreign Policy and the Conservation of Natural Resources," p. 59.
27. Ibid.
28. Ibid.
29. Ibid.
30. Larry Tye, "Winning One for the World's Forests," *Boston Globe,* April 10, 1989, p. 14.
31. Ibid.
32. Conversation with Stuart Hudson, National Wildlife Federation, International Affairs Division.
33. Conversation with Jason Clay, Research Editor, Cultural Survival, Inc.

34. Ashoka, *ChangeMakers,* pamphlet, October–November 1988, p. 1.

35. John Bierman, "Murder in the Amazon," *Maclean's,* January 9, 1989, p. 21.

36. Ibid.

37. Ibid.

38. Ibid.

39. "Maria Allegretti-A Profile,"*Action for Children,* vol. 3, 1988, p. 1.

40. Ibid.

41. Ibid.

42. Tropical Forestry Program, Program Design and Description of Ongoing Projects, The World Wildlife Fund and the Conservation Foundation, January 1989.

43. William K. Reilly, "The New Context for Conservation in Latin America," *Vital Speeches of the Day,* October 15, 1986, pp. 27–28.

44. Leslie Roberts, "Hard Choices Ahead on Biodiversity," *Science,* September 30, 1988, p. 1761.

45. Ibid.

46. Ibid.

47. Reilly, "The New Context for Conservation in Latin America," pp. 28–29.

48. Jeffrey P. Cohen, "Creating a Conservation Ethic," *Americas,* November-December 1985, p. 14.

49. Ibid., p. 12.

50. Ibid., p. 15.

51. Ibid., p. 14.

52. Tropical Forestry Program.

53. Ibid.

54. Conversation with Vice-Dean David Smith, Harvard Law School.

55. Conversation with Stuart Hudson.

56. "Financing Ecological Destruction," paper prepared for a World Bank–International Monetary Fund meeting, September–October 1987, p. 6.

57. Ibid.

58. Ibid.

59. "Reprieve for the Rain Forest?" p. 35.

60. Ibid.

61. Dianne Dumanoski, "Plan Urges World Bank to Swap Conservation for Nations' Debts," *Boston Globe,* July 28, 1987, p. 8.

62. "Action Alert #33," *Rainforest Action Network,* January 1989.

63. Charles Secrett, "Last Chance for the Timber Trade," *Friends of the Earth International,* April 1986, p. 8.

64. Tropical Forestry Program.

65. Secrett, "Last Chance for the Timber Trade," p. 8.

66. Stowe, "United States Foreign Policy and the Conservation of Natural Resources," p. 60.

67. Barbara Bramble, "Swapping Debts for Nature," *International Banks Newsletter,* September–October 1987, p. 7.

68. Joseph Palca, "High-Finance Approach to Protecting Tropical Forests," *Nature,* vol. 328, July 30, 1987, p. 373.

69. "Summary of National Energy Policy Act of 1989," prepared by Senator Timothy E. Wirth's office.

70. "Saving the Rain Forest," *Denver Post,* February 5, 1989, editorial, p. 26.

71. "Brazil Balks at International Pressure to Save Environment in Industrializing," *Wall Street Journal,* February 13, 1989, p. A–11A.

72. John Goshko, "Baker Urges Step on Global Warming," *Washington Post,* January 31, 1989.

1-2

DELTA ENVIRONMENTAL AND THE ADVANCE OF THE GREENS

*This case was written by Alfred A. Marcus, Associate Professor,
Curtis L. Carlson School of Management, University of Minnesota.*

Delta Environmental Consultants, Inc., founded in 1986 by four former employees in the environmental department of a large midwestern engineering and testing firm, offers nationwide consulting and project management services aimed at environmental problems. Its project managers consult with clients and coordinate activities with subcontractors and regulatory agencies. Among the areas in which Delta offers services are Hazardous Waste Site Cleanup Design and Contracting, Health Risk Assessments and Toxicology Services, and Water Resource Management and Development. Delta has a broad subcontractor network and relies on highly qualified subcontractors to do work it cannot perform in-house.

By 1989, it had enjoyed phenomenal growth. From twenty employees in 1986 there were 190 in August 1988, and the expectation of 325 employees by January 1990. Sales went from $450,000 in 1986 to nearly $12 million in 1988. Headquartered in St. Paul, Minnesota, Delta had offices throughout the United States.

Delta has tried to develop innovative policies in human resources. For example, its human resource management philosophy describes the company as an "adaptive organization, a problem-solving medium, and an educational institution—that for its own economic growth and survival must increase the psychological, professional, and economic competence of the people who work for it." Its strategic planning project, called "Project 2000," investigates political trends and the business climate in geographical areas outside the United States in the short (to 1992), medium (to 1998), and long (to 2005) term. The company is especially interested in Europe.

This case is designed to give some background on the environmental movement in Europe and to raise questions about the strength and influence of the Greens on environmental policies in Europe in the coming years.

THE GREENS IN EUROPE

In most European countries the environment is a principal element in the political debate.[1] This is due largely to the growth of the Greens following the major battles over the environment that occurred about twenty years ago. When one considers the Greens in the twelve countries that constitute the European community, one usually thinks first about the West German party, that explosive mixture of pacifists, antinuclear activists, environmentalists, feminists, and believers in alternative lifestyles. However, the Green parties in Europe today are a broader, more conservative movement.

In the early 1980s the movement mainly signified opposition to U.S. military power, the military presence in Europe and nuclear weapons. At that time it had a pro-Moscow bent and included among its ranks militant Communists opposed to the capitalist system. Now, the movement is much broader and there is confusion as to where it lies on the political spectrum. Some commentators are viewing it as a conservative movement.

The ecology movement in Europe began in the 1970s with the energy crisis. Ecologists were opposed to the rapid and intensive development of nuclear power. To them, the atom was evil incarnate. Large-scale demonstrations in 1975 against the construction of the Wyhl nuclear power station in Bade-Wurtemberg (right across the Alsatian border from France) included French as well as West German activists. In Italy, demonstrations took place outside Toscane, the site of Montalto-di-Castro, the first large-scale nuclear power station to be constructed in Italy. Attention then switched to Brokdorf in the extreme north of West Germany, where German ecologists swore they would nip in the bud once and for all the growing presence of nuclear energy in Europe. Encouraged by the success of the German ecologists (the Schleswig-Holstein authorities suspended construction at Brokdorf), the ecologists of Europe let loose a furious outburst of demonstrations in 1977 against the construction of plants at Grohnded in Basse-Saxe, Kalkar in Rhenanie-Westphalie, and Creys-Malville in France.

Two of these plants, Kalkar and Creys-Malville, were advanced commercial breeders. In the United States, President Carter had decided not to go through with the commercialization of the breeder. Besides the increased danger of the technology, unlike the conventional reactor, it was capable of producing plutonium for atomic weapons.

Winning Political Power

European ecologists began to realize that political power was the only way to influence decision making. It was this realization that led the West German movement to found the Green party in 1980. Their intention was not to support a protest candidate with no chance of winning (as many French ecologists did in 1974 when they supported Rene Dumont in the presidential elections); nor was it to elect a single candidate to Parliament (as occurred in Switzerland in 1979 when Daniel Brelaz became the first political figure in Europe with strong ecological sympathies to be elected to a national legislature). Rather, the West German Greens wanted to develop a truly national movement with a full slate of candidates that would have a real chance of taking power.

In 1981 the Belgium Greens elected six candidates to Parliament. Soon there were national parties in Ireland (the Green Alliance) and in Portugal (the Organization of Greens). Never very successful in attracting voters, they did prove by their very existence, however, that they could play a major role in the politics of their countries.

French ecologists were unable to rally around a candidate for the 1981 presidential elections. They gave only token support to Brice Lalonde, an activist for Friends of the Earth and a partisan of the "happy ecology" orientation which was at odds with the more militant West German conception. The left wing of the movement challenged Lalonde's ascendancy and succeeded in removing him from the leadership. The sympathies of the Left were with the militant demonstrators who had staked everything in their determination to defeat nuclear power. The Left also was stridently antimilitary and accused the more moderate faction of compromise and weakness. Demobilization and demoralization set in, and 1982 marked a low point in the development of the French movement. No longer were there large-scale demonstrations. Rather, isolated militants and obscure combatants continued the struggle without much success.

In contrast, in West Germany the year 1982 marked a period of rapid growth as a consequence of opposition to the deployment of American missiles. For the first time the West German Greens elected candidates to the Bundestag. After the March 1983 election they held twenty-eight seats. Their success sparked the creation of other Green parties in Europe. In 1983 parties were founded in Denmark, Spain (the Green Alternative in Catalonia), Luxembourg (the Green Alternative), and the Netherlands. In 1984 national parties were formed in Spain and in France. In Great Britain, the Greens did not organize at the national level until 1985, and 1986 saw the creation of the Italian Green Federation. Only Greece did not have a single national party, although a coalition of ecologists did present a list for the 1989 European elections.

Continued Protest

Protest against nuclear power continued. In West Germany, it was at the Wackersdorf site in Bavaria, where a fuel retreatment center for nuclear waste was being constructed. Protestors from Luxembourg were jailed in France because of their opposition to the French reactor at Cattenom (Moselle), which in case of an accident could spread radiation throughout their country. In Spain, where protest was rare, the sole object was the nuclear power industry. The reactor site at Lemoniz in the Basque area saw its first demonstration in 1978; in 1981 an engineer was assassinated and the military were brought in to restore order. Portuguese ecologists opposed the construction of a Spanish reactor at Sayago, 12 km from the Portuguese border. Greenpeace became active after a decision to deposit nuclear waste in the Mediterranean Sea. In Britain, where Greenpeace and Friends of the Earth traditionally had led the fight against nuclear power, the catastrophe at Chernobyl energized the small Green party. The elections following Chernobyl quadrupled the vote for the Greens and permitted the party to gain for the first time two deputies in district councils. Only in France did the Greens fail to win additional support. The 1989 municipal elections around plant sites at Nogent-sur-Seine, Cattenom, and Creys-Malville did not show the Greens gaining any ground.

Other Issues

Although the foundation for Green political organization was the struggle against nuclear power, nuclear power was not the only issue in Europe. Increasingly in the 1980s other issues came to the forefront. In West Germany financial scandals tainted the established parties and politics took on a moralistic tone. The atmosphere was perfect for the Greens to make their claims. In addition to the American missiles, the declining West German forests, an issue dramatic in the extreme, forced the existing parties to integrate the environmentalists' concerns into their existing programs. Other campaigns broadened the environmentalists' base, including industrial and chemical wastes and the destruction of the ozone layer.

In the Netherlands the Greens could always count on the pollution of the Rhine to attract support. The river collected waste from many countries, including deadly chemicals from German and Swiss factories. Other issues aroused Dutch feeling, such as the death of seals in the North Sea in the summer of 1988 and the greenhouse effect, which threatened a warming trend that would lead to the flooding of most of Holland. Belgians were stirred by plans to expand the super-fast French railroad (TGV). With destinations in Great Britain, the TGV was supposed to pass through densely populated Flanders. Belgian ecologists exploited the local fears provoked by the planned expansion.

In Italy the ecologists began a campaign against hunters (there are more than 1.6 million in Italy) who were accused of wanting to shoot anything in their path that budged. Three different times (1973, 1980, and 1984) they tried to impose a referendum on the population but were rebuffed by the established parties. However, in 1989, supported by Communists and Socialists, the ecologists came close to succeeding.

In Spain campaigns have been against the creation of a military training camp in the province of Ciudad-Real south of Castille and against a Spanish equivalent of the TGV. Efforts have been made to come up with a workable solution for the intolerable air pollution that hangs over Madrid and Barcelona. Portuguese environmentalists have been mobilized to fight against industrial plantations which are rapidly doing away with the country's eucalyptus forests for the purpose of manufacturing paper. A demonstration in the north ended in confrontations with the police.

The Greek government finally agreed to prevent an aluminum smelter from emitting fumes at the site of the ancient Delphi. To preserve tourism, it has accepted the idea of a zone of protection around several beaches on the Island of Zante in the Ionian Sea. Similarly, the Irish Greens are trying to preserve historic sites from the threat posed by intolerable industrial fumes. In the spring of 1989 several thousand demonstrated at Westport on the west coast of Ireland. Those who viewed the demonstration said there had been nothing like it in Ireland since the uprising against the English in 1921.

Successes and Setbacks

The European environmental movement failed to prevent the deployment of the Pershing missile, and it has not stopped the rapid expansion and development of nuclear power. In France over fifty nuclear reactors are supplying over 70 percent of the country's electrical needs, and France exports electricity to all its neighbors. In contrast, nuclear power expansion in the United States has been halted and U.S. reactors supply only about 18 percent of U.S. electric power.

Nonetheless, European environmentalists can claim success in the political arena. With Gorbachev, for example, the general feeling is that the time for disarmament has arrived; and since Chernobyl enthusiasm for nuclear power has been on the wane. Other successes include the following:

- The Belgians have decided against constructing an eighth nuclear reactor. They will return to natural gas to provide future electrical needs.
- West Germany is having trouble operating its existing nuclear power stations because of the constant scrutiny. It has decided not to proceed with a fuel retreatment facility it had planned to build at Wackersdorf.
- Denmark has excluded any further recourse to nuclear energy.
- The Netherlands will maintain its two existing stations but has cancelled plans to build three additional plants.
- Italy in a 1987 referendum said no to nuclear power and has stopped construction of two reactors.
- In Spain production has stopped at the country's only nuclear station. Plans to build an additional five reactors have been shelved.
- England no longer envisions creating a new retreatment facility at Ecosses.
- France, the country most committed to nuclear power in Europe, has decided not to proceed with construction at Plogoff and is planning no new construction activity.

In other areas of environmental concern results vary. If the Greens have been unable to prevent the construction of new highways and rail lines (some environmentalists favor rail as an alternative to the automobile), they have at least made it more difficult to do so. In France the government was forced to suspend construction of a dam, Serre-de-la-Fare, in Haute-Loire, and it annulled a license to construct a high-tension electric utility wire to Spain. In West Germany environmentalist pressure led to the adoption of the catalytic converter as a requirement on autos.

In Italy, pressure from environmentalists has resulted in the prohibition of automobile traffic in the center of Florence and Bologna. There has been a highly successful campaign against the use of plastic bags, and in many Italian cities environmentalists are instituting recycling programs for glass, paper, aluminum cans, and organic material.

Supported by Queen Beatrice, environmentalists in the Netherlands have raised public consciousness about the decline of the planet, forcing adoption of many specific measures. Even Dutch farmers, long regarded by the environmentalists as laggards, have come forward with a plan to rely less on intensive agriculture, which requires large amounts of pesticides and fertilizers. And the Lubber government, which at one time almost collapsed because it wanted to implement a very costly program inspired by the Greens, has now made the Greens program the central element in its political strategy.

For the European ecologists, the 1980s were a remarkable decade. Today, government and industry contemplating large-scale projects can expect a reaction from environmentalists. Even the countries of southern Europe, poorer and traditionally less concerned about environmental issues, have developed an acute environmental sensibility.

If anything emerges from the greater integration of Europe it will be a stronger environmental movement, more united and potentially more capable of exerting influence throughout the European community. Europeans have much to thank the environmentalists for—less auto and industrial pollution and cleaner skies. On the other hand, they have had to put up with unruly political disturbances and demonstrations that sometimes threatened to get out of control. The moralistic tone of the environmentalists could have a destabilizing effect if it resulted in increased polarization in the European community.

Political Achievements

One thing is clear—the environmentalists have already achieved a certain degree of political power in their host countries and they aim to use the European Parliament as an arena for forging greater cohesiveness and discipline among the different national movements (see Table 1-2-1).

Belgium. The first time a Green party elected candidates to a legislature was in Belgium. In 1979 the party ECOLO (Verts de Wallonie) obtained 5.1 percent of the popular vote and in 1981 had 6 seats in the legislature. In 1984 ECOLO won 9.8 percent of the popular vote, but only 6.8 percent in 1987.

Denmark. In Denmark, the Greens have never exceeded 1.3 percent of the popular vote. The other parties argue that they support an ecological perspective. This has never been contradicted, and has thus confined the Danish Greens to marginality.

Spain. The Spanish Greens are divided into various regional factions. In the 1987 national elections they were able to obtain only 0.4 percent of the popular vote. For the 1989 Europeanwide elections they presented a common front for the first time, uniting behind the Andalouse activist Purificacion Garcia.

France. The French ecologists received only 3.9 percent of the popular vote in the 1981 presidential election with candidate Brice Lalonde. In 1988, seven years later, with candidate Antoine Waechter, they still got only 3.8 percent of the vote. Their performance improved, however, in regional and local contests in 1988 and 1989. In municipal contests in 1989 they attained 30 percent of the vote in some areas; overall they won 8 percent of the vote. They have elected 1,400 municipal counsellors, of whom about a dozen have become mayoral assistants in important cities.

Table 1-2-1

European Parliament Election Results: 1979 and 1984
(Percentage of popular vote)

	Greens		Communists & Extreme Left		Social Democrats		Conservative & Christian Democrats		Extreme Right	
	'79	'84	'79	'84	'79	'84	'79	'84	'79	'84
Italy	0.7	1.4	35.5	36.7	15.3	13.7	42.6	45.6	5.4	6.4
G. Britain					31.6	34.8	61.0	57.3		
W. Germany	3.2	8.2	0.4	1.7	41.2	37.4	55.2	50.8		0.9
France	4.4	3.4	23.6	14.8	23.5	24.1	43.9	43.0	1.3	11.0
Netherlands	5.1	6.9			39.4	36.0	55.0	54.1		2.5
Spain		0.4		7.9		39.4		36.2		
Belgium	3.4	8.2	3.9	1.5	23.4	30.4	54.0	45.4		
Portugal				11.5		27.0		52.9		2.8
Greece			18.1	15.0	40.1	41.3	39.9	40.0	1.2	2.3
Ireland			3.3	9.2	14.5	8.4	81.5	81.9		
Luxembourg		6.1	5.5		35.1	30.3	64.4	56.5		

Source: Phillippe Pottie-Sperry, "Les Forces Politique Pays Par Pays: Resultats des Scrutins de 1979 et 1984," *Le Journal des Elections*, No. 8, Juin/Juillet 39, pp. 36–37.

Greece. Today there are over 100 ecological groups in the country, divided up into eleven different organizations, almost all of which came into being after 1985. The most active is the Alternative Ecological Movement, which put together the coalition that presented candidates for the Europeanwide elections in 1989.

Ireland. The Green Alliance never has achieved more than 2.3 percent of the vote in the districts in which it is represented. Overall it constitutes about 0.6 percent of the national vote.

Italy. Italy has seen a proliferation of groups concerned with the protection of nature, including the Friends of the Earth, the WWF (130,000 members), Italia Nostra (12,000 members), and the League for the Protection of Birds (20,000 members). The only political movement has been the League for the Environment, created in 1980 as a marginal element within the Italian Communist party. Today the League has brought together older Communists with militants on the extreme Left, including the Radical party and the party of the Democratic Proletariat. As part of this coalition, the first Greens to run for the national parliament (in 1987) were only able to obtain about 2 percent of the vote. However, candidates sympathetic to environmental positions ran for other parties, such as the group "Verdi," which won eleven deputies in the Assembly.

Luxembourg. In Luxembourg the Green Alternative has won 6 percent of the national vote in the last two elections and has two deputies in the National Chamber.

Netherlands. In this country where Greenpeace has over 350,000 contributors, the Greens have yet to make proportional gains. The Groene Partij, founded as an offshoot of the Radical party, is the dominant but not the only Green party. The Green Coalition (The Groene Progressif Akkord), which presented candidates for the European elections in 1984, was able to obtain 5.6 percent of the vote and elect two delegates, who have played a leading role as part of the rainbow coalition in the Strasbourg (all-European) Parliament.

Portugal. The Green party of Portugal has not been able to field a list of its own in the national elections. It is an ally of the Communist party and the Group for Democratic Intervention, which obtained 14 percent of the vote in the 1987 general elections and won two seats in the National Assembly.

West Germany. The Greens had twenty-eight deputies in the Bundestag in 1983 and seven deputies in the European Parliament in 1984. In the 1987 national elections they won 8.3 percent of the popular vote and sent forty-four deputies to the Bundestag, which is the strongest representation of Greens in the Parliament of a European nation.

Great Britain. In Great Britain, the Greens have never elected a member of Parliament, where 7 percent of the vote is needed. Their 133 candidates in 1987 received only 90,000, votes and in only three districts surpassed 2.5 percent of the vote. For the 1989 European elections the Greens were very cautious, presenting candidates in only seventy-eight districts, because unless these candidates obtained more than 5 percent of the vote, the party would not be reimbursed by the government for campaign expenses. The Greens have elected only eleven district counsellors. Even though they present a rather severe aura to the public, membership rose in 1988–89 from 7,500 to 10,000. They now have as many supporters as the Communists.

Right or Left?

Where to place the Green parties in the political spectrum is a question that has aroused some debate. They are at the confluence of movements. On the one hand, they are part of the antimilitary and antinuclear movements, traditionally close to the Left. On the other hand, they are part of a naturalist and apolitical tendency which has been hostile to the Left. Thus, the Greens tend to vary from one country to the next and from one group to another. Nonetheless, in general, one is likely to find among them a number of constants: the struggle for respect for the environment and for limiting pollution accompanied by opposition to nuclear power, rapid industrial development, and the heavy use of pesticides and chemicals in agriculture. These tendencies are combined with a moralistic tone which accompanies the Greens' political pronouncements, whether they deal with national or international issues. Political scandals such as illegal campaign contributions, as well as opposition to war and militarism, have played as much a role in the success of the West German Greens as the efforts to protect Germany's forests. The aspiration for an "ecological society" has led Greens to all sorts of political and economic theories, some more traditionally associated with the Right than with the Left.

In France, after the election of Antoine Waechter, a naturalist who in all respects is a moderate, there was a transformation of the movement away from the militants of the extreme Left who violently opposed the growth of consumerism and a consumer-style society like the United States. In Europe, Green parties have become the repository for all those who feel they are without a party and who have nowhere else to turn. Some of these are traditional conservationists and naturalists, but some are from the most conflictual elements on the Left. These groups wish to end the slavish seeking of productivity improvements and betterment in standards of living at all costs, which have come to dominate the aspirations of most Europeans in the postwar period.

On certain issues the French Greens have been further to the left than the standard parties. For example, with regard to New Caledonia and the alleged rights of the Palestinians, the Greens admit to being "to the left of the Left." Antoine Waechter is the only head of a major French party who personally met with Arafat prior to the Palestinian's meeting with Mitterand in France in the spring of 1989.

The Greens in Europe today tend to support the philosophy of works like Our Common Future, written by ex-Norwegian prime minister Harlem Brundtland. In France, Pierre Radanne, one of the most well-known Green theoreticians, has endeavored to diffuse the ideas found in

Brundtland's book. These ideas deal mostly with sustainable or durable development, which is supposed to be the only type of development that will permit human survival in an age of environmental limits. Radanne maintains that countries in the Northern Hemisphere, that is, the developed world, have been strangling the underdeveloped countries in the South; he reproaches them for not showing sensitivity to the environment. For Radanne, there is no difference between the social struggle and the struggle for the environment. He has argued that ecologists have to be strongly anticapitalist.

Alain Lipietz, another French ecologist, maintains that the only major difference between the ecologists and the Communists is with regard to the question of economic growth. Growth at all costs traditionally has been a core value of the Left and of workers' parties throughout Europe. The Greens, according to Lipietz, totally reject this view in favor of quality of life.

Even if all Greens do not want to consider themselves part of the Left, most apparently do. Nonetheless, it is interesting to observe that the extreme Right, jealous of its new rival, has begun to view the environment as an issue upon which it too can capitalize. In December of 1988 at a Europeanwide meeting of the extreme Right, the Italian professor Alessandro Di Pietro declared that ecology and conservation have always been core values of the Right, which it has defended even at the expense of economic progress. The Left has appropriated the issue solely for political ends as an instrument of propaganda to gain political advantage. The Right must respond by creating in all of the European countries its own organizations for the environment which will oppose the Leftists, Greens, and the eco-pacifists, who exist not to protect nature but to enhance Communism.

The implications are that environmental values have become universal in Europe. They belong neither to the Left nor to the Right; instead, their espousal has become a precondition for political success of any kind.

Political Alliances and the Temptation of Power

Could the Greens become part of a ruling coalition?[2] Are they capable of assuming the reins of power and governing? The possibility exists in all the European countries, but is most likely in West Germany. The participation of the Greens in governing coalitions at the local level is accepted as a reality. Coalitions exist between the Social Democrats and "alternative" forces in West Berlin and Frankfort. What attracts attention in foreign capitals is the eruption of the extreme Right in West Germany, which began with the West Berlin election in January of 1989. The electoral advances of the Greens in the West German local politics came about as a result of a campaign centered on the threat of auto pollution and the need to encourage the greater use of public transport.

The entry of the Greens into the regional government of Hesse in 1985 in a power-sharing arrangement with the Social Democrats was viewed as a major development. The German establishment had seen the Greens as a temporary phenomenon that would quickly dissipate without making a lasting mark on the future of West German politics. Today, the Greens are an accepted part of the political landscape. Contrary to what was thought at the beginning, the Greens have not faded away. Rather, they have pressed strongly for their positions on the environment and disarmament, pushing even the Liberal party of Chancellor Kohl in directions they favor. Public disputes between more moderate (the realists) and more militant (the fundamentalists) fringes within the environmental movement have not hurt the support environmentalists have received from influential elements in the West German populace.

The rupture of the coalition in Hesse, caused in large part by the Social Democrats who were unsure of aligning themselves with the Greens, suspended for a number of years discussion about the impact of the Greens' participation at the highest levels of power. Not only have the Greens needed the time to stabilize their image as being less threatening and less chaotic, but so too have the Social Democrats needed time to end disputes in their ranks about whether to cooperate with the Greens. The Social Democrats have decided that in all negotiations with the Greens they should insist that the Greens accept three principles: (1) no immediate and total withdrawal of allied forces and unilateral surrender of the allied cause; (2) the recognition that state-sanctioned public authorities have a monopoly with regard to the legitimate use of force; and (3) automatic adoption by West Berlin of the laws of the West German Federal Republic.

It has not been entirely evident that under these conditions all factions within the Greens would support participation in power. The Hesse eruption was viewed as temporary by many in the movement who felt compromised by holding power. The question of whether to cooperate with the established parties dominated internal discussions.

At the highest levels the movement is led by activists who had been involved in the violent demonstrations of the 1970s and for whom the prospect of holding power was not particularly appealing. However, the local leadership in the municipalities and cantons had a taste of power sharing and responsibility and this experience provided a different perspective which was lacking when the movement started.

The movement in West Germany is divided into three local centers which have very different orientations. The Hamburg Greens are the most radical. In Hamburg in 1987 the fundamentalist wing blocked the creation of the power-sharing arrangement with the Social Democrats over the question of whether the state should have a monopoly over the legitimate use of violence. The Hamburg movement continues to be dominated by the extreme Left. This is not true of the movement generally, even though a potential in this direction exists even among the West Berlin "alternatives" who have taken their part in regional government. In spite of serious confrontations with the police on May Day 1989, provoked by West Berliners seeking autonomy from the Federal Republic, the coalition of the Reds and Greens so far has held together. In Frankfort, West Germany's financial center and the headquarters for the realist faction among the Greens, the Greens have won three positions in the municipal government. One was held by Daniel Cohn-Bendit, sixties radical, who headed an office which dealt with the government's relations with the immigrant community. The idea of threatening investments of polluting industries, once advanced with particular vehemence against the chemical industry, has been softened, and the pragmatism displayed by Joshka Fischer, another sixties radical, has calmed fears about what it would signify if the Greens held power.

The 1989 European Elections

In the Europeanwide elections held in June 1989 there were three big surprises (see Table 1-2-2), all of them related to the Greens as they continued to become an important political force. First was the defeat of the Conservative party in Britain, partially a consequence of Labor's and Neil Kinnock's more moderate tone, and partially a consequence of the emergence of the Greens as a power to be reckoned with in British politics. For the first time the British Greens won substantial electoral support. The second big surprise was the growth of extreme right-wing parties in West Germany and the Netherlands, where support for the Greens has apparently peaked. The third is the large increase in the vote for the Greens in France. The French Greens broke the 10 percent vote barrier for the first time, surpassing the German Greens and becoming the most popular Green party in continental Europe. Where does the vote for the French Greens come from? Most likely the young and intermediate ranks of the professional class (see Table 1-2-3). Ideologically, the French Greens tend to be on the Left.

Table 1-2-2

European Parliament Election Results: 1989
(Popular vote change from 1984)

	Greens	Communists & Extreme Left	Social Democrats	Conservative & Christian Democrats	Extreme Right
G. Britain	15		40	35	
Change from 1984	+15		+5.2	-22.3	
W. Germany	8.4		37.3	43.3	7.1
Change from 1984	+0.2		-0.1	-7.5	+6.2
France	11.9	9.7	23.6	37.3	11.7
Change from 1984	+8.5	-5.1	-0.5	-6.7	+0.7
Netherlands	7.0		36.2	48.2	5.9
Change from 1984	+0.1		+0.2	-5.9	+3.4

Source: Data taken from *Le Monde*, June 20, 1989.

Table 1-2-3

The Nature of the French Ecology Vote

	Social Democrats %	Ecologists %	Moderate Right %
Age			
18–34	40	47	27
35–49	25	28	26
50+	35	25	47
Profession			
Agriculture	2	3	6
Commercial	2	5	7
Management	4	5	6
(intellectual professions)			
Professional	32	40	24
(intermediate-level employees)			
Worker	17	13	8
Unemployed, Retired	43	34	50
Partisan Preference			
Left	94	34	12
Ecological	2	49	4
Right	2	11	78
No response	2	6	6

Source: Enquetes *Sofrres,* based on 4,000 interviews conducted between April 22 and May 15, 1989; reprinted in *Le Monde*, May 28–29, 1989, p.6.

THE EFFECT OF THE GREENS ON DELTA ENVIRONMENTAL

In considering the effect of the Greens on the business prospects of Delta Environmental in Europe in the next five to ten years, a number of issues are relevant.

1. Many of Europe's environmental problems are transnational in character. Will the Green parties be able to form coalitions with other parties in the Europeanwide Parliament that meets in Strasbourg? Will it be able to pass legislation that is binding on all the member states in the emerging European community? What type of legislation, and how might this legislation impact Delta's business prospects?

2. The strength of the Greens seems tied to economic development. The Greens are generally stronger (electorally) in countries that are economically more advanced (West Germany and France), and generally weaker in countries that are economically less developed (Spain and Greece). Does this suggest a particular business strategy for Delta? What if the economic tide in Europe turns and the economies weaken? Will the Greens command as much support?

3. How broad is the support for the Greens? Will these parties peak at about 10 percent of the electorate in the economically most advanced countries in Europe, or can they move even further in winning political support? How would they have to change their strategy and tactics to win broader support? What would the possible changes in Greens' strategy and tactics mean for Delta's business prospects?

4. Given the internal divisions in most of the Green parties (the split between radicals and moderates), will it be possible for the Greens to hold together and maintain a common front? Will it be possible for them to develop a broader, more comprehensive philosophy, one that is more inclusive and is capable of attracting additional support?

5. Will Europeans support a Green foreign policy? What would such a foreign policy look like? What would have to happen with regard to East–West and North–South relations for the Greens to gain greater influence?

6. Is the real influence of the Greens limited to the pressure they can apply on the other parties? Will the Greens ever hold power?

7. Are the Greens for most Europeans simply an alternative to the conventional parties? When Europeans vote for the Greens are they simply making a protest vote that could be equally lodged with other unconventional parties such as those found in Europe on the extreme left and extreme right?

8. What about the differences between environmental movements in the United States and Europe and the future of environmental legislation in light of these differences? In the United States, the environmental movement is large and very active, but because of our two-party system, it is confined to being a protest movement and pressure group. Although an environmental figure, Barry Commoner, has run for president, and American presidents going back to Teddy Roosevelt have portrayed themselves as environmentalists, it is unlikely that the American environmental movement will ever be organized as a political party and be successful in electoral politics. Unlike Europe it is almost certain that the ideals and main themes of the American environmental movement will be absorbed (albeit in less radical form) by the conventional parties. Will this difference mean greater power and influence for the European movement?

9. Environmental problems generally are more visible in Europe (because of denser population levels, an aging industrial base, and years of neglect) than in the United States. Does this mean, along with the particular character of the environmental movement, that European nations will take the lead in developing innovative environmental policies and programs? What would this development signify for Delta?

10. What particular innovations are likely to occur in Europe? What issues will emerge? Already the issues that preoccupy Europeans are somewhat different from those that preoccupy Americans. Will these differences become more pronounced in the future? If so, what will they signify with respect to the global strategy of a company like Delta?

Discussion Questions

1. What countries in Europe offered the best hope for market development by Delta?
2. With the growing unification of the countries in the European Economic Community (EEC), would the influence of the Greens expand or contract? What impacts would the Greens have on the policies of the EEC and on the policies of the EEC member states?
3. What kind of legislation was likely to be in place in the EEC and in the EEC member states? Would this legislation provide a particular niche for the kind of expertise Delta had developed in the United States?
4. Should Delta make an effort to establish a presence in Europe?
5. What would Delta have to do to go about establishing such a presence? What practical steps would it have to take?

NOTES

1. Roger Cans, "La Saga des Verts Europeans," *Le Monde*, June 1, 1989, p. 1.
2. Henri de Bresson, "La Tentation du Pouvoir," *Le Monde*, June 1, 1989, p. 9.

1-3

THE BIG SPILL: OIL AND WATER STILL DON'T MIX

This case was written by Rogene A. Buchholz, College of Business Administration, Loyola University of New Orleans.

Alaska is North America's last frontier. The state contains areas of natural beauty with panoramic peaks and rushing rivers. Most of its pristine land is populated with an abundance of game, fish, and fowl. Complementing its diverse wildlife is its wealth of resources such as oil, gas, coal, and timber. These natural riches are beginning to be exploited to support the population of the lower forty-eight states, which require ever more resources to sustain their demanding lifestyle. Initially, Alaskans welcomed development. It meant a stronger economy. It was assumed that the two Alaskas— one wild and the other industrial—could exist in harmony.

Alaska's most recent resource development boom began in 1968 when large quantities of oil were discovered at Prudhoe Bay. In 1969 the state auctioned the bay's oil drilling leases, bringing $900 million into its coffers. Income from oil leases and other oil-related activities has helped the state to build schools, roads, and other public projects. The abundance of oil-related money has made state personal taxes unnecessary and has even enabled the state to pay an annual oil dividend to each resident. In 1988 this dividend amounted to $826.93 per person. Even at today's prices, the state gets 85 percent of its revenues from the petroleum industry.[1]

The trans-Alaska pipeline runs 800 miles from Prudhoe Bay to the port of Valdez. The United States depends on Alaskan oil for 25 percent of its domestically produced oil supply. About half of this oil is carried in large tankers. When the pipeline was being planned, builders assured concerned officials and citizens that the chances of a major oil spill in Prince William Sound, where Valdez is located, were extremely remote. Builders argued that the normal safety precautions used for the domestic tanker trade provided sufficient protection to waters off the Alaskan coast. No special efforts were needed, such as double-bottom tankers and special ballast tanks, which were some of the additional precautions suggested.[2]

THE ACCIDENT

The Exxon supertanker Valdez entered the port of Valdez on March 22, 1989, riding high in the water because its cargo chambers were empty. Tugs guided it into the dock at the Alyeska oil terminal (Alyeska is the name of a consortium of oil companies which formed to operate the terminal). The tanker Valdez, only two years old and built in the San Diego shipyards, cost $125 million. It was one of the best equipped vessels that hauled oil from the port of Valdez, having collision avoidance radar, satellite navigational aids, and depth finders.[3]

Fully loaded, the tanker carried 61 million gallons of crude oil. But since winter loading limits were in effect when it arrived at the Alyeska terminal, the Valdez was loaded with 52 million gallons. The loading would take sixteen hours to complete and, given that an Exxon policy prohibits drinking only on board its vessels, the crew spent much of this time drinking in town. After loading, the vessel would be headed for Long Beach, California, a five-day trip under normal conditions.[4]

Captain Joseph Hazelwood, of Huntington, New York, was the commander of the Exxon Valdez. Hazelwood was a 20-year Exxon veteran and had been commander of the Valdez for twenty months. In 1985 Hazelwood was convicted of drunk driving in Long Island, New York. During that year, Hazelwood informed Exxon about his drinking problem and the company immediately sent him to an alcohol rehabilitation program. In September 1988 Hazelwood was found guilty in New Hampshire of driving while intoxicated. In the span of five years Hazelwood's automobile driver's license was revoked three times. At the time of the Valdez spill Hazelwood was still not permitted to drive an automobile even though he retained his license to command a supertanker.[5] Exxon claimed it was not aware that Hazelwood's alcoholism had persisted.

On Thursday, March 23, the tanker Valdez was eased out into the harbor by the port pilot, which is customary practice in most shipping facilities. The pilot noticed alcohol on Hazelwood's breath but no impairment of the captain's judgment or faculties. The port pilot turned command of the Valdez over to Hazelwood and descended over the side of the tanker to a waiting boat. At some point after the port pilot left the tanker, Hazelwood left his command post and went below to his cabin, violating company policy which requires the captain to stay in command of the ship until it is in open water. Third Officer Gregory Cousins was left in charge, even though Cousins lacked Coast Guard certification to pilot a tanker in Alaskan coastal waters. The tanker Valdez increased its speed to 12 knots and entered the waters of Prince William Sound. It was the 8,549th tanker to safely negotiate the sound's narrows since the first tanker left the port fully loaded in August 1977. No serious accidents had happened during that time.[6]

As the tanker made its way through the sound, it detected icebergs in the outgoing ship lane. The tanker radioed the Coast Guard for permission to steer a course down the empty incoming lane to avoid the icebergs. Permission was granted and the Valdez altered course. The tanker was in trouble almost immediately; it was heading due south on a collision course with Busby Island five miles away.[7]

The Coast Guard station that tracked vessels through the sound did not notice the Valdez's potential collision because the tanker disappeared from its radar screen. Two years ago the Coast Guard replaced its radar with a less-powerful unit. During the time the Valdez disappeared from the radar it rode over submerged rocks off Busby Island and minutes later plowed into Bligh Reef and began spilling its cargo. The reef tore eleven holes in the Valdez's bottom, some as large as 6 by 20 feet. Eight cargo holds, each big enough to swallow a 15-story building, were ruptured. While a command had been given to change the course of the Valdez to avoid disaster, it came too late to have an effect. At 12 knots it takes about half a mile for a rudder change to substantially alter the course of a 987-foot ship.[8]

On Friday, 12:28 a.m., the Coast Guard station in Valdez was notified of a vessel run aground. About 1 a.m. a Coast Guard pilot boat headed for the accident site, following a tugboat which had been previously dispatched. At 3:23 a.m. they arrived on the site and saw the tanker losing oil at a rate of 1.5 million gallons an hour. At 5:40 a.m. the Valdez had lost 210,000 barrels of oil, or more than 8.8 million gallons. There are 42 gallons in a barrel of oil, which is the standard industry measure. At 7:27 a.m. spotters aboard an Alyeska plane reported that the oil slick was 1,000 feet wide, five miles long, and spreading. Earlier a passing boat reported encountering an oil slick about half a mile south of Bligh Reef. Later it was estimated that the Valdez released about 240,000 barrels of oil into the sound, equivalent to 10.1 million gallons.[9]

Nine hours after the collision Hazelwood's blood was tested for alcohol. The test revealed that Hazelwood still had a blood-alcohol level of 0.06, which is higher than the 0.04 the Coast Guard considers acceptable for captains. Hazelwood's blood-alcohol level at the time of the accident was estimated to be about 0.19, assuming he had nothing more to drink after the accident and that his body metabolized at the normal rate. The 0.19 level is almost double the amount at which most states consider a motorist to be legally drunk. After learning of these test results Exxon fired Hazelwood. The state of Alaska filed criminal charges against him for operating a ship under the influence of alcohol, reckless endangerment, and criminally negligent discharge of oil. The maximum penalty for the combined charges was twenty-seven months in jail and a $10,000 fine. The state also issued a warrant for his arrest.[10]

Hazelwood fled Alaska to avoid arrest but later turned himself in near his Long Island home. His initial bail, set at $500,000, was subsequently reduced to $25,000 on appeal. The judge who set the initial bail, himself a lover of the sea and wildlife, said the misdemeanors committed by Hazelwood were of a magnitude unparalleled in this country: "We have a manmade destruction that probably has not been equaled since Hiroshima." The judge apparently overstepped his legal bounds, given that another judge reduced Hazelwood's bail a day later, but no one took issue over his outrage at the disaster.[11]

Hazelwood was released. Meanwhile, the FBI investigated, charging him with violations of the Clean Water Act. It was reported that Hazelwood was more remiss than initially thought. Instead of simply handing the tanker over to the third mate, Hazelwood may have left the vessel on autopilot when he changed course into the incoming sea-lane. When the third mate realized the tanker was headed for the reef he may not have been able to reset the course.[12]

A day after the accident, the oil slick grew to eight miles long and four miles wide. It was now the worst oil spill in U.S. history. By the end of the week, the slick covered almost 900 square miles to the southwest of Valdez, threatening the marine and bird life in the sound and spreading to the Chugach National Forest. Almost a week after the accident, the slick began taking its greatest toll on wildlife when oil began washing up on the beaches of Knight and Green islands. Scientists found blackened animals dead or huddled on the beaches. Scores of birds were barely distinguishable from the oil-covered sand and gravel.[13]

The oil slick continued to spread, covering more than 1,000 square miles and hitting hundreds of miles of inaccessible beaches. The spill drifted into the Gulf of Alaska where it threatened the port of Seward and the delicate shoreline of Kenai Fjords National Park. The area covered by the spill was now larger than the state of Rhode Island. The slick eventually spread 100 miles out into the Gulf of Alaska, forcing federal officials to develop a second front in their battle to contain its advancement.

Scientists estimated that about half the oil lost by the Valdez left Prince William Sound and entered the gulf, creeping south at about 15 to 20 miles a day.[14] Before it reached Kodiak Island, however, the slick was breaking up and dissipating. Exposure to the natural elements was transforming the oil into tar balls that sank to the bottom of the ocean. Rain and snowstorms also helped to break up the floating oil and cleanse a number of shores.[15]

PREVIOUS WARNINGS

Environmentalists had warned of an accident in Prince William Sound and asked what would happen if one occurred. In response, the oil companies said the chances of an accident in either the sound or at the terminal were one in a million. The danger of an accident, according to Alyeska, was further reduced because the majority of the tankers calling on the port were of American registry; these vessels are piloted by licensed masters or pilots. In almost twelve years of shipping out of Valdez, there had not been a major incident. People were lulled into believing an accident could not happen.[16]

In the event of an accident, the oil companies claimed they could control a spill with booms, skimmers, and chemical dispersants. The 1,800-page cleanup plan, developed by the oil companies for Alyeska, involved storing skimmers and oil-containment booms at the port of Valdez. According to the plan, immediate access to this equipment would allow a 36-member crew to respond within five hours after an accident. The plan, which detailed how Alyeska would respond to a 200,000 barrel spill in the sound, was filed with the federal government. The Coast Guard and the Alaska Department of Fish and Game expressed skepticism about the plan and the claims made by the oil companies, but no changes were made.[17]

Local citizens were also skeptical and offered to supplement company equipment. The mayor of Valdez offered to stockpile cleanup equipment, but the city's offer was turned down by Alyeska who assured the mayor it had an adequate supply of equipment. The city then tried to impose a property tax surcharge on Alyeska to create its own cleanup fund, but because state law prohibits taxing oil companies at higher rates than other property owners, it was barred from spending the money. Later, when Alyeska came under fire for responding slowly to the spill and not having enough equipment on hand, it claimed it could not keep cleanup gear near every place along the hundreds of miles of tanker routes where an accident might occur.[18]

Warnings were issued about problems caused by icebergs in the sound. In 1977 a U.S. Geological Survey Report indicated that the Columbia Glacier showed increased signs of instability and could potentially shed icebergs into the port. The report said icebergs had migrated into the Valdez area more frequently than suspected, and because the tanker route passes within 8 miles of the glacier's terminus, they could pose problems for tanker traffic. Suggestions were made to contain the icebergs behind a rope barrier until they melted, but since the cost was estimated to be between $30 and $35 million, nothing was done. On the night of March 22, 1989, the tanker Valdez tried to avoid icebergs from the glacier by altering its course.[19]

THE CLEANUP EFFORT

Shortly after the accident, a second tug that had left for the site was called back to port to pick up lightering equipment—the gear needed to transfer oil from one tanker to another. At 4:14 a.m. the Exxon Baton Rouge was ordered to head for the site and take on the Valdez's stranded cargo. More than two thirds of the Valdez cargo was still on board and it was important to transfer it before further damage occurred. As one observer commented, "If this is what 210,000 barrels looks like, then, God, I don't want to see what a million looks like."[20]

Calls went out from Alyeska's Emergency Response Center for boats, equipment, and manpower. Containment booms would be needed along with oil skimmers, chemical dispersants, spray planes, and helicopters. However, many employees could not be reached since they were out of town for the Easter weekend. Moreover, Alyeska had only one barge—an important piece of equipment needed for the initial cleanup. The barge was out of commission due to a hole that needed repair. Nonetheless, it was pressed into service but before it could be used it had to be reloaded. In order to reload the barge, a 70-ton crane had to be moved from a neighboring dock. All this maneuvering cost precious time and as a result booms did not reach the stranded tanker until ten hours after the accident.[21]

It took eighteen hours to get the first boom in place, and by late Saturday, the main slick was nowhere near containment. Just encircling the tanker with containment booms took a day and a half, and by that time the spill covered a 12-square-mile area. Alyeska's contingency plan, however, called for getting the containment boom into place within five hours of the mishap. The spreading spill made skimming difficult, and by the end of the second day only 1,200 barrels were recovered. However, in its contingency plan, Alyeska claimed that as much as half of a

200,000-barrel spill could be recovered by skimming operations. Some of Alyeska's skimming machines were ten years old and broke down frequently. In addition, replacement parts for some of its British models were unavailable. The tanks on the skimmers filled up rapidly and the oil had to be transferred to nearby barges, taking a great deal of time.[22]

Exxon later claimed that ringing the stricken tanker with a containment boom too quickly after the accident could set off an explosion that would destroy the vessel. Exxon claimed that oil spewed so rapidly from the tanker that a huge cloud of volatile vapor had formed over the stricken ship. A containment boom would have intensified this cloud and a spark would have set off an explosion, thus tearing the ship apart and releasing the remaining oil into the sound. Whether this was a response to criticism for not getting the containment booms into place earlier is not known, but the admission was evidence that the company was unprepared to handle a spill of this magnitude.[23]

The Exxon Baton Rouge, lashed bow-to-stern to the Valdez, attempted to lighten the damaged tanker's load so that it might float free of the reef. Eventually, three smaller tankers were used to hold the remaining 984,000 barrels of oil on the Valdez. Once empty, on-site repairs would be attempted before towing it to a shipyard. On April 5 Exxon reported that the transfer of remaining oil on the Valdez was complete and it would begin efforts to refloat the vessel. This oil transfer effort had been the most ambitious ever attempted and prevented the spill from becoming four times as worse. Exxon anticipated towing the Valdez to a dry-dock facility in Portland, Oregon, but city officials had not decided whether it would welcome the tanker to its facilities. The alternative was to use a shipyard in the Far East. The repair job was estimated to cost $12 million and employ as many as 200 workers.[24]

Exxon promised it would persist with its cleanup efforts for months, if this was necessary, and boasted it would leave the sound "the way it was before." The company said crews of workers would rake the beaches to get congealed oil into a pile that could be hauled away, use high-pressure hoses to blast sludge off the rocks and back into the water where skimmers could collect it, and use absorbent rags to wipe off any remaining splotches. The company vowed to pick up all the oil that was spilled.[25]

Frank Iarossi, president of Exxon Shipping Company, arrived from Houston the Friday night after the accident to take command of the cleanup. At that time, chemical dispersants could not be used because the sound's water was too calm for them to be effective, as these chemicals depend on wave action to disperse the slick.[26] But even if it had been possible to use dispersants effectively, Exxon did not have an adequate supply of them on hand. On the day of the wreck, the company had 4,000 gallons on hand, even though its own guidelines required 500,000 gallons to fight a spill of this size. Six days later there were still only 110,000 gallons of dispersants on hand.[27]

On Sunday, as a result of 70-mile-per-hour winds, boats were hindered from laying booms and skimming the oil off the top of the water. The winds also grounded planes from dumping dispersants on the spill. The strong winds whipped the oil into a froth known as mousse, and attempts to spread a napalmlike substance on the oil and ignite it with laser beams did not succeed.[28] On the fifth day after the accident Exxon sprayed 11,000 gallons of dispersants on the slick, but by then most of the volatile fractions of the crude had vaporized, leaving behind the mousse, which does not readily yield to dispersants. By this time only mechanical skimmers proved useful to collect oil trapped by containment booms. Some 2,000 barrels a day was being skimmed in this fashion.[29]

On the fourth day after the accident fishermen from Cordova and Valdez formed a fishermen's strike force and attempted to save the region's three salmon hatcheries. These hatcheries anchor the area's $75 million salmon industry. The fishermen deployed containment booms at the hatcheries and saw some successes for their efforts. At Port San Juan, for example, 117 million pink-salmon fry were due to be released into the sound. When the slick reached the hatchery, the booms deflected it away and saved the salmon fry from destruction. Eventually, ten skimmers were concentrated in the Port San Juan area to keep oil from fouling the hatchery.[30]

Other countries offered to help with the cleanup effort. The Soviet Union sent a skimmer ship and Norway sent five environmental experts. Cleanup crews were sent to beaches to hand-wipe rocks and boulders and skim tide pools with shovels, spades, or their bare hands. It was absurd work, as the round trip from Valdez took six hours, which left workers barely six hours to work at the cleanup site. When they were finished, the incoming tide buried their work under more oil. About 100 workers were working seven days a week to mop up a few million gallons by hand. The company realized the futility of these efforts, but was responding to pressures to put somebody out there doing something.[31]

At mid-week a team from Washington, D.C., that included Transportation Secretary Samuel Skinner, Environmental Protection Agency Administrator William Reilly, and Coast Guard Commandant Paul Yost, arrived at the scene. The team reported to President Bush that Exxon's cleanup effort was progressing adequately and the federal government did not need to assume control over the process. Essentially, the team recommended that Exxon remain in control of the cleanup. Such a statement may have been a way for the federal government to keep out of the effort and thus avoid sharing the blame for what the president was calling a major tragedy.[32]

In an unusual public apology, Exxon placed an advertisement signed by Chairman L.G. Rawl in about 100 national magazines and newspapers, admitting its responsibility for the accident. The company promised to meet its "obligations to all those who have suffered damage from the spill." Under federal law, the company was obligated to pay the first $14 million of cleanup costs and then could draw on a fund set up by the Trans-Alaska Pipeline Act for an additional $86 million. The law limits a company's liability to $100 million, but that limit has no effect if a company is found guilty of negligence. Because of the behavior of Captain Hazelwood and the failure of Exxon and Alyeska to respond quickly to the incident, such a finding was not beyond possibility.[33] Exxon was exposed to potentially huge punitive damage claims, but it had at least one insurance line that covered it against claims based on negligence for up to $400 million.[34]

At hearings held by the Senate Commerce, Science, and Transportation Committee, the Chairman of Exxon restated his company's intention to take full responsibility for the spill and pay for all cleanup costs. One committee member pointed out that when Japanese companies cause serious accidents, their executives resign their positions in a show of public remorse. The suggestion was made that the disaster caused by Exxon called for that kind of response. Chairman Rawl replied that the Japanese are also known for committing suicide, and he refused to take that action.[35]

During the first eight days after the accident Exxon officials stated that more than 1,100 tons of cleanup supplies and equipment had been shipped into Valdez aboard forty-nine cargo jet airplanes. Twelve oil-skimming boats had been deployed and more than 16 miles of absorbent floating boom had been deployed or was being held ready. But such efforts seemed to have little effect on the volume of oil that was still floating on the sound.[36] Later, an Alyeska spokesperson conceded that its spill contingency plan may have been unrealistic given the consortium's inability to quickly bring the spill under control. Alyeska further admitted it had violated a requirement of its cleanup plan when it failed to notify the state Department of Environmental Conservation that the barge used to string oil containment booms had been taken out of service for repairs. The barge had been in dry dock for two weeks prior to the accident because Alyeska could not locate a licensed welder to repair a hole in the side of the vessel.[37]

Edinburgh Napier
University Library

After almost a week of cleanup work the state of Alaska not only condemned Exxon's cleanup effort but asked the Coast Guard to take over the process. A House Interior and Insular Affairs Committee member stated that Exxon was merely managing failure and that its cleanup claims were fraudulent. The governor of Alaska believed the Coast Guard would be better able to coordinate and manage the cleanup. Exxon was thought to be too bureaucratic and many believed that a military system was needed to get things accomplished. However, President Bush maintained that federal management of the cleanup effort was unnecessary. Costs of the cleanup were running $1 million a day. It was better to have Exxon cover these costs than to declare a federal cleanup and have taxpayers bear the expense.[38]

On Thursday, April 6, acting under pressure from the state of Alaska, the Bush administration reversed itself and increased Coast Guard authority over the cleanup. Admiral Paul Yost, Jr., the Coast Guard commandant, was appointed to lead the effort. Also, the military was ordered to prepare about 1,500 army troops from Ft. Lewis, Washington, to cleanse oil from birds and marine animals and help clean the oil stained beaches. The Pentagon created a joint task force that was to coordinate the use of military oil-skimming equipment including twenty boats and 22,000 feet of oil-trapping booms.[39] Additionally, the president called for a summer program to enlist volunteers to assist in the cleanup effort and ordered a nationwide review of plans to deal with environmental emergencies.

Exxon came in for more criticism when Dennis Kelso, commissioner of Alaska's Department of Environment Conservation, charged that the company's efforts to clean up the beaches have been "entirely inadequate." At that time, only about 9 percent, or 21,000 barrels, of the total spilled had been recovered. More than 160 sea otters and 1,300 birds were estimated to have died as a result of the spill. It was also disclosed that Exxon's slow response to the accident may have been partly the result of cost-cutting efforts in the mid-1980s which affected its spill management personnel. The company had lost nine of its top environmental and spill-control officers during this period.

Also at this time former Exxon employee Bruce Amero went public with claims that Hazelwood, the captain of the tanker Valdez, was often drunk on duty. Amero, who had worked under Hazelwood from 1980 to 1982, was suing Exxon for $2 million, charging that Hazelwood's "abuse and harassment" had caused him to suffer a nervous breakdown.[40] A short time later tapes of radio messages for the Valdez showed that Hazelwood attempted to rock the tanker free from the reef, a move that

the Coast Guard said would have sunk the ship and possibly spilled the rest of its cargo.[41]

By the end of April the cleanup effort had all the makings of a military operation. Exxon had mobilized 460 vessels, 26 aircraft, and the first 2,850 members of what was expected to be a 4,000-person cleanup force. But in spite of these numbers, only 3,300 feet of beach had been cleaned, leaving about 304 miles of shoreline in Prince William Sound alone still contaminated. Meanwhile, the toll on Alaskan wildlife continued to mount. The actual count of 458 otters and 2,889 dead birds was believed to represent only a fraction of the total casualties. Up to 2,000 otters may have perished and some 33,000 birds may have died in the sound. The fishing seasons for herring, herring roe, and pot shrimp were cancelled, and the salmon season was still in doubt.[42]

During the first part of May Exxon presented a revised cleanup plan that left some of the cleanup work to nature. The company held to its September 15, 1989, deadline for cleaning the sound's soiled beaches, despite lowering the estimates of workers needed to cleanse the beaches, and conceded that weather might cut in half the number of days it could access the oil-soaked areas. The plan left the cleanup of 191 miles of "moderately soiled" shoreline to wave action and nature. The plan was immediately criticized for being unrealistic and for not addressing cleanup of beaches outside the sound. By some estimates, as many as 100 miles of beaches in Kenai Fjords National Park may have been soiled, and oil had begun to wash up on the beaches of Katmai National Park more than 250 miles away.[43]

EFFECTS OF THE SPILL

Nearly all previous oil spills had occurred in areas of moderate climate where the waves, currents, and ocean winds helped to disperse the oil. The Valdez spill, however, was the first to occur in an enclosed body of frigid water where these effects do not exist. The fjordlike topography of Prince William Sound was expected to magnify the effects of the spill many times over. Much of the oil became entrapped where the oil's residence time was high and contamination widespread. Because the oil may biodegrade less readily in the sound's subarctic waters, marine life may be slower to return.

Some experts claim that only about 10 percent of the oil in a spill of this magnitude can be recovered. The rest will either evaporate or turn into a thick black gunk that eventually sinks to the ocean floor. These deposits could turn loose harmful hydrocarbons for years after the spill occurred. The contaminants will first enter microorganisms, then the smaller fish that feed upon them, and then the larger sea creatures which feed upon smaller fish, and on up the food chain. Such a process could ruin catches of shrimp, salmon, herring, and crab, wiping out the livelihoods of fishermen.[44]

One of the first effects of the spill was to indefinitely postpone the shrimp and sablefish fishing season. Fishermen reacted bitterly. Questions arose as to whether the herring roe season would be canceled because of the spill. Herring roe, which are herring eggs, are a delicacy in Japan and bring high prices to fishermen, creating an economic boost which carries them through to the summer salmon season.[45] The fishermen feared that the floating kelp beds where herring lay their eggs would be smothered by the oil slick. Other fishermen were concerned for the millions of salmon fingerlings which were to be released from the hatcheries to begin a two-year migration cycle. The fingerlings feed on plankton which may have been poisoned by the oil, thus beginning a contamination that would continue up the food chain. Clams and mussels were expected to survive the spill, but hydrocarbons would probably accumulate in their body tissues, which would then endanger any species that fed upon them.[46]

Before long, waterfowl by the tens of thousands would finish their northward migrations and settle in summer nesting colonies in the sound. More than 200 different species of birds were reported to be in the sound, some 111 of them water-related. The Copper River delta, located at the east end of the sound, is home to an estimated 20 million migratory birds, including one fifth of the world's trumpeter swans. It was later estimated that thousands of sea birds (e.g., cormorants, loons) died, either because oil destroyed their buoyancy or because they were poisoned.[47]

Emergency cleanup teams found ducks coated with crude and sea lions with their flippers drenched in oil clinging to a buoy located near the damaged tanker. Environmentalists feared that a significant part of the sound's sea otter population of 12,000 would be wiped out by the spill. Sea otters die of hypothermia when their fur becomes coated with oil. They may also sink under the surface of the water and drown.[48] Many different kinds of animals were threatened by the spreading oil slick (see box).

Fishermen saw their livelihoods threatened by the spreading oil slick. They called Exxon's cleanup efforts "pathetic" and organized small boat armadas with borrowed or commandeered equipment to help fight the slick. Press conferences held by Exxon turned into town meetings where

Exxon spokespersons were drowned out by the shouts of fishermen. They vilified Exxon for promising them that the oil industry would be ecologically benign. Now the company was making bold promises to clean up the sound and return it to its pristine condition, a claim the fishermen saw as hollow.[49]

Alaska's Menagerie of Catastrophes

The flood of crude fouling the marine reserve encompassing Prince William Sound and its islands is threatening sea life from zooplankton to seals. Thousands of animals have been exposed to the oil; only a few have been brought to rescue centers. The impact of the oil:

Sea Otters: The mammals most vulnerable to an oil spill. Because they have so little body fat for insulation, once petroleum coats their fur, sea otters quickly lose heat and can freeze to death. According to one Alaskan biologist, the 10,000 or so otters that live in the region of the spill could be completely wiped out by the oil spreading from the Exxon Valdez.

Birds: A whole aviary, ranging from cormorants to ducks and terns. Even a speck of oil on its feathers can poison a bird if it ingests it during preening. Thousands of birds have been exposed to the Alaskan oil spill. In previous spills, up to 90 percent of the affected birds were saved by volunteers who had washed the birds in detergent.

Other Mammals: Whales, seals, walruses. Dozens of seals are huddling on buoys to avoid the slick; others are leaping from the water in a desperate attempt to break free of the oil. As yet, there are no reliable figures on their mortality.

Herring: A multimillion-dollar industry. Roe floating on kelp will almost certainly be smothered by the oil; Japanese buyers have already canceled orders. Some fishermen have written off the entire herring run.

Salmon: More spawn in the waters around Valdez than anywhere else on earth. Fishermen managed to protect at least three hatcheries, raising hopes that fry will make it to sea without being contaminated.

Source: "Smothering the Waters," *Newsweek*, April 10, 1989, p. 57.

Petroleum prices soared after the tanker accident, as the spill temporarily halted shipment of crude oil out of Valdez. Producers scaled back production at some of their Prudhoe Bay fields by as much as 60 percent, and talked about halting production altogether if the port was not quickly reopened. Storage facilities, holding oil already shipped through the Alaskan pipeline, were expected to be filled to capacity by the early part of the first week after the accident. Shipments on the pipeline were stopped altogether for four days after the spill, and then resumed at a rate of 800,000 barrels a day. The normal flow through the pipeline is two million barrels a day.[50]

The impact was greatest on the lower 48's West Coast, where refiners depend on Alaskan oil for 60 percent of their needs. Prices at the pump immediately rose 10 cents a gallon and further increases were expected; some independents faced wholesale price hikes of 20 cents a gallon. For several days after the accident, not a single tanker arrived at ARCO's facility on Long Beach where oil is then delivered to the firm's Carson refinery. The 230,000 barrel-a-day refinery normally gets two to three tanker shipments a week.

An Orange County, California, group filed a lawsuit against Exxon asking that the company repay consumers for the higher cost of gasoline following the accident. Consumers felt they were not responsible for the accident and believed Exxon should absorb the costs of increased prices. Exxon responded that it was not gouging the public but was passing on real costs connected with the shortage of oil for West Coast consumers. Meanwhile, the price of gasoline continued to rise, reaching its highest level in three years.[51]

Traffic in the Prince William Sound resumed a few days later, but movement of tankers was significantly limited. The Coast Guard allowed only one ship at a time to enter the sound during daylight hours. Industry officials estimated that 10 to 12 million barrels of crude production had been lost to the market since the oil slick slowed tanker traffic.[52] The pipeline was restored to its normal daily flow on Wednesday, April 5, 1989, almost a week after the accident, even though the Alaskan governor made threats to close it down entirely unless the owners of the pipeline met his terms for improved safety and cleanup measures.

People were frustrated with Exxon and some vented their anger by destroying their credit cards. The New York *Village Voice* urged readers to return their Exxon credit cards to the company in sealed plastic bags filled with oil. Some boycotts were attempted in New York State when Suffolk County ordered its 400 employees to surrender their Exxon cards.[53] Environmentalists later staged a national day of protest against the company and pleaded with customers to boycott Exxon gasoline and destroy their credit cards. Ralph Nader and other speakers called for Exxon to establish a $1 billion trust fund to deal with the disruption the spill caused in the lives of Alaskan natives and in restocking otter populations. But such actions were not expected to have much effect on Exxon. The company stated that only 10,000 out of 7 million outstanding cards had been returned.[54]

A long-term effect of the Valdez spill might be a shift in the balance of power between the oil industry and environmentalists. Alaskan environmentalists lost no time in getting their message out regarding oil and gas exploration on the state's North Slope. While they were unable to prevent development of the North Slope fields, the Valdez disaster gave them new ammunition in their fight against developing the Arctic National Wildlife Refuge (ANWR), which lies between Prudhoe Bay and the Canadian border. As the name implies, the area teems with wildlife and environmentalists want to keep the oil industry out of this preserve.[55]

The ANWR is estimated to have reserves of 3.2 billion barrels of oil. This would allow oil to flow down the trans-Alaskan pipeline for thirty more years after Prudhoe Bay begins to run dry at the end of the century. Also, the area is believed to hold some 30 trillion cubic feet of natural gas, a resource that could be tapped in the future. The Bush administration planned to permit drilling on the coastal plain of the 19 million acre refuge, and in March 1989 the Senate Energy Committee reported out a bill which opened up the ANWR to oil and gas exploration. However, the Valdez disaster put this issue on hold for the session.[56]

Industry lost the trust of the Alaskan public who had believed the oil companies' claims of protecting the environment and now felt betrayed. Because of this betrayal, people are now less likely to believe the Arctic can be developed in a responsible manner. State lawmakers, wanting assurances that industry operations would not further harm the environment, feel state regulation is necessary to enforce industry compliance. The State Senate's president, for example, developed plans for a Spill Response Corps to be organized and maintained by the state but paid for by the oil companies. And the governor insisted that Alyeska put together a believable plan for handling oil spills.[57]

Federal officials began talking about stricter enforcement of existing laws as well as new requirements for tankers to be equipped with double hulls for added protection. Other suggestions deal with tougher personnel rules that would ban drunken drivers from commanding tankers, and proposals for updating the training standards for tanker crews. One of the most controversial proposals deals with testing employees for drug and alcohol abuse.[58] Also considered is allowing the Coast Guard access to the national driver register—used for checking airplane pilots' and locomotive engineers' automobile driving records—for seamen applying for Coast Guard licenses.[59]

Discussion Questions

1. Why was Alyeska not better prepared to deal with an oil spill? What happened over the years to create an attitude of complacency? How can companies guard against this attitude and keep themselves alert to potential accidents?

2. Did Exxon accept responsibility for the spill? In what ways? Why did they get such bad coverage from the media and criticism from the state government and environmentalists? Was it deserved? How could they have responded differently?

3. Is it possible for there to be a balanced approach to industrial development and preservation of the environment? Can industry and the environment live with each other in harmony? How can such a balance be achieved? What policies would you recommend to achieve such a balance?

4. Who are the stakeholders in this case? What rights do they have? What does Exxon owe to each of them? How shall the rights of these stakeholders be balanced against each other? Do the animals whose lives are threatened have any rights? If so, how shall these rights be recognized?

5. Was the federal government right in not taking over the cleanup operation? Would the federal government have been more effective in carrying out the cleanup operation? Why or why not? Did the state government play a constructive role? What could it have done differently?

6. What should be done to prevent such a disaster from occurring again? What technologies exist that may help achieve this objective? What new policies should be instituted on the part of government and oil companies? What about alcohol testing? Should this kind of testing be required of all ship captains? What about rights of privacy?

Notes

1. Michael D. Lemonick, "The Two Alaskas," *Time*, April 17, 1989, p. 63.

2. Larry Pryor, "Grounding of Tanker Caps Lengthy Debate over Risks," *Los Angeles Times*, March 26, 1989, p. I–1.

3. William C. Rempel, "Disaster at Valdez: Promises Unkept," *Los Angeles Times*, April 2, 1989, p. I–20.

4. Ibid.

5. George J. Church, "The Big Spill," *Time*, April 10, 1989, p. 39.

6. Rempel, "Disaster at Valdez," p. I–20.

7. Ibid.

8. Ibid., p. I–22.

9. Ibid., p. I–21.

10. Church, "The Big Spill," p. 40.

11. George Hackett, "Environmental Politics," *Newsweek,* April 17, 1989, p. 18.

12. Lemonick, "The Two Alaskas," p. 57.

13. Mark Stein, "FBI Starts Probe of Valdez Spill as Toll Mounts," *Los Angeles Times,* April 1, 1989, p. I-1.

14. Larry B. Stammer and Mark A. Stein, "New Front Opened in Oil Spill Battle," *Los Angeles Times,* April 8, 1989, p. I-23.

15. Jordan Bonfante, "Nature Aids the Alaska Cleanup," *Time,* May 8, 1989, p. 84.

16. Church, "The Big Spill," p. 40.

17. Rempel, "Disaster at Valdez," p. I-20.

18. Sharon Begley, "Smothering the Waters," *Newsweek,* April 10, 1989, p. 56.

19. Pryor, "Grounding of Tanker Caps Lengthy Debate," p. I-6.

20. Pryor, "Disaster at Valdez," p. I-21.

21. Ibid.

22. Mark A. Stein, "Alaskans Try Impossible Job: Cleaning Up Oil," *Los Angeles Times,* April 4, 1989, p. I-1.

23. Ken Wells and Charles McCoy, "Exxon Says Fast Containment of Oil Spill in Alaska Could Have Caused Explosion," *Wall Street Journal,* April 5, 1989, p. A-3.

24. Mark A. Stein, "Ship Refloated: Former Skipper Gives Self Up," *Los Angeles Times,* April 6, 1989, p. I-1.

25. Begley, "Smothering the Waters," p. 57.

26. Church, "The Big Spill," p. 40.

27. Begley, "Smothering the Waters," p. 56.

28. Church, "The Big Spill," p. 40.

29. Begley, "Smothering the Waters," p. 56.

30. Ibid.

31. Mark A. Stein, "Alaskans Try Impossible Job: Cleaning Up Oil," *Los Angeles Times,* April 4, 1989, p. I-1.

32. Church, "The Big Spill," p. 41.

33. Ibid.

34. Ken Wells and Marilyn Chase, "Paradise Lost: Heartbreaking Scenes of Beauty Disfigured Follow Alaska Oil Spill," *Wall Street Journal,* March 31, 1989, p. A-1.

35. Lemonick, "The Two Alaskas," p. 57.

36. Stein, "Alaskans Try Impossible Job," p. I–1.

37. Ken Wells, "Alaska Begins Criminal Inquiry of Valdez Spill," *Wall Street Journal,* March 30, 1989, p. A–3.

38. Stein, "Ship Refloated," p. I–1.

39. James Gerstenzang, "Bush Vows Greater Federal Role in Oil Cleanup," *Los Angeles Times,* April 8, 1989, p. I–22.

40. Barbara Rudolph, "An Oil Slick Trips Up Exxon," *Time,* April 24, 1989, p. 46.

41. "Captain Tried to Rock Exxon Valdez Free of Reef, Tapes Show," *Wall Street Journal,* April 26, 1989, p. B–5.

42. Jordan Bonfante, "Nature Aids the Alaska Cleanup," *Time,* May 8, 1989, p. 84.

43. Ken Wells, "Exxon's Revised Plan for Spill Excludes Firm's Cleanup of Less-Soiled Beaches," *Wall Street Journal,* May 3, 1989, p. A–4.

44. Church, "The Big Spill," p. 39.

45. Mark A. Stein, "Arrest of Missing Tanker Captain Sought by Alaska," *Los Angeles Times,* April 2, 1989, p. I–1.

46. Wells and Chase, "Paradise Lost," p. A–1.

47. Ibid.

48. Begley, "Smothering the Waters," p. 57.

49. Ibid., p. 54.

50. Allanna Sullivan, "Alaska Oil Spill Sparks Big Rise in Crude Prices," *Wall Street Journal,* March 28, 1989, p. A–2.

51. Donald Woutat, "Flow of Oil to State Rises; So do Gas Prices," *Los Angeles Times,* April 1, 1989, p. I–1.

52. Wells, "Alaska Begins Criminal Inquiry of Valdez Spill," p. A–3.

53. Andrea Rothman, "Who's that Screaming at Exxon? Not the Environmentalists," *Business Week,* May 1, 1989, p. 31.

54. Wells, "Exxon's Revised Plan for Spill Excludes Firm's Cleanup of Less-Soiled Beaches," p. A–4.

55. Michael Satchell, "Tug of War over Oil Drilling," *U.S. News & World Report,* April 10, 1989, p. 48.

56. Ibid.

57. Lemonick, "The Two Alaskas," p. 63.

58. Ibid., p. 66.

59. Charles McCoy and Ken Wells, "Alaska, U.S. Knew of Flaws in Oil-Spill Response Plans," *Wall Street Journal,* April 7, 1989, p. A–3.

1-4

SAVE THE TURTLES

This case was written by Rogene A. Buchholz, College of Business Administration, Loyola University of New Orleans. Research assistance was provided by Carol Zajicek, an M.B.A. student at Loyola University.

The Endangered Species Act was originally passed in 1973 to protect animal species threatened with extinction. It marked the first time a law had been passed in the United States which recognized that animals have a right to exist for their own sake, and that animals must be protected both from human beings and from projects that threaten their existence. The law was based in part on the notion that animals have an intrinsic value apart from their value for human welfare. As such, a law was needed to protect this value as well as give animals a haven from extinction. Since the law's passage, various animals have been placed on the endangered list when their species have become threatened for one reason or another.[1]

Since 1978 all six species of sea turtles found in U.S. waters have been labeled threatened and have been placed on the endangered list to protect them from further decimation. Sea turtles are powerful and imposing creatures which evolved about the time of the dinosaurs. They are fascinating in their own right, and some people are loath to see them disappear. Turtle populations in North America have declined in recent years due to the development of beaches where they breed; butchery of nesting females and theft of eggs from their nests; oil slicks; eating plastic garbage; and nets used to catch fish and shellfish.[2]

The Kemp Ridley sea turtle nests only on one beach—near Rancho Nuevo, Mexico—and is one of the world's most threatened species of sea turtles. The Kemp Ridley's population has declined from 40,000 nesting females a day in the late 1940s to 10,000 in 1960 to little more than 500 in the 1980s. The decline continues at an annual rate of about 3 percent. Their nesting beach is now protected by a detachment of Mexican marines who guard the site against poachers. Shrimp nets are the major suspect in their continuing decline. According to some estimates, approximately 48,000 sea turtles are caught each year on shrimp trawlers in the southeast, and about 11,000 of these turtles die because of drowning, since they must come to the surface every hour or so to breathe. About 10,000 of the turtles that die are Loggerheads, and 750 are Kemp Ridleys.[3]

The Kemp Ridley has a diameter of about 32 inches and may weigh as much as 85 pounds. The breeding season starts in early April and lasts through the first week of September. During this period biologists from the United States and Mexico, together with a contingent of volunteers from both countries, work at the Rancho Nuevo site to improve the turtles' reproduction rate. After a female turtle digs her nest in the sand and lays her 100 or so eggs, she leaves the scene and heads out to sea the moment her clutch has been buried. When left unguarded, the nest may be victimized by predators. To protect the eggs, volunteers transfer them to nests in a nearby corral guarded by the marines.[4]

The shrimping industry disputes government figures showing a close correlation between the number of dead turtles found on beaches and the number of trawlers working in the vicinity. While any one boat may not catch many turtles, the cumulative impact of approximately 7,000 offshore commercial vessels towing 4 to 5 million hours per year can be serious. Shrimpers claim dead turtles are mostly victims of pollution or disease rather than shrimpers' nets. There is evidence supporting both points of view, but there is no doubt that shrimpers are killing a number of turtles along with other nonshrimp organisms. For every pound of shrimp caught, 9 pounds of fish, such as juvenile trout, redfish, whiting, and flounder, are dumped dead over the side of the boat in what is called the by-catch.[5] The by-catch has become more of a problem as shrimping has increased.

Americans eat an average of 2.4 pounds of shrimp a year, making it the most popular seafood in the country. In 1988, 331 million pounds of shrimp, worth $506 million, were caught. The shrimping industry provides jobs for many people in the southeastern part of the United States. More than 30,000 commercial fishermen and their families rely on shrimp for their livelihood, and many more work in shoreside processing plants.[6] Many shrimpers are second and third generation, following in the paths of their fathers and grandfathers. As such, the industry has great social as well as economic value, and any threat to the industry is likely to be met with great resistance.[7]

THE SOLUTION

Such a threat appeared in the form of Turtle Excluder Devices (TEDs), which act as trapdoors in the nets of the shrimpers. The TED is a panel of large-mesh webbing or a metal grid inserted into the funnel-shaped nets of the shrimpers. When these nets are dragged along the bottom of the ocean, shrimp and other small animals pass through the TED and into the narrow bag at the end of the funnel where the catch is collected. Sea turtles, sharks, and other marine species too large to get through the panel are deflected out the trapdoor. The problem is that some of the shrimp escape as well, as much as 20 percent or more of the catch, according to some estimates.[8]

Some fishermen call the TEDs a Trawler Elimination Device. They claim the TEDs, which are about 3 feet in diameter, are dangerous, wasteful, expensive, and unnecessary, and often lead to wholesale losses of catch. "Would you all like to go to work with a big hole in the back of your pants?" asked the wife of a Louisiana fisherman. "That's what they're asking us to do. We can't pull a TED." Many shrimpers simply refuse to use TEDs in spite of laws requiring their installation.[9]

Ironically, TEDs were developed to save the shrimp industry. Since the law requires that endangered species in the public domain be protected regardless of cost, the industry was in danger of being totally shut down if environmental groups were to sue the industry or the federal government. To prevent a total shutdown, the National Marine Fisheries Service (NMFS) sought a technological solution. Between 1978 and 1981 the NMFS spent $3.4 million developing and testing the TED device. By 1981, the agency was promoting voluntary usage of the device and in 1983 began distributing free TEDs to further encourage shrimpers to use them. However, shrimpers rejected the TEDs, claiming they were difficult to use and lost a significant percentage of the shrimp catch.[10]

As more dead turtles washed ashore, environmental groups like Greenpeace and the Center for Marine Conservation demanded an end to the killing. Since the voluntary approach to TEDs had failed, the U.S. Fish and Wildlife Service mandated the use of TEDs, and the Center for Marine Conservation threatened to sue the NMFS and close down the industry completely. Industry representatives agreed to phase in use of TEDs, but rank-and-file fishermen rose up in rebellion. They vowed civil disobedience against what they saw as a threat to their survival, and filed lawsuit after lawsuit, which were all eventually lost in court.[11]

The fight then moved to Congress where the Endangered Species Act was up for renewal. It was hoped that Congress would not require the devices until a study was done to determine (1) whether the turtles to be protected were really endangered, (2) if so, whether the TEDs would protect them, and (3) whether there were better ways, such as increased use of hatcheries, to protect the sea turtle population.[12] After prolonged debate, amendments were passed in early fall 1988 which made the use of TEDs mandatory by May 1, 1989, but only in offshore waters, with the exception that regulations already in effect in the Canaveral, Florida, area remain in effect. Regulations for inshore areas were to go into effect by May 1, 1990, unless the secretary of commerce determined that other conservation measures were proving equally effective in reducing sea turtle mortality by shrimp trawling. Further testing was to be done on TEDs under inshore conditions, but until 1990, inshore turtles had virtually no protection.[13]

FURTHER CONTROVERSY

Disaster struck almost immediately after the amendments were passed. Record numbers of dead turtles began washing up on beaches from Georgia to New Smyrna Beach, Florida. From October to December 1980–1986, 32 Kemp Ridleys had washed ashore, but during these same months in 1988, 70 dead Kemp Ridleys washed ashore along with several other species of sea turtles. Altogether, 201 dead turtles were counted, and since there were 150 to 200 boats working in the area, shrimpers were again blamed.[14] In December 1988 environmentalists pressured the state of Florida into requiring emergency use of TEDs in state waters off Florida's northeast coasts. Florida's mandated use of TEDs was now set for an earlier date than required by the federal government.[15]

As the May 1 federal deadline for implementing TEDs drew closer, fishermen in Louisiana rallied to oppose installation of the device. Officials from across the South pledged to help stop TED legislation from being implemented. Governor Roemer of Louisiana said that state wildlife agents should boycott TED laws until studies showed conclusively that the device worked. Roemer said he would take his concerns to Washington, D.C., and tell George Bush to "read my lips."[16]

Louisiana congressional representatives persuaded the secretary of commerce, who was responsible for implementing TED regulations, to further delay their implementation. This would allow shrimpers additional time to buy and install the devices. Only warnings would be issued through the end of June while a National Academy of Sciences committee studied the issue.[17] However, shrimpers who were caught many times not pulling a TED would be branded flagrant abusers of the new law and could be held liable for civil penalties of up to $12,000 per violation.[18] When the warning period ended, penalties as high as $10,000 would go into effect and the catch confiscated. Criminal violators—those who repeatedly thumbed their noses at the law—could be convicted of a felony and fined $20,000 in addition to losing their catch. Emotions ran high in some Louisiana communities, and many shrimpers vowed to break the law by not pulling TEDs, and dared officials to haul them off to jail. Some vowed to shoot the man that tried to take away their living.[19]

In order to comply with the regulations, many shrimpers installed and tried to use the device. Then nature struck with the largest bloom of seaweed in several years, which clogged the excluder panels and prevented much of a shrimp catch from being taken. Shrimpers who had installed TEDs cut them out of their nets, and the Coast Guard temporarily suspended the regulations for Louisiana coastal waters. Representatives from the state hoped that the secretary of commerce would make the suspension permanent.[20]

Then the secretary of commerce, after initially telling the Coast Guard not to enforce the law, reversed himself. When the shrimpers heard this, they streamed into port to protest, blocking shipping channels in Galveston and Corpus Christi, Texas, as well as several Louisiana locations. The blockade in Galveston halted all ship and ferry traffic, although by midafternoon the shrimpers agreed to let ferries pass through the blockade. The blockade threatened to shut down Houston's oil refineries. There was some violence. An Alabama man was arrested after firing a semiautomatic rifle from his boat in Galveston, and two men were arrested in Corpus Christi for throwing an object through a window of a 41-foot Coast Guard patrol boat. Angry fishermen set fire to a huge pile of TEDs on shore.[21]

The secretary of commerce then announced that he was suspending the use of TEDs until the National Academy of Sciences completed its study. Environmental groups filed suit, claiming that the secretary had caved in to terrorism and had put the Bush administration on a collision course with the Endangered Species Act. Robert E. McManus, president of the Center for Marine Conservation, said the secretary of commerce's decision "is a capitulation to organized violence, assaults against government and private property and individuals, and legitimizes organized efforts by a minority of shrimpers to promote illegal activity."[22]

Meanwhile, researchers for the National Marine Fisheries Service released the results of their research which showed that nets equipped with TEDs resulted in only a 2 to 5 percent reduction in the shrimp catch. These results were at considerable variance with the 20 to 50 percent loss claimed by shrimpers. The results were based on 1,555 hours of trawling off the coast of Louisiana, which produced 12,185 pounds of shrimp in nets equipped with TEDs and 12,391 pounds of shrimp in nonequipped nets. Shrimpers accused the researchers of fudging their data to keep sea turtle research money flowing into their organization.[23]

Experts on the use of TEDs defended their results and accused the shrimpers of refusing to learn how to use the devices correctly. They argued that if TEDs were installed properly the shrimp catch could even be increased. But shrimpers, as victims of a depressed economy which resulted in an increase in the number of competing boats thus contributing to stagnant prices, believed they were fighting for their lives. TEDs were seen as the death-blow to a dying industry, and research data regarding the use of TEDs was rejected. With such a hardened position, nothing short of a court-ordered settlement seemed likely to resolve the issue.[24]

With respect to the lawsuit filed by environmental groups, a federal judge refused to immediately force offshore shrimpers to use TEDs, but directed the secretary of commerce to enforce some immediate turtle protection until he ruled on the TEDs issue. The judge stated that the secretary of commerce's decision to suspend the use of TEDs left sea turtles totally unprotected, but it was not the court's responsibility to determine what protection was appropriate. The secretary then published regulations that required shrimpers to limit their tows to 105 minutes so that any sea turtles caught would not drown. Environmental groups were unhappy with these results, and said they would appeal the judge's decision, arguing that restricting tow times is not nearly as effective in protecting the turtles as TEDs. They claimed that turtles could not survive even 90 minutes underwater.[25]

In order to enforce the trawl limits, the secretary of commerce planned to embargo shrimping altogether for 30 minutes after each 105-minute period. The normal trawl times for shrimpers ranged between 2 and 6 hours. Shrimping would be banned for 11 half-hour periods during a 24-hour day. This fixed routine would allow Coast Guard officials to spot violators. Fishermen who pulled TEDs, however, would not have to adhere to this schedule.[26]

After the Coast Guard reported that 88 percent of the shrimp fleet was not complying with the shorter tow times, the secretary withdrew the limited tow times and required TEDs to be installed once again.[27] The new regulations were to go into effect Friday, September 8, 1989, but until September 22 violators would not be fined if they immediately installed a TED upon being caught. Violators caught between September 22 and October 15 would be eligible for reduced fines if they purchased and installed TEDs, otherwise the fines ranged between $8,000 and $20,000 depending on the circumstances. Agents of the federal government could also confiscate both the boats and their catch.[28]

When President Bush visited New Orleans in September 1989 to address the U.S. Hispanic Chamber of Commerce and the National

Baptist Convention, shrimpers and their families lined his motorcade route protesting the use of TEDs, and more than fifty shrimpers blocked nearby waterways. Instead of confronting the shrimpers, the Coast Guard issued citations that could have amounted to $55,000 per vessel. Shrimpers, who sealed off Belle Pass in Lafourche Parish and the Intercoastal Waterway near Intercoastal City, were cited under two little-used maritime laws. Many shrimpers were cited for one count of anchoring in and blocking a narrow channel and two counts of violating a safety zone as designated by a port captain.[29]

Shrimpers then protested an editorial which appeared in the *Times-Picayune* under the headline "Shrimpers as scofflaws." The protest took place outside the newspaper's main offices in downtown New Orleans. The shrimpers resented being compared to outlaws and wanted the newspaper to listen to their side.[30] The president of Concerned Shrimpers of America then said his groups might sue the federal government for cash compensation for losses caused by being forced to use TEDs. Comparisons were made with ranchers who are subsidized by the federal government if endangered animals feed on their cattle. These payments are designed to stop ranchers from killing the endangered species.[31]

To protect shrimpers from an unfair competitive advantage given to countries that did not require the use of TEDs or other actions to protect endangered sea turtles, Congress considered a law barring these cheaper imports. Even though imports constitute 80 percent of shrimp consumption in this country, the law was not expected to have much of an impact. Most of the shrimp imported into the United States are produced by an aquaculture industry that relies on shrimp farming. China and Ecuador, for example, each of which accounts for about 104 million pounds of shrimp imports, run aquaculture industries. The import provision was inserted into a spending bill by U.S. Senators J. Bennett Johnston and John Breaux, both from Louisiana. The measure ordered the state department to negotiate agreements with countries that do not protect sea turtles to institute similar turtle protection measures to those found in the United States.[32]

In February 1990 shrimpers sued the federal government again, saying TED laws placed an unconstitutional burden on their businesses. The suit was filed in federal court in Corpus Christi, Texas, and sought immediate suspension of the regulations requiring the use of TEDs for offshore shrimpers. Attorney Robert Ketchand, who filed the suit on behalf of the Concerned Shrimpers of America, called the TED laws "regulatory taking" of shrimpers' profits.[33]

The controversy had now come full circle, with the shrimpers pursuing their cause through the courts as they did before the amendments to the Endangered Species Act were passed. Nothing yet has been resolved, and a solution to the problem seems nowhere in sight.

Discussion Questions

1. Is there a technological solution to this problem, or is the nature of the controversy so political at this point that the parties to the controversy have ceased to believe a technological solution exists? If so, what kind of a political solution will work to resolve the controversy?

2. Should the fishermen be paid compensation for the losses they claim because of using TEDs? How should these losses be determined? Who should pay for the protection of endangered species? What is a fair resolution of this issue?

3. Is the on-again, off-again nature of the regulations a serious problem? Was the secretary of commerce right in suspending TED regulations when shrimpers blockaded ports along the Gulf Coast? What else could have been done at this point?

4. What should be done now? Is our system structured in such a way that it can resolve conflicts of this nature? What makes this conflict different from others that seem to get resolved without resort to violence or stonewalling tactics that drag on forever?

NOTES

1. Roderick Frazier Nash, *The Rights of Nature: A History of Environmental Ethics* (Madison: University of Wisconsin Press, 1989), pp. 175–179.

2. Jack and Anne Rudlow, "Shrimpers and Lawmakers Collide over a Move to Save the Sea Turtles," *Smithsonian,* December 1989, p. 47.

3. Ibid.

4. "TEDs Couldn't Keep Gilbert from Attacking Turtle's Beach," *Times-Picayune* (New Orleans), September 20, 1988, p. A–4.

5. Rudlow, "Shrimpers and Lawmakers Collide," p. 49.

6. Ibid., p. 47.

7. Ibid., p. 49.

8. Ibid., p. 45.

9. Christopher Cooper, "La. Shrimpers get Break on TEDs," *Times-Picayune* (New Orleans), July 11, 1989, p. B–1.

10. Rudlow, "Shrimpers and Lawmakers Collide," p. 50.

11. Ibid.

12. Susan Finch, "Congress May Delay TEDs Date," *Times-Picayune* (New Orleans), July 16, 1988, p. A–13.

13. Endangered Species Act Amendments of 1988, Conference Report 100–928 to Accompany H.R. 1467, House of Representatives, 100th Congress, 2d Session, p. 5.

14. Rudlow, "Shrimpers and Lawmakers Collide," pp. 50–51.

15. Ibid., pp. 52–53.

16. Christopher Cooper, "Shrimpers Vow to Defy Law on TEDs," *Times-Picayune* (New Orleans), April 9, 1989, p. B–1.

17. Rudlow, "Shrimpers and Lawmakers Collide," pp. 52–53.

18. Christopher Cooper, "TED Honeymoon May Be a Short One," *Times-Picayune* (New Orleans), May 6, 1989, p. B–2.

19. Christopher Cooper, "Furious Shrimpers Flouting TEDs Law," *Times-Picayune* (New Orleans), July 9, 1989, p. B–1.

20. Cooper, "La. Shrimpers Get Break on TEDs," p. B–1.

21. Christopher Cooper, "Shrimpers' TEDs Protest Turns Violent," *Times-Picayune* (New Orleans), July 23, 1989, p. A–1.

22. Christopher Cooper, "Environmentalists Plan Legal Challenge of TEDs Suspension," *Times-Picayune* (New Orleans), July 26, 1989, p. B–1.

23. James O'Byrne, "Research Disputes Shrimpers' Claims," *Times-Picayune* (New Orleans), July 27, 1989, p. A–1.

24. Ibid.

25. Rick Raber and Christopher Cooper, "Judge Refuses to Force Shrimpers to USE TEDs," *Times-Picayune* (New Orleans), August 4, 1989, p. A–1.

26. Christopher Cooper, "Trawling Schedules Start for Shrimpers," *Times-Picayune* (New Orleans), August 8, 1989, p. A–1.

27. Rudlow, "Shrimpers and Lawmakers Collide," p. 55.

28. Christopher Cooper, "Commerce Department Reinstates TED Regulation," *Times-Picayune* (New Orleans), September 6, 1989, p. A–1.

29. Christopher Cooper, "$55,000 Fines Are Urged for TEDs Blockage," *Times-Picayune* (New Orleans), September 13, 1989, p. B–1.

30. Christopher Cooper, "Shrimpers Picket Newspaper to Protest Blockade Editorial," *Times-Picayune* (New Orleans), September 22, 1989, p. B–5.

31. "Shrimpers May Sue U.S. for Losses," *Times-Picayune* (New Orleans), October 4, 1989, p. B–5.

32. Rick Raber, "TED Provision OK'd for Shrimp Imports," *Times-Picayune* (New Orleans), October 21, 1989, p. A–4.

33. Christopher Cooper, "Shrimpers File Federal Suit against TEDs," *Times-Picayune* (New Orleans), February 22, 1990, p. B–1.

─────────PART II─────────

PUBLIC POLICY, ECONOMICS, AND THE ENVIRONMENT

This background note was written by Alfred A. Marcus and Gordon P. Rands, both of the Curtis L. Carlson School of Management, University of Minnesota.

Federal, state, and local government agencies play major roles in resolving environmental problems. Sometimes all three levels of government are involved, greatly complicating the task of reaching effective solutions. Cost–benefit analysis is often useful, but usually political solutions are necessary. As in Part I, the cases illustrate these issues. The first two concern clean air legislation. Case 2-1 describes the role of Congress and the Ford administration in passing the original Clean Air Act, the complexity of the legislative procedure, and how politics dictate outcomes. The next case provides an interesting contrast—how the 1990 clean air legislation impacted one company, Du Pont, and the political and implementation strategies involved. Case 2-3, about Los Angeles' response to groundwater contamination, illustrates the force of public opinion in getting government agencies to act on environmental issues. Case 2-4, about Ocean Spray Cranberries, Inc., describes how difficult it is to resolve an environmental issue once it has reached the litigation stage. The last two cases in this section concern waste disposal. Case 2-5 is about the cleanup of hazardous waste sites in New Jersey. It shows how delays and increased costs can result when public and private sector cooperation breaks down. Case 2-6 discusses the complex public policy responses to solid waste disposal problems in Rhode Island.

Public policy and economics provide an analytical alternative to the environmentalists' perspective. Rather than limits to growth, the emphasis is on the role of human ingenuity in overcoming these limits. Rather than the benefits afforded by environmental protection, there is emphasis on the costs. Rather than the effectiveness of government programs in cleaning up the environment, there is an emphasis on the limitations of government programs. Rather than scientific information being adequate to the task of providing information to resolve environmental disputes, there is an emphasis on the insufficiency of this information. The public policy and economic approaches intend to introduce a sense of realism into the debate about environmental protection.

In forging solutions to natural resource and environmental problems, society must balance competing ends and invest scarce resources in numerous endeavors. For this reason, the public policy–economic perspective is useful. Society needs to know the true extent of resource limitations. It needs methods to estimate the risks from environmental contaminants and the expense of cleaning up these contaminants. It must have knowledge of the strengths and weaknesses of the solutions offered to environmental problems.

The public puts an immense burden on science to give definitive answers to questions such as, what is the potential for generating energy from solar technologies? or what are the risks to exposed populations from various chemicals? But rarely does science completely stand up to this challenge. Thus, these approaches also compel society to consider how scientific knowledge is generated and how it is used in debates about environmental issues.

ARE THERE LIMITS TO GROWTH?

Environmentalists offer arguments to show that there are limits to growth (Mann and Ingram 1985). They appeal to the historical record noting that numerous ancient civilizations were destroyed because they abused the environment. They use the laws of physics, in particular the notion of entropy, to demonstrate how society systematically dissipates highly concentrated forms of energy, converting them into waste that cannot be used again. Environmentalists use the laws of biology to show that the earth has a limited ability to tolerate the disposal of contaminants. They draw on engineering and management to argue that exceedingly complex and dangerous systems cannot be managed by humans without disastrous consequences. They project current resource use and environmental degradation into the future to demonstrate that civilization is running out of critical resources; the earth cannot tolerate additional contaminants; a crisis and collapse is inevitable; and this crisis will occur in the immediate future. The conclusion that environmentalists draw is that human intervention, in the form of technological innovation and capital investment complemented by substantial human ingenuity, will be insufficient to prevent this outcome unless drastic steps are taken immediately. A doomsday scenario, according to the environmentalists, is possible as early as the late twentieth century.

Policy analysts and economists counter these arguments by pointing out that market forces provide for technological adjustment. The traditional economic view is that production is a function of labor and capital (Kneese 1989). In theory, resources are not necessary since labor and capital are infinitely substitutable for resources. Impending resource scarcity results in price increases which lead to technological substitution for capital, labor, or other resources in scarce supply. Price increases also create pressures for efficiency-in-use, which leads to reduced consumption. Thus, resource scarcity is reflected in the price of a given commodity. As resources become scarce, their prices rise accordingly. Increases in price induce substitution and technological innovation. People turn to less-scarce resources which fulfill the same basic technological and economic needs provided by the resources no longer available in large quantities. The energy crises of the 1970s (the 1973 price shock induced by the OPEC embargo and 1979 price shock following the Iranian Revolution) were solved by these very processes: higher prices leading to the discovery of additional supply and to conservation. By 1985, energy prices in real terms were lower than they were in 1973.

What the environmentalists do not adequately consider is the political, sociological, and psychological nature of the human response to signals of scarcity and degradation. Government programs express the public's collective sentiments, and social movements readjust the public's expectations, attitudes, and values. These feedback loops, expressive of human change as a result of information about resource scarcity and environmental degradation, are not adequately factored in to the doomsday models.

Back at the end of the eighteenth century prophets of doom like Thomas Malthus made predictions about the limits to growth. Today, technological innovation and substitution are responses to societal signals, not to calamity brought about by resource exhaustion. In general, the prices of natural resources have been declining, despite increased production and demand, due to discoveries of new resources and innovations in the extraction and refinement processes. Policy analysts and economists question the motives of the doomsday prophets. The interests of the well off are frequently served by closing the channels to those who are less well-off via arguments that additional growth is limited. A triad of the affluent—"members of the leisure class, intellectuals, and professionals" (Rostow 1978, pp. 146–48; as quoted by Mann and Ingram 1985)—may increase social tension and decrease the prospects for peaceful and democratic settlement of national and international conflicts because of their antigrowth pronouncements.

BALANCING THE BENEFITS AND COSTS

Some environmentalists believe that the total elimination of risk is possible and desirable, but economists and policy analysts argue that the benefits of risk elimination need to be balanced against the costs. Measuring risk is very complicated. It involves determining the conditions and levels of exposure, the adverse effects, and the overall contamination, and must consider long latency periods and the impact of background contamination. Simple cause-and-effect statements are out of the question. The most that can be said is that exposure to a particular contaminant *is likely* to cause a particular disease. Risk is stated in terms of probabilities, not certainties. It has to be distinguished from safety, which is a societal judgment about how much risk society is willing to bear. When comparing technological systems, different types of risks (e.g., mining, radiation, industrial accidents, and climate impacts) may have to be compared, further complicating the judgments that must be made.

Reducing risk involves asking to what extent are the proposed methods of reduction likely to be effective, and at how much cost? In theory, decision making could be left to the individual. Government could provide people with information (e.g., warning labels) and each person would decide what to do, that is, whether to purchase a product or service depending upon the environmental and resource consequences. However, relying upon individual judgments in the market may not adequately reflect society's preference for an amenity such as air quality. Thus, social and political judgments must be made. Science reduces uncertainty in making social and political judgments, but gaps in knowledge remain. Scientific limitations open the door for political and bureaucratic biases that may be irrational. In some instances politicians have framed legislation in ways that seriously hinder, if not entirely prohibit, the consideration of costs (e.g., the Delaney Amendment and the Clean Air Act). In other instances (e.g., the president's Regulatory Review Council) politicians have explicitly forced cost factors to be considered.

Cost factors can be considered in different ways. Analysts can carry out a cost-effectiveness analysis in which they attempt to determine how to achieve a goal with limited resources, or they can carry out formal risk–benefit and cost–benefit analyses in which they quantify both the benefits of risk reduction and its costs.

Economists and policy analysts admit that formal, quantitative approaches to risk assessment do not eliminate the need for qualitative judgments. The commonly used cost–benefit analysis was originally developed for water projects where the issues were not of the same caliber that society faces today (Kneese 1989). For example, how does society assess the value of a magnificent vista obscured by air pollution? What is the loss to society if a given genetic strain of grass or animal species becomes extinct? How does society assess the lost-opportunity costs of spending vast amounts of money on air pollution that could have been spent on productivity enhancement and global competitiveness?

Neither can interpersonal and intergenerational equity issues be ignored when doing a cost–benefit analysis. The costs of air pollution reduction may have to be borne disproportionately by the poor in the form of higher gasoline and automobile prices. The costs of water pollution reduction, on the other hand, may be borne to a greater extent by the rich because these costs are financed through public spending. Regions dependent on high-sulfur coal may ask for help from regions free from high-sulfur coal to pay for scrubbers. The scrubbers save coal mining jobs in West Virginia but impede the development of the coal mining industry in the West where large quantities of clean burning coal are located.

Future generations have no current representatives in the market system or political process. How their interests are taken into account ultimately amounts to a philosophical discussion about altruism: To what extent should current generations hold back on their own consumption for the sake of posterity? Should Bentham's "achieving the greatest good for the greatest number" be modified to read "sufficient per capita product for the greatest number over time"? These questions about intergenerational equity are particularly poignant given that most people today do not have "sufficient per capita product," and to ask them to reduce their consumption for the sake of some future generation may be asking for too great a sacrifice. Also, achieving moral consensus in a world of diverse cultural values would be extremely difficult. The extent to which political coercion should play a role in achieving global consumption and procreation standards has to be considered. Economists and policy analysts have no simple answers. These are ethical issues that require choosing some appropriate ethical rule.

The ethical issues have numerous rules that can be used for their resolution. Economists offer the Pareto Optimum which is often formulated as a situation where no one can be better off without making someone worse off. John Rawls creates a contemporary liberal philosophy around the following: "Each person is to have an equal right to the most extensive basic liberty compatible to similar liberty for others"; and "social and economic inequalities are to be arranged so that they are both: (a) reasonably expected to be to everyone's advantage and (b) attached to offices and positions open to all." (From John Rawls, *A Theory of Justice* (Cambridge, MA: Harvard University Press, 1971) as cited by Tom Beauchamp and Norman Bowie, *Ethical Theory and Business* (Englewood Cliffs, NJ: Prentice Hall, 1983), p. 603.) Robert Nozick formulated the contemporary libertarian position as "any act that improves an individual's (or several individuals') well-being and harms no one is then moral or 'right.'" These rules are in conflict. They cannot be easily reconciled. (From Robert Nozick, *Anarchy, State, and Utopia* (New York: Basic Books, 1974), as cited by Beauchamp and Bowie, p. 610.)

MARKET AND GOVERNMENT FAILURES

Ordinarily, markets are a superior means for fulfilling human wants. Deals are struck when both parties believe they are likely to benefit. Society gains from the aggregation of the many individual deals because the parties involved believe they are likely to benefit. The wealth of a society grows by means of a "hidden hand" that offers spontaneous coordination with a minimum of coercion and explicit central direction. Policy analysts and economists justify government intervention only under special conditions: (1) Markets are not perfectly competitive; (2) market participants are not fully informed; and (3) property rights are not appropriately assigned. It is this last condition that provides the main justification for government intervention for the sake of natural resource and environmental protection. Nature often lacks a discrete owner. Its rights can be violated by market exchanges between consenting parties. It is a "common property resource" which is subject to overuse and degradation. If not for government, nature would be inadequately protected from deals affecting it. The term that economists and policy analysts use to describe this process is an externality. A nonconsenting third party who is not involved in the deal is unintentionally harmed by it. The consenting parties are able to damage the third party without compensating it. Thus, the exchange does not adequately reflect the true costs to society. When the third party is a large and diverse group, it cannot easily pursue remedies in the courts. In attempting to gain compensation for the damage done, it suffers from the problems of collective action. It is not sufficiently in the interest of any single member of the group to sue. Thus, government intervention is needed to protect what has been harmed.

Government involvement, however, is not always effective. In the same manner that there are market failures, there are government failures. With respect to voters and politicians, the signals that are sent may be inadequate. Voters may not understand the issues well enough to formulate options for politicians; or decision making may be dominated by interest groups, partisanship, ideology, financial deals, or personal arrangements. In some cases, civil servants cannot successfully implement the laws because the goals are too diverse, the problems are intractable, the resources are insufficient, the political opposition is too great, other issues gain higher priority, and bureaucratic in-fighting sabotages the effort. Economists and policy analysts speak of a "deadweight cost" of any government program which must be balanced against the proposed benefits. Wolf (1988) proposes the term "'internalities,' i.e. the inefficiencies derived from the very nature of the public decision-making system."

THE USE AND MISUSE OF SCIENTIFIC INFORMATION

One of the main causes of government failures is the lack of adequate information to make good decisions. Unveiling scientific assumptions behind public policy debates need not lead to undue cynicism. To use the technical language of economics, the most important choices are made under conditions of "residual risk," implying that complete knowledge of probabilities is not available nor is the decision made entirely random. Some knowledge exists but it is not perfect. Moreover, the knowledge that exists changes. Choices concerning policy and implementation are made and remade in response to a process of sorting out what is known and unknown; a process that depends on the imperfect capabilities of individuals, groups, and organizations to perceive risk and to act on the basis of their perceptions.

Implicit in this process is an evaluation of "societal negligence." Derived from the classic formulation of Judge Learned Hand, this concept postulates that in evaluating risk, a "reasonable" person considers (1) the probability of injury, (2) the gravity of the injury should it occur, and (3) the burden of taking adequate precaution (Cooter and Ulen, 1988; Landes and Posner, 1987). Judge Hand argued that if the expected injury exceeds the costs of precaution and the defendant takes no action, then the defendant is negligent. Extended to society at large, the costs of precaution arising from a risk are balanced against the probability of harm multiplied by the costs of harm as follows:

1. If the probability of harm multiplied by the costs is greater than the costs of precaution, then there is negligence if the actions to prevent the harm are not taken.
2. On the other hand, if the costs of precaution are greater than the expected harm, then there is no negligence even if actions to prevent the harm are not taken.

Different groups in society make this trade-off differently. Social movements (environmentalists), for example, are likely to emphasize the probability and costs of harm while downplaying the burdens of precaution. This is because they are unlikely to obtain support if they admit the likelihood of harm is low or the uncertainties about the probable danger are great. Also, the actions that need to be taken when the expected danger is great are frequently in accord with these movements' philosophies of more government involvement, slower growth, and simpler living. Corporations, on the other hand, are likely to focus on the burdens of precaution. They will downplay both the probability and costs of harm because the burdens of precaution that affect them have far-reaching implications for products and how these products are made. The government, in contrast, should be guided by rational and scientific judgments, but because the uncertainties are great, both elected officials and bureaucrats can be swayed by the viewpoints of social movements and corporations.

The evolution of policy often depends on the attention span of various publics. Broad social movements lose the capacity to follow an issue once it moves from policy formulation and the symbolic enactment of new legislation to the details of policy implementation and the carrying out of the legislation. During the enactment stage, the public policy process can be captured by social movements with their exaggerations about the likely harm to befall the public if action is not taken. On the other hand, it is industry that has the advantage during implementation. After all, industry has to make the changes needed to make the legislation effective. If it balks and refuses to act, there is little that public officials can do to coerce it. Industry's advantage during the implementation stage lies in its ability to make claims about the costs of precaution. It has the staying power to be involved with an issue through both the enactment and implementation stages, a staying power that the social movements, which require a broad public to be mobilized, cannot sustain.

This view ignores the fact that public policy issues are inherently difficult to resolve with certainty. The social movements and industry groups are both contributing information, albeit of a limited form, to the debate. Broadly, this debate concerns the matter of "societal negligence." The social movements contribute information about the expected harms. The industry groups contribute information about the costs of precaution. Public officials are caught in the middle. They tilt at one moment toward the social movements and at another moment toward industry. Their limitation is that they appear to pay serious attention to only one side of the equation at any point in time. Resolution of this uncertainty is as much what the debate is all about as is the effort to capture public officials for the ends of either social movements or industry.

REFERENCES

Robert Cooter and Thomas Ulen, "An Economic Theory of Torts," *Law and Economics* (Glenview, IL: Scott, Foresman, 1988).

Allen Kneese, "The Economics of Natural Resources," in M. Teitelbaum and J. Winter (eds.), *Population and Resources in Western Intellectual Traditions* (The Population Council, 1989), pp. 281–309.

William M. Landes and Richard A. Posner, *The Economic Structure of Tort Law* (Cambridge, MA: Harvard University Press, 1987).

Dean Mann and and Helen Ingram, "Policy Issues in the Natural Environment," in H. Ingram and R.K. Goodwin (eds.), *Public Policy and the Natural Environment* (Greenwich, CT: JAI Press, 1985), pp. 15–47.

Charles Wolf, Jr., *Markets or Governments: Choosing Between Imperfect Alternatives* (Cambridge, MA: MIT Press, 1988), p. 66.

2-1

THE AUTO EMISSIONS DEBATE: THE ROLE OF SCIENTIFIC KNOWLEDGE

This case was written by Alfred A. Marcus and Mark C. Jankus,
both of the Curtis L. Carlson School of Management, University of
Minnesota.

On February 10, 1970, President Nixon delivered his "Message on the Environment" in which he proposed that environmental protection and natural resource programs be combined in a new Department of Natural Resources.[1] The president delegated to the Advisory Council on Executive Organization, better known as the Ash Council, the responsibility of working out the details of his proposal. The Council, headed by Roy Ash, a former Litton Industries executive, hoped to merge existing departments and agencies and create four "super-departments"— Community Development, Economic Affairs, Human Resources, and Natural Resources. However, elements in Congress and the administration opposed this plan, and what emerged was a much more modest proposal to create the Environmental Protection Agency (EPA). The EPA began operations on December 2, 1970.

THE 1970 CLEAN AIR ACT

In his statement Nixon stressed the need to merge pollution control programs in order to manage the environment "comprehensively"; but his plan for comprehensive management did not come about. At the time Nixon was reorganizing environmental programs in the EPA, Senator Edmund Muskie, Democrat from Maine and head of the powerful Senate Subcommittee on Air and Water Pollution, was considering amendments to the Clean Air Act. With public concern over air and water pollution rising, Muskie was an attractive contender for the presidency.[2] A speaker at April Earth Day rallies, Muskie was generally respected within the ranks

80

of the environmental movement. Because of his national exposure as a vice presidential candidate, he was a front-runner among Democratic presidential contenders, and his activities were scrutinized daily by reporters who covered national issues. In May 1970 the national media publicized accusations hurled at the senator by a Ralph Nader study group.[3] These accusations evoked commitment to a stronger Clean Air Act from Muskie. After the Nader report appeared, Muskie directed the Senators in his subcommittee to search for "handles" that would force the automobile industry to achieve air quality goals by a specific date.

The search for "handles" addressed a problem of regulatory administration which scholars have called "vague delegation of authority."[4] According to this argument, the typical regulatory statute has indefinite provisions. In effect, Congress says to the bureaucracy, "Here is the problem—deal with it." The regulatory agency does not have the binding authority it needs to coerce industry into achieving statutory goals. The remedy for problems attributable to vague and ill-formed legislation is to draft statutes that have clear goals and explicit means of implementation. The 1970 Clean Air Act, passed into law on December 31, 1970, mandated that auto manufacturers achieve a 90 percent reduction in hydrocarbon and carbon monoxide emissions by 1975, and a 90 percent reduction in nitrogen oxide emissions by 1976.

According to Lester B. Lave and Gilbert S. Omenn, the foundations of this law were fundamentally "flawed."[5] To start with, the air quality goals were "based on incomplete data and large margins of safety."[6] Moreover, the rollback model, which assumes a reduction in emissions will result in an equivalent improvement in air quality, was too strict.[7] The required 90 percent reductions were taken from calculations of the highest levels of carbon monoxide emissions ever recorded in Chicago, the highest levels of nitrogen oxide emissions ever recorded in New York, and the highest levels of hydrocarbon emissions ever recorded in Los Angeles.

These technical and scientific considerations, however, were not what motivated Senator Muskie. During the conference committee sessions the automobile manufacturers—through the intervention of Health, Education, and Welfare Secretary Elliot Richardson—tried to extend the 1975–1976 deadlines to 1980–1981, but Muskie did not want to appear as if he were caving in to industry. He believed that government needed to apply pressure to get the automobile industry moving. A five-year deadline, even if scientifically unsound and technically unfeasible, would force the manufacturers to reduce pollution as fast as they could by whatever means available. Muskie took pride in the "strong, tough" air pollution legislation he helped draft.[8] The questioning of his environmental record by the Nader group elicited a commitment to stringent legislation.

ENERGY SHORTAGES

Meanwhile, President Nixon warned the American people about the possibility of energy shortages. On June 4, 1971, in his first energy message to Congress, Nixon argued that the rate of energy consumption was outpacing the production of goods and services, and the American people could no longer take their energy supply for granted. In August 1971, largely in response to presidential initiatives, Congress authorized research and development in superconducting transmission, energy storage, solar energy development, geothermal resources, and coal gasification.[9] The president also created a Special Energy Committee of senior White House advisers and a National Energy Office to identify issues and coordinate analysis.

In the early 1970s a petroleum shortage afflicted much of the country. According to industry, price controls instituted by the Nixon administration to fight inflation were the cause of the winter 1971–1972 heating oil shortage. The gasoline shortage in the summer of 1973 was due to price controls as well as the tax depletion allowance and import quotas and fees.[10] In April 1973 Nixon noted that the United States had only 6 percent of the world's population but it used one third of the world's energy. As a consequence, the energy shortages and higher prices were likely to continue. In June of that year, at the urging of Roy Ash, then director of the Office of Management and Budget, the president established a White House Energy Policy Office. He also proposed that Congress create the Energy Research and Development Administration (ERDA). ERDA would combine the research and development activities of the Department of Interior and the Atomic Energy Commission (AEC), while the AEC's regulatory and licensing functions would be transferred to the newly created Nuclear Regulatory Commission. In September 1973 President Nixon urged that Congress pass bills that would provide for the construction of the Alaskan pipeline and deep-water ports for petroleum-carrying ocean tankers. He also called for new surface mining standards and proposed that natural gas prices be deregulated.

THE ARAB OIL EMBARGO

Although there had been shortages of oil prior to the fall of 1973, no one anticipated that the Organization of Petroleum Exporting Countries (OPEC) would impose an embargo. On October 6, 1973, the Syrian and

Egyptian armies launched a surprise attack on the state of Israel, and oil shipments from the Arab oil-producing oil countries to the United States and the rest of the free world were severely curtailed. In the United States consumers experienced two- to three-hour waits in line for gasoline, truck drivers blockaded highways to protest fuel shortages and price increases, and in some states the National Guard had to be called out to maintain order. The embargo resulted in an approximate 10 percent cut in the total oil supply and wrought a tremendous change in the nation's way of life.[11]

In a televised address to the nation on November 7, 1973, President Nixon urged the American people to engage in such voluntary conservation measures as lowering thermostats, driving slower, and eliminating unnecessary lighting. He also launched the much vaunted "Project Independence" to free the United States from dependence on foreign oil; and, on December 4, 1973, established the Federal Energy Office (FEO) in the White House to consolidate federal energy-related efforts, allocate reduced fuel supplies, and control prices. Former deputy secretary of treasury William Simon became the nation's first "energy czar" as head of the FEO. Simon was assisted by ex-OMB official John Sawhill, who eventually replaced Simon when Simon became secretary of the treasury.

MODIFICATIONS IN THE CLEAN AIR ACT

Before delivering his January 1974 State of the Union address, Nixon presented a special report on "The Nation's Energy Future." Calling for the establishment of the Federal Energy Administration (FEA) to replace the FEO and coordinate new resource development and conservation efforts, he proposed that Congress allocate $10 billion for research and development. He urged Congress to modify the Clean Air Act, saying that the interim 1976–1977 auto emissions standards should be extended so that manufacturers could concentrate on fuel economy, and smokestack emissions standards should be altered so that it would be easier for oil-burning facilities to switch to coal.

The automobile emissions deadlines had already been extended once. In April 1973 the EPA granted a one-year extension for hydrocarbons and carbon monoxide, and in July it granted a year extension for nitrogen oxides. These extensions came after the United States Court of Appeals for the District of Columbia found in February 1973 that economic considerations had to be taken into account despite claims to the contrary by the EPA's administrator William Ruckelshaus. In June 1974 Congress passed the Energy Supply and Environmental Coordination

Act, which extended the emissions deadline for yet another year.[12] Congress also gave auto manufacturers the right to ask for still another one-year extension. Now the final reduction in emissions would not be required until the 1977 models, with the prospect that auto manufacturers could ask for still another extension.

To meet the emissions standards then in effect, auto makers had taken a number of steps that reduced the fuel economy of 1973–1974 autos by about 10 percent over that of 1970's autos.[13] For compacts, the reductions were 6 percent and for standard- and luxury-size vehicles, the reductions were 15 percent. However, a large percentage of the losses in fuel economy of 1973 and 1974 automobiles was caused by the retarded spark timer used to control hydrocarbons and carbon monoxide emissions and the exhaust gas recirculation system that controlled nitrogen oxides. EPA officials believed that if the auto companies used catalytic converters instead of these techniques there would be virtually no fuel penalty. In a 1974 report the National Academy of Sciences found that the original 90 percent reductions could be met by auto companies equipped with catalysts without sacrificing fuel economy. By switching to catalysts rather than using techniques for engine tuning the auto companies could improve fuel economy at the same time that they reduced pollution.[14]

THE ACID EMISSIONS PROBLEM

Shortly after the 1974 Energy Supply and Environmental Coordination Act was passed, the Ford Motor Company asked for a third one-year extension of the auto emission deadline. Ford's reason was that sulfuric acid emissions had been discovered in the discharges of the catalytic converters. Ford brought the problem of "acid emissions" to the EPA's attention in February 1973. This issue, however, remained dormant until the fall of 1973 when John Moran, an EPA research scientist, held an unauthorized press conference which alerted the public to the "danger." Moran, a health effects researcher located at Research Triangle Park—the EPA's scientific complex near Durham, North Carolina—made public a study he had done showing that although catalysts reduced hydrocarbons and carbon monoxide, they caused significant amounts of sulfuric acid to be emitted with probable adverse effects on public health. Moran's study pointed out that the catalytic converter, which was supposed to eliminate the health hazards caused by air pollution, actually caused a health problem. The catalyst tended to convert the small amount of sulfur emitted from the engine as SO_2 into SO_3. The SO_3 then combined with water vapor in the exhaust stream to form sulfuric acid, H_2SO_4, and other acid sulfates. Emissions of these sulfates by automobiles was minute, but in regions of high traffic density Moran was concerned that the level of sulfur emissions could become hazardous to health.

Moran's statements were attacked by EPA staff. EPA staff held their own unauthorized press conference where they accused Moran of leaking information about health risks because he wanted EPA headquarters to continue funding his emissions testing program. They claimed that only under special circumstances were the emissions of sulfuric acid significant; otherwise sulfuric acid emissions were too small to make a difference. Only at sufficiently high concentrations were adverse health effects associated with sulfuric acid, but these high concentrations were not likely to occur.

The unauthorized press conferences took place during a transition period between William Ruckelshaus, who left the EPA as administrator, and Russell Train, who had been designated to succeed Ruckelshaus. Train confronted questions about the conflict during his nomination hearings and agreed to launch a program to resolve the issue of the health effects of sulfuric acid emissions. After Train became administrator, Moran's lab in North Carolina was given the authority to determine the comparative health effects associated with sulfuric acid emissions in relation to the health effects associated with hydrocarbon and carbon monoxide emissions.

PRESIDENT FORD'S RESPONSE

On December 28, 1974, President Ford proposed that interim standards on HC and CO be reduced to 0.9 and 9 grams respectively on 1977 to 1981 models, with the final 90 percent reduction to be achieved only in 1982. His justification for the new delay was the finding that catalysts might produce sulfuric acid mist: "If the auto emissions standards are further lowered, then changes in the catalytic converter control system would be mandatory. This could produce substantially more sulfuric acid which my advisors believe we should not accept."[15] The president was also aware that tightened exhaust standards might have adverse impacts on his administration's energy and economic policies. In his statement the president said that tighter controls on auto exhausts would reduce the mileage per gallon of gasoline and that the catalytic converter would raise the price of cars and discourage new-car sales. FEA administrator Zarb mentioned the gas mileage issue at a later briefing and suggested that it had affected the decision to delay the exhaust cleanup. "It became clear," Zarb said, "that moving to these standards would require a penalty in fuel."[16]

In essence, the president endorsed Ford Motor Company's request for a delay without the benefit of new technical information being compiled by the EPA, and he did not consult with Train prior to his endorsement of the delay. On January 30, 1975, the EPA released the results of a study which estimated that the health risks from sulfuric acid emissions would exceed the benefits from reduced hydrocarbon and carbon monoxide emissions after four model years. The media again ran stories on the "acid emissions" problem, and Train felt that he had no choice but to grant auto manufacturers the additional extension. Train also supported an amendment to the 1974 law that would postpone achievement of the 1977 standards for hydrocarbons and carbon monoxide to 1982 and give EPA and industry more time to resolve the "acid emission" controversy. Predictably, environmentalists criticized Train's decision as a sell-out, but surprisingly, General Motors was disappointed. Unlike Ford and Chrysler, GM had spent hundreds of millions of dollars on catalyst research, built an expensive plant for the fabrication of catalysts, and signed long-term contracts for obtaining the precious metals used in the catalyst.

THE 1975 CONGRESSIONAL HEARINGS

In 1975 Congress held hearings to determine the appropriate balance between the clean air, energy, and economic goals of the country, as reflected in the existing Clean Air Act of 1970 (CAA).[17] All the participants in this debate—environmentalists, industry, representatives of the administration, and experts who were called to testify—used the language and rhetoric of science to advance their positions. Each interest group's arguments were buttressed by some form of scientific study.[18] As the hearings progressed, however, it became clear that the state of technology and scientific knowledge did not provide definitive answers to the congressmen's questions. Studies by reputable scientific organizations came to conflicting conclusions, and some of the scientific experts who testified stated bluntly that conclusions could not be based on such inadequate information.

On March 13, 1975, the House Subcommittee on Health and the Environment began hearings on issues related to amending the 1970 CAA.[19] The decision on whether to recommend an extension of the statutory deadlines for auto emissions, in line with the Ford administration proposal, was not simple. The committee had to sort out a number of complicated policy issues concerning energy, the economy, and the environment. The technical nature of the related issues meant that committee members had to make sense of the scientific evidence that was conflicting and inconclusive. The main issues were:

1. Would air pollution be a significant health problem if emissions standards were frozen at the 1975 levels for three to five years?
2. Should the EPA set a sulfate emissions standard? What should it be? When should it be instituted?

   Just how serious a health threat was the sulfuric acid emitted by catalytic converters?

   How should the relative benefits and risks of using catalysts be balanced?

   Was desulfurization of the gasoline supply a feasible solution to the problem?

   Was there sufficient low-sulfur gasoline available to blend with higher-sulfur gas so that the problem could be mitigated while desulfurization proceeded?
3. Were nitrogen oxides a health threat at current standards? If not, what should the standards be?
4. Was the technology for the production of cars available to meet the final statutory standards?

   Did that technology have to be catalysts?
5. Could industry meet the 40-percent-increase-in-fuel-economy goal if the schedule for meeting the statutory standards was not relaxed?
6. What would the costs to the consumer be under the different alternatives?
7. What would the costs to industry be?
8. How credible was the industry position, given its track record of protesting that advances were impossible yet accomplishing them nevertheless?
9. How reliable were the scientific data on the issues?

RUSSELL TRAIN'S TESTIMONY

Russell Train represented the EPA at these hearings. He began his testimony by praising the intent of the 1970 CAA, as did most of those who testified.[20] Train's position on the issues is paraphrased as follows:[21]

Auto emissions have been decreasing, and will continue to decrease as new cars replace the older, uncontrolled cars. Current standards are 83 percent below the pre-1970 level, and "very substantial progress" has been made towards cleaning up the air.

EPA scientists have concluded that sulfate emissions represent "a very real threat" and the threat to the health of the public will exceed the benefits that the catalysts provide within two to four years. A sulfate standard for the 1979 models is necessary and will be proposed within two months.

Desulfurization of the fuel stocks is not a feasible option because it would cost the refining industry billions in capital costs, would extract a significant energy penalty at the refining point, and could not be done before the 1978 cars that need it are produced.[22] Refining oil to remove sulfur results in a 1/2%–2% energy penalty, or decrease in the amount of gasoline produced, depending on the degree of desulfurization. According to Train's testimony, the costs of desulfurizing fuel to a meaningful level (30-50 ppm) would cost $8–$24 billion, extract a 1-1/2%–2% energy penalty, and take four years to complete. There is enough low-sulfur fuel to use for blending for two years; after that, supply would lag behind demand.

The NOx standard should be frozen at 2 grams per mile in order to allow industry time to develop alternative engine designs that are fuel efficient and meet the statutory standards.

The technology to meet the statutory standards is available, and there is a good deal of evidence that catalysts are not required to meet the current 1975 standards; U.S. auto makers chose to use them, but many foreign manufacturers did not.

The president's fuel economy goal is achievable under the EPA's proposed timetable.

As for the industry's credibility, Train said, "We are not privy to all of the research effort going on in industry—and I don't know if there is any way to really become fully informed on everything going on in industry—and I am reasonably sure that given competitive and other reasons, the industry isn't going to be doing things it doesn't have to in terms of meeting regulatory standards."[23] Train admitted that the studies upon which the EPA based its decisions were not perfect, but nevertheless provided the best data. The information was made public and there was no real disagreement with it. The decision to grant an extension of the deadlines and request further extensions was based solely on the sulfate threat. Health issues were the only relevant consideration. The decision was made without consultation with the FEA or any other agency.

FRANK ZARB'S TESTIMONY

In his testimony Zarb repeatedly expressed his interest in reaching a compromise that would protect the environment as well as reduce the energy and economic penalties caused by meeting the emissions standards. The key points of his formal statement were that

1. there was a growing dependence on foreign oil;
2. conservation was important because motor vehicles consumed one fifth of all U.S. energy; and
3. President Ford's agreement with the auto industry to improve fuel economy by 40 percent by 1980 in return for a five-year freeze on standards would conserve a significant amount of energy and reduce foreign imports of oil by 10.6 percent by 1980.[24]

With regard to EPA administrator Train's proposals to freeze emissions standards at more lenient levels and to set a sulfuric acid standard, Zarb said:

> We are assessing Mr. Train's recommendation in relation to a 40 percent fuel economy improvement by 1980. We are hopeful, that at the levels proposed by Mr. Train, the automobile manufacturers will still be able to meet the 40 percent fuel economy improvement goal. We plan to meet with representatives from Department of Transportation and EPA to explore this matter further.
>
> While catalysts allow for re-tuning of the engine, which contributed to the 1975 model year increase in fuel economy, we concur with Mr. Train's findings that the potential exposure of the public to increased sulfuric acid mist may prove to be significant in the long term. We also concur that his proposed standards can be attained by technologies other than the catalyst.[25]

Although, as his statement indicates, the FEA agreed that the sulfuric acid problem was significant, it was not in the FEA's interest to have the sulfuric acid problem be determined significant enough to warrant scrapping catalyst technology. Without catalysts, the emissions standards could only be met, if at all, by tuning the engines in such a way that fuel economy would be significantly decreased.

In order to counter the EPA study which suggested that the sulfuric acid threat was significant enough to warrant action, the FEA commissioned Tabershaw/Cooper Associates, an independent consulting group, to reassess the study. The language used in the FEA's "Request for a Proposal" suggested what conclusions the agency was looking for in the reassessment:

> The subject EPA document represents a compendium of health research which strongly implicates atmospheric sulfate with mortality and morbidity . . . . Review by FEA staff and several EPA personnel indicates that there are grave reservations in accepting the estimates and associations presented in the above EPA document . . . . A critique is proposed that . . . should delineate clearly the scientific uncertainties and technical weakness involved in making national estimates . . . derived from epidemiological evidence. Not only should the critique be scientifically valid, but it should stand as a public document representing an independent appraisal of EPA work."[26]

Tabershaw/Cooper was awarded the contract on a noncompetitive basis. The major findings of the Tabershaw/Cooper study were

1. The environmental and medical evidence published by the EPA did not support conclusively the position of the EPA with respect to the health effects of sulfur oxide emissions.
2. The assumption that the health effects of sulfur-bearing air pollutants were largely due to the formation of sulfates was theoretical in that no quantitative cause-and-effect relationship had been demonstrated and the promulgation of quantitative criteria and standards based on this assumption was unwarranted and unsubstantiated in light of present knowledge.[27]

Train disagreed with the conclusions of the Tabershaw/Cooper study when he testified before the Senate committee, stating that there was "absolutely no question whatsoever" that there was a basis for concern over the sulfate issue.[28]

The Tabershaw/Cooper study, which most of the committee members had not yet seen when Zarb testified, took a lot of criticism from members of the committee as well. Senator Jennings Randolph pointed out that the EPA study had taken eighteen months to complete and was undertaken by the government's own scientists, while the FEA turned to outsiders who had taken only two months to complete their analysis. Randolph questioned the motivation for seeking an outside consultant's opinion:

> Randolph: "Then you, Mr. Zarb, turned to an organization outside of the federal government. Someone might say that you wanted a tailormade report; however, I am not saying that."

Zarb: "Who might say that, Senator?"

Muskie: "Senator, you certainly put those unthinkable thoughts out for the public to view."

Randolph: "But I do say that here was 18 months of work—"

Muskie: "I just said, I couldn't have done better myself."[29]

Zarb was put on the defensive concerning the study and qualified his support for the study's findings, saying, "I just thought it was in the best interest of all concerned to make it available freely, so we could all look at it and judge its contribution for whatever it is worth."[30] The FEA's attempt to discredit the EPA study was itself cast into doubt.

Discussion Questions

1. How were environmentalists likely to interpret this debate? What were they likely to do?

2. What impact would the environmentalists have on Congress?

3. What was Congress likely to do? What was the EPA likely to do? What was the FEA likely to do? Would the president intervene?

4. What about the different companies in the automobile industry—what should they do? Should they act individually (recall that GM had a very different view of catalysts than Ford or Chrysler) or in concert through their trade association? If they had different positions that they publicly expressed with respect to catalysts and their health impact, would this hurt their cause? Would this damage their credibility?

5. What should the members of the Manufacturers of Emission Controls Association do? Should they align themselves with the environmentalists? Should they align themselves with industry? Which companies in industry should they approach? Should they commit themselves to commissioning another scientific study? What should they do in order to be most effective?

6. What does this debate say about the way policy deliberations are carried out in Washington? What does it say about the role of scientific knowledge?

7. What about the role of the scientific and technical community in this debate—how would you evaluate it?

8. Does this tale of air pollution policy in the Ford administration give you more or less confidence about the ability of the democratic political process to grapple with complicated scientific issues?

NOTES

1. Alfred Marcus, *Promise and Performance, Choosing and Implementing an Environmental Policy* (Westport, CT: Greenwood Press, 1980), pp. 31–53.
2. Alfred A. Marcus, "Environmental Protection Agency," in James Q. Wilson, *The Politics of Regulation* (New York: Basic Books, 1980).
3. John C. Esposito, *Vanishing Air* (New York: Grossman, 1970) pp. 287-298.
4. See Roger Noll, *Reforming Regulation: An Evaluation of the Ash Council Proposals* (Washington, D.C.: The Brookings Institution, 1971); and Theodore Lowi, *The End of Liberalism* (New York: W.W. Norton, 1969).
5. Lester B. Lave, and Gilbert S. Omenn, *Clearing the Air* (Washington, D.C.: The Brookings Institution, 1981), pp. 30–31.
6. Ibid., p. 30.
7. Ibid., p. 31.
8. *Congressional Record* (December 15, 1970), pp. 520597–99.
9. Jack M. Holl, "The Nixon Administration and the 1973 Energy Crisis: A New Departure in Federal Energy Policy," in George H. Daniels, and Mark H. Rose, *Energy Transport: Historical Perspectives on Policy Issues* (Beverly Hills: Sage, 1982), p. 152.
10. David Davis, *Energy Politics* (New York: St. Martin's Press, 1978), pp. 91–92.
11. Ibid., p. 91.
12. *Energy Supply and Environmental Coordination Act of 1974*, P.L. 93-319 (88 Stat. 248), 1974.
13. *Report on Automotive Fuel Efficiency* (Washington, D.C.: EPA, February 1974).
14. John Quarles, *Cleaning Up America* (Boston: Houghton Mifflin, 1976), p. 194; and Committee on Motor Vehicle Emissions,

Semi-Annual Report (Washington, D.C.: National Academy of Sciences, February 12, 1973).

15. Theodore Bogosian, *Automobile Emissions Control: The Sulfate Problem* (Cambridge, MA: Harvard University, Kennedy School of Government, Case C15-76–077, 1975), p. 14.

16. Ibid., p. 14.

17. P.L. 91-604 (84 Stat. 1676), December 31, 1970.

18. See Samuel Hays, "Clean Air: From the 1970 Act to the 1977 Amendments," *Duquesne Law Review*, Vol. 17, No. 1, 1978–79, p. 40.

19. U.S. Congress House of Representatives, Subcommittee on Health and the Environment of the Committee on Interstate and Foreign Commerce, *Hearings on the Clean Air Act Amendments 1975, Part 1*, 94–25, 94th Congress, 1st Session, March 13–26, 1975.

20. Ibid., transcript, p. 34.

21. Ibid., condensed and paraphrased from Train's testimony; see transcript at 34–137, 1165–1209.

22. Ibid.

23. Ibid., transcript, p. 1188.

24. Ibid., transcript of testimony, pp. 138–206; and U.S. Congress, Senate, Subcommittee on Environmental Pollution of the Committee on Public Works, *Hearings on the Implementation of the Clean Air Act—1975*, 94-H10, 94th Congress, 1st Session, 1975, pp. 282–672.

25. See Zarb's testimony, Senate Subcommittee on Environmental Pollution, p. 345.

26. Ibid., p. 353.

27. Ibid., pp. 401–402.

28. Ibid., p. 289.

29. Ibid., p. 293.

30. Ibid, p. 294.

2-2

THE 1990 CLEAN AIR ACT
AND DU PONT

*This case was written by Mark C. Jankus under the editorial
guidance of Alfred A. Marcus, Associate Professor, Curtis L. Carlson
School of Management, University of Minnesota.*

By the time Congress recessed for the 1990 Memorial Day holiday it was
clear that new clean air legislation would soon be passed, legislation that
would have a greater impact on Du Pont than any legislation ever had.[1]
Both the House and Senate had passed amendments to the nation's Clean
Air Act, and after the holiday lawmakers would reconvene in a conference
committee to reconcile the two versions, as well as to accommodate the
Bush administration's concerns. That would be Du Pont's last chance to
influence the legislation, if it chose to do so.

As one of the ten largest companies in the United States and, according to government reports, the nation's fifth largest polluter, E.I. Du Pont
de Nemours and Company had more at stake than perhaps any other
company. The question now facing Du Pont was which strategy to adopt
with respect to the new legislation. Du Pont could simply prepare to
adapt to the coming legislation, for there would be winners as well as
losers within the company; but this meant leaving important business
decisions entirely in the hands of the politicians. Clearly, the strategy
chosen would have wide-ranging consequences.

THE CLEAN AIR ACT

The Clean Air Act (CAA), enacted in 1970, was intended to protect people and property from the ill effects of air pollution.[2] The three titles of
the law dealt with pollution from both stationary (industrial plants,
buildings, and factories) and mobile sources (cars, trucks, buses, and airplanes). The CAA originally required the nation's air to be clean by 1975.
However, this proved impossible, and the law was amended in 1975 and
1977 to allow more time for industry to either comply or deal with newly

discovered pollutants and ambiguities in the law. By 1982 most of the nation's air quality control regions had met the set limits for four of the six major pollutants: lead, nitrogen oxides, particulates, and sulfur oxides. Ozone and carbon monoxide proved more intractable, and some parts of the country had failed to attain the standards set for these pollutants by the end of the decade. Progress had been made overall, though. The EPA reported that between 1978 and 1987 the level of carbon monoxide had dropped 32 percent; lead by 88 percent; nitrogen dioxide by 12 percent; ozone by 16 percent; particulate by 21 percent; and sulfur dioxide by 35 percent.

Environmentalists, however, were not satisfied with this progress, citing the threats that airborne pollutants posed to forests, waterways, and wildlife when precipitated out of the atmosphere in the form of "acid rain." Their efforts to amend the CAA in the 1980s failed, largely because of the deregulation ideology of the Reagan administration. But by 1990 the political situation had changed. The Senate finally passed a clean air bill in April 1990, and the House completed voting on its version one day in late May. The new clean air bill covered smog, alternative fuels, toxic emissions, and acid rain (see boxes).

Much rested on the final form the amendments took after the conference committee finished its deliberations. The administration estimated that the bill would cost U.S. industry—already spending $33 billion a year on air pollution control—at least another $21.5 billion annually; more than the 1989 earnings of General Motors, General Electric, Ford Motor, IBM, and Exxon combined.[3] The amendments designed to combat acid rain could mean double-digit electricity rate increases for the heavily industrialized Midwest. The nation's coal miners could expect to lose thousands of jobs. Antipollution equipment could raise the price of a new car by $600. On the other hand, the estimated expected benefits were also significant: air pollution was contributing to the premature deaths of over 50,000 people per year and costing the nation $10 to $25 billion annually in health care.[4] In the ranks of industry there would certainly be both winners and losers. For each company that would have to spend some of the upwards of $20 billion that the air act was supposed to cost, there would be other companies that would win substantial dividends as the recipients of that spending.[5]

Smog

Some ninety six areas missed the deadline for meeting health standards for ozone, a main ingredient of smog. The new bill requires that all but nine areas comply by November 1999, all but Los Angeles, Baltimore, and New York by 2005, Baltimore and the NYC area by 2007, and Los Angeles by November 2020.

Areas that are moderately polluted or worse must cut smog 15 percent within six years. After that areas that are seriously polluted or worse must make 9 percent improvements every three years until they meet the standards.

Tougher tailpipe standards are phased in starting with 1994 models to cut nitrogen oxides by 30 percent and hydrocarbons by 40 percent. Even deeper cuts are required for 2003 models if the EPA finds they are cost-effective and needed. These standards have to be maintained for ten years or 100,000 miles.

Warranties on pollution control equipment must last eight years or 80,000 miles for catalytic converters and electronic diagnostic equipment and two years or 24,000 miles for other pollution gear.

Special nozzles are required on gasoline pumps in almost sixty smoggy areas. Also, fume-catching canisters are to be phased in on all new cars, starting in the mid-1990s. Gauges are also required on cars to alert drivers to problems with pollution-control equipment.

Industrial polluters that emit as little as 10 or 25 tons of smog-forming chemicals a year may have to make cuts, depending on the severity of smog in their areas. The present law sets the limit at 100 tons a year. Forty-three other categories of smaller pollution sources, including printing plants, are also regulated.

Alternative Fuels

Beginning in 1995 all gasoline sold in the nine smoggiest cities must be cleaner-burning, reformulated gasoline that cuts emissions of hydrocarbons and toxic pollutants by 15 percent. By the year 2000 the reductions must equal 20 percent.

Starting with 1998 models, fleets of ten or more cars in the two dozen smoggiest cities must run 80 percent cleaner than today's autos. Trucks must be 50 percent cleaner. Requirements could be delayed three years if clean vehicles are not available.

By the model year 1996, car makers must begin producing at least 150,000 super-clean cars and light trucks annually under a California pilot program designed to launch vehicles that can run on non-gasoline fuels, such as natural gas and methanol. By the year 2001 even cleaner models must be produced.

Toxic Emissions

Only seven chemicals have been regulated since 1970, but over the next ten years the majority of polluting plants must use the best technology available to reduce their emissions of 189 toxic chemicals by 90 percent.

For any remaining cancer risks, the EPA is required to set health-based standards that produce ample margins of safety—a cancer risk of not more than about one in 10,000—for people living near factories. Coke ovens are eligible for extensions until 2020 if they made extra-stringent reductions in the first round.

The alternative fuels program should significantly reduce toxic emissions from vehicles. Additional cuts from cars or fuel is required after an EPA study. Benzene and formaldehyde must be controlled.

Acid Rain

In the first phase, the 111 dirtiest power plants in twenty-one states must cut sulfur-dioxide emissions by 1995 for a total cut nationwide of 5 million tons. Two-year extensions can be given to plants that commit to buy scrubbing devices that allow continued use of high-sulfur coal.

In the second phase, more than 200 additional power plants must make sulfur-dioxide cuts by 2000, for a total nationwide cut of 10 million tons. This deadline can be extended until 2004 for plants that use new clean-coal technology.

An innovative trading system is created in which utilities that make extra-deep pollution reductions get credits they can sell or swap to utilities that want to increase their emissions. Bonus pollution credits are awarded to dirty utilities that install scrubbers and to power plants in high-growth and extremely low-polluting states plus the hard-hit Midwest.

A nationwide cap on utility sulfur-dioxide emissions is imposed after the year 2000.

Utilities must cut nitrogen-oxide emissions by 2 millon tons a year, or about 25 percent, beginning in 1995.

No help is provided for ratepayers beyond changes in the trading system. Coal miners and others put out of work because of clean-air rules may qualify for extra weeks of unemployment pay under a $250 million five-year job assistance program.

DU PONT AND THE NEW CLEAN AIR ACT

The new legislation, which experts called economically more significant than any ever passed, would have profound consequences for Du Pont. The corporate giant, founded in the early nineteenth century as an explosives manufacturer, had $35.5 billion in sales in 1989, 10 percent higher than in 1988 (see Tables 2-2-1 and 2-2-2). The company had made a name for itself by harnessing science for commercial purposes. Du Pont's laboratories were the birthplace of Nylon, Teflon, Orlon, Dacron, Lycra, and Kevlar. Du Pont helped General Motors develop Freon® (see Case 3-7), and became the first producer of the ubiquitous chemical. The company produced a wide range of products, from pesticides to biomedical equipment. The new CAA had economic implications for most of Du Pont's businesses, but the chlorofluorocarbon, chemical, coal, and gasoline businesses were particularly affected.

CHLOROFLUOROCARBONS

Chlorofluorocarbons (CFCs) are a group of chemical compounds prized by industry for their stability, economy, nontoxicity, and wide range of uses: for example, coolant in refrigerators and air conditioners, foaming agents in many types of insulation, and solvents for cleaning electronic equipment (see case 3-7).

Du Pont's Freon® Products Division is the largest producer of CFCs in the world, supplying half the U.S. demand and 25 percent of demand worldwide. Though CFC sales are significant (Du Pont's sales are about $750 million), their future is limited because of the threat they pose to the earth's stratospheric ozone layer, which protects the planet from harmful ultraviolet radiation. In 1974 a wave of concern following the discovery of this threat led to a 1978 ban on the use of CFCs as aerosol propellants in the United States, Canada, and several Scandinavian countries. But concern waned until 1985 when the "ozone hole" over Antarctica was discovered. When stratospheric ozone measurements showed that the ozone layer was being depleted faster than the best models had predicted, political leaders from around the world agreed to phase out CFCs, an agreement codified in the Montreal Protocol in 1987. The Protocol calls for a cap on the production of CFCs at 1986 levels by the year 1989, and a 50 percent reduction in production by 1998.

In 1988 Du Pont—acting on its pledge to stop production of CFCs if proved harmful—vowed to completely stop its production of CFCs in 2000. The company shifted its attention to developing a marketable substitute, spending $5 million in 1985, more than $30 million in 1988, and

Table 2-2-1

Summary of Results

	1989	1988	1987
Sales	$ 35,534	$ 32,360	$ 29,931
Net income	2,480	2,190	1,786
Earnings per share	3.53	3.04	2.46
Dividends per share	1.45	1.23⅓	1.10
Net return on equity	15.7%	14.6%	12.9%

Dollars in millions, except per share
Source: 1989 Annual Report.

Table 2-2-2

Industry Segments

	Sales			After-Tax Operating Income		
	1989	1988	1987	1989	1988	1987
Industrial products	$ 3,702	$ 3,082	$ 2,636	$ 629	$ 355	$ 319
Fibers	5,966	5,465	5,012	729	676	601
Polymers	5,581	5,423	4,783	455	531	475
Petroleum	12,314	10,995	10,560	538	391	277
Coal	1,818	1,757	1,770	223	226	157
Diversified business	6,153	5,638	5,170	307	275	271
Total company	$ 35,534	$ 32,360	$ 29,931	2,881	2,454	2,100
Interest and other Corporate expenses Net of tax				(401)	(264)	(314)
Net income				$2,480	$2,190	$1,786

Dollars in millions
Source: 1989 Annual Report.

planning to spend more than $1 billion on the effort by 2000. Known substitutes like propane, carbon dioxide, or pentane were dangerous, inferior, or more expensive. A promising possible substitute that Du Pont called 132b had to be scrapped when it was discovered the compound caused sterility in male rats.

By early 1990 the company rested its greatest hopes on a class of chemicals called HFCs and HCFCs. These chemicals performed many of the same tasks as CFCs, but because their molecular composition allowed them to break down before they reached the upper atmosphere, they had either zero (HFCs) or only 2 to 10 percent (HCFCs) of the ozone-depleting capacity of CFCs. In 1987 Du Pont estimated that these compounds could be produced at two to five times the cost of CFCs. Though more expensive, they were not prohibited under the Montreal Protocol and appeared to be the most viable alternative. But while the Montreal Protocol did not restrict HCFC use, the new House and Senate bills would. The bills would freeze production of most HCFCs in 2015 and ban nearly all production in 2030. Both dates were decades earlier than the 2030 to 2050 time frame Du Pont had determined reasonable.

This posed a serious obstacle to Du Pont's plans for the substitute chemical. Customers would be hesitant to adapt to a substitute that would itself be phased out. For example, HCFC-22 could be used in automobile air conditioning systems, but only if the systems were substantially redesigned to handle the higher operating pressures necessary to use HCFC-22. General Motors executives estimated the necessary retooling would cost their company $600 million.

Up until 1986 Du Pont had disputed the scientific basis for the ozone threat and led the effort to oppose restrictions on CFC production. The company was instrumental in forming the Alliance for Responsible CFC Policy, an industry trade group that lobbied for an approach to CFC regulation that took into account the economics and usefulness of the compounds. But when new scientific information on the ozone hole appeared in 1986, Du Pont changed its strategy and came out in favor of an international approach to the ozone problem. The company was concerned that the United States might undertake unilateral limitations on CFC production, giving a competitive advantage to foreign CFC producers.

The new CAA bills again raised the threat of unilateral action, but this time with respect to HCFCs. In March 1990, citing competitive issues, the company sent a letter to its Freon® customers urging them to contact their congressmen to protest the legislation for an earlier-than-planned phase-out of HCFCs. Nonetheless, both House and Senate bills mandated the early phase-out. Publicly, Du Pont executives were silent on how the company would respond. But even before debate on the issue began, Du Pont had designed its first new commercial-size HCFC plant to initially produce only small quantities of the chemical, in case a market did not develop.

Du Pont managers were now faced with hard decisions about where to focus the CFC and CFC substitute divisions' energies. How hard should it lobby Congress to end the early ban on HCFCs? To what extent should it redirect its research and development efforts to other possible substitutes? Did these substitutes exist?

If Du Pont was going to lobby Congress and redirect its corporate development strategy, it needed an assessment of the scientific and technical issues that was clear, understandable, and definitive. However, scientific and technical knowledge was in such a state of flux that coming up with such a statement would not be easy.

CHEMICALS

Two major provisions of the proposed CAA legislation had substantial implications for Du Pont's chemical operations (Du Pont was the largest U.S. chemical company; eighty or more plants could be affected). First, the Senate bill would require chemical plants to stop production unless they reduced toxic emissions to the point where people living near the plant face no more than a one-in-ten-thousand risk of getting cancer from these emissions. Several Du Pont plants in Texas and Louisiana, emitting carcinogens like carbon tetrachloride (which is used to produce synthetic rubber), had been cited by the EPA for posing an unacceptable cancer risk to nearby residents. Some of these cited plants already controlled their toxic emissions through state-of-the-art technology, and additional safety measures to further reduce emission levels would be very expensive. Achieving the mandated risk level would be difficult, and proving it even more so. Risk analysis is a tricky business. Different groups of experts use different assumptions, which can be contested not only in the legal system but in the court of public opinion as well, where estimates of risk raise emotions and arouse both public concern and controversy.

Unlike the Senate bill, the House did not specify an acceptable level of risk; instead it relied on the EPA to conduct further risk-assessment studies and make recommendations to Congress. These studies could take years to complete and digest, time Du Pont could use to plan for the needed changes. Du Pont favored the House bill, but was unsure what if anything it should do to pressure Congress. Becoming too identified with the House's position might backfire. Environmentalists could use industry backing as a tactic to obtain more stringency from Congress.

The second major provision, contained in both versions of the bill, required that every production line nationwide install the best available emissions control technology. The measure was designed to reduce toxic fumes by 90 percent. If a company could not on its own meet the 90 percent reduction, EPA would set the standards for that company, defining what the best available control technology would be and requiring the company to install it.

Toxic fumes are blamed for 2,700 potential cancer cases annually (0.2 percent of all reported cases) as well as other health problems. The cost to industry of the best-technology requirement was pegged at $5 billion per year. However, Du Pont, acting on its own, had already begun spending hundreds of millions of dollars to reduce its emissions by 60 percent (from 1987 levels) by 1993. This was in addition to their ongoing reductions in air pollutants, tracked since the early 1970s. If Du Pont were to continue with its own plan, it might be able to meet the 90 percent reduction guideline, which would exempt it from EPA-specified emissions control measures. On the other hand, if it failed, millions of dollars would have been spent on control equipment that did not meet the EPA requirement. Whether to continue or wait for EPA regulations to be clarified was a key issue for the chemicals division.

COAL

After a decade of debate Congress and the administration were ready in 1990 to combat acid rain. Formed when sulfur and nitrogen oxides precipitate out of the atmosphere, acid rain damages forests and lakes, particularly in the Northeast. A major culprit is the high-sulfur coal used by some coal-burning energy utilities and industrial plants. Du Pont's Consolidated Coal subsidiary is one of the two biggest high-sulfur coal producers in the country, with high-sulfur coal accounting for 60 percent of its production.

Congress and the administration were largely in agreement on the provisions that would address the acid rain problem. Under the plan, utilities would be forced to cut sulfur dioxide emissions by 10 million tons per year by 2000, at a cost of about $4.1 billion per year. The president's proposal included an innovative pollution-trading system which would allow utility companies that cut their emissions by more than the required amount to sell their "unused" pollution rights to utilities that could not meet the standards.

Because many utilities would find it cheaper to buy low-sulfur coal than to invest in costly emissions control technology, Consolidated executives estimated that up to $40 to $50 million in annual revenue would be lost, up to 750 to 800 company coal miners would lose their jobs, and perhaps half of the company's four high-sulfur coal mines would be forced to close starting in 1995. Again, it was unclear what Du Pont should do. Protesting to Congress at this late date was likely to be futile. There seemed to be little opportunity for creative adjustment to this change in government policy, other than adjustment to lost revenues.

GASOLINE

The proposed CAA amendments that dealt with gasoline seemed to offer the most opportunity for Du Pont's Conoco subsidiary, stemming from the fact that a gasoline meeting the standards proposed for the mid-1990s had not yet been developed. Both the Senate and House versions of the legislation would require that cleaner-burning gasoline be sold in nine of the nation's smoggiest locations: Los Angeles, New York City, Houston, Chicago, Milwaukee, Baltimore, San Diego, Philadelphia, and much of Connecticut.[6] Together, these areas comprise 25 percent of the U.S. gasoline market, but a very small portion of Conoco's market. The Senate version specified what the reformulated gasoline should contain, while the House version allowed refineries more leeway as long as they met the minimum performance standards. If the oil industry failed to persuade lawmakers to change the reformulation requirement, there would be a large market for any company that came up with an acceptable, workable formulation. Conoco researchers started working on the problem shortly after President Bush unveiled his clean air proposal requiring cleaner fuels. Should Du Pont support Congress despite the oil industry's opposition?

When the Senate passed the reformulation amendment, industry trade groups and companies were caught off guard. They then undertook an unprecedented, multimillion-dollar lobbying effort to defeat a similar amendment in the House.[7] Conoco neither contributed nor initiated its own effort. A $1 million newspaper ad campaign attacked both the gasohol lobby, which was pushing for the reformulation provision, and Congressman Bill Richardson (New Mexico), who sponsored the provision. Several oil companies set up 800 numbers, encouraging shareholders to call or send prepaid mailgrams to Congress protesting the amendment. Employees and dealers were urged to deluge Congress with mail on the subject. The American Petroleum Institute, an industry trade group, circulated API-financed research that discounted the benefits of reformulated gasoline.

The lobbying blitz backfired. According to an environmental lobbyist involved with the legislation, not only did the oil industry lack credibility, but House members were irritated by its heavy-handed tactics.

Consequently, the barrage of mail and attention on the issue confirmed the belief of many lawmakers that Congress needed to define exactly how gasoline should be reformulated, rather than leave it to the oil industry to decide.

Should Du Pont support the efforts of Congress at the cost of alienating the oil industry? Could the benefits of supporting Congress' desire to define exactly how gasoline was to be reformulated be traded for congressional aid on other aspects of the proposed Clean Air Act that were of interest to Du Pont (e.g., HCFCs)? If Du Pont was to support Congress' effort, should it provide its expert assistance and technical help in advising Congress with respect to its own research about gas reformulation? Would doing so in any way reveal trade secrets that might be used by its competitors?

WHAT NEXT?

The CAA amendments in their final form would substantially determine how Du Pont would spend its environmental equipment budget, which was slated to be $500 million by 1991. But other costs would increase as a result of the legislation as well, for example, the company's electric bill. By some calculations, Du Pont—which uses about 0.5 percent of all the electricity generated in the United States—could expect to spend up to $40 million more per year in energy costs alone. There were opportunities as well. Du Pont's fledgling environmental services business was projected to expand tenfold during the 1990s, up to $1 billion per year. Management first had to develop a strategy for the upcoming conference committee: how to approach the legislation in the short term and how to prepare for its implementation in the long term.

Discussion Questions

1. What should Du Pont's strategy be vis-a-vis the proposed legislation?

2. What type of scientific and technical information does it need in order to develop a strategy?

3. What type of economic information would be persuasive with Congress and with the American public?

4. How should Du Pont approach environmentalists? Should it attack or try to work with them on this bill? How can it work with the environmentalists given the stake it has in these issues?

5. What about health and safety? How persuasive is the government's case? Should Du Pont do anything to counter the government position?

6. Should Du Pont suspend all lobbying at this late date (after two bills have been passed and Congress is simply in the process of resolving disparate items in the two bills) and concentrate on the strategic changes it will have to make in its operations in response to the coming passage of a new Clean Air Act?

7. What types of changes in Du Pont's business strategy will the CAA signify? What opportunities are there for Du Pont with the passage of this bill? How will it affect Du Pont's position vis-a-vis its competitors?

NOTES

1. Barbara Rosewicz and Richard Koenig, "How Clean Air Bill Will Force Du Pont into Costly Moves," *Wall Street Journal,* May 25, 1990, p. A–1.

2. Clean Air Working Group, "The Clean Air Act: A Primer & Glossary," pamphlet.

3. Barbara Rosewicz and Rose Gutfeld, "Clean Air Legislation Will Cost Americans $21.5 Billion a Year," *Wall Street Journal,* March 28, 1990, p. A–11.

4. David Wessel, "Air Bill's Cost–Benefit Data Look Very Foggy Close Up," *Wall Street Journal,* May 25, 1990, p. A–7.

5. Rose Gutfeld, "Firms, Environmentalists Gear Up for Crucial Round," *Wall Street Journal,* May 25, 1990, p. A–7.

6. Allanna Sullivan and Rose Gutfeld, "Bill Would Require Oil Companies to Sell Advanced Fuel," *Wall Street Journal,* May 25, 1990, p. A–7.

7. Jill Abramson, "Big Oil May Have Misfired in Heavy Lobbying Drive," *Wall Street Journal,* May 25, 1990, p. A–6.

2-3

GROUNDWATER CONTAMINATION: A CITY WITH PROBLEMS

This case was written by Rogene A. Buchholz while the Visiting Hilton Professor of Business Ethics at Loyola Marymount University, Los Angeles, California. The author acknowledges the assistance of Lloyd B. Dennis, Executive Director of Public Affairs, and Sandra S. Tanaka, Manager, Information Systems for the Public Affairs Division of the Los Angeles Department of Water & Power, who provided information for the case and who read early drafts making suggestions for improvement.

The City of Los Angeles receives its water supply from three sources. About 80 percent comes via aqueduct from the Owens River and Mono Basin watersheds. These areas, located about 300 miles north of Los Angeles, contain abundant streams fed by snowmelt from the eastern slopes of the Sierra Nevada mountain range. Another 15 percent comes from the San Fernando Valley Groundwater Basin, which provides enough water to supply five to six hundred thousand people. This basin is made up of layers of clay, sand, and gravel which naturally contain large quantities of water. The water is drawn from wells located throughout the valley. The remaining 5 percent of the city's water supply comes from the Metropolitan Water District, which delivers water wholesale from the Colorado River or the Sacramento River delta via the State Water Project.[1]

In addition to supplying annual water needs, the San Fernando Valley Groundwater Basin holds large quantities of stored water, which is extracted during droughts and replenished during years of surplus water supplies. The basin has an estimated total groundwater storage capacity of 3.2 million acre feet, and is estimated to contain approximately one million acre feet of usable stored groundwater.[2] The estimated annual value of groundwater produced from this basin, based on current rates, is $15 million, and based on water replacement costs of new water supplies, $30 million.[3]

The basin is an important source of drinking water for Los Angeles as well as for Burbank, Glendale, and San Fernando, and for the unincorporated area of La Crescenta. While only 15 percent of Los Angeles' water supply comes from this basin, it provides nearly all of San Fernando's and about half of La Crescenta's requirements. This resource will become increasingly important in the future, due to the expected loss of imported surface water supplies. It must be protected and not allowed to become contaminated.

THE PROBLEM

In late 1979 the California Department of Health Services (DHS) requested that all major water purveyors using groundwater conduct tests for the presence of certain industrial chemicals. This request was part of a statewide groundwater quality surveillance effort. The initial tests were completed in the spring of 1980 and showed that hazardous substances such as trichloroethylene (TCE) and perchloroethylene (PCE) were present above state action levels in a number of San Fernando Valley water production wells. The primary contaminant, TCE, was found at concentrations exceeding the state action level in forty-seven of the valley's 120 production wells. In addition, PCE concentrations above state action levels were found in thirty-nine valley wells.[4]

TCE and PCE are widely used for machinery degreasing, dry cleaning, and metal plating. Some of the current contamination was traced back to the period between 1940 and 1967 when disposal of large quantities of chemical wastes was unregulated and the effects of the disposal unknown. After it became apparent that these chemicals posed significant risks to human health, the state set temporary guidelines, or action levels, for contaminants in drinking water at five parts per billion (ppb) and four ppb for TCE and PCE respectively.[5] The five-ppb standard is the level that may cause one additional cancer per million people if they all drank two liters of water a day for seventy years. TCE was virtually eliminated in 1966 when restrictions were placed on its use, but PCE continued to be used in dry cleaning establishments and in industry.

In response to the test findings, the Los Angeles Department of Water and Power (DWP) and the Southern California Association of Governments (SCAG) received funds from the Environmental Protection Agency (EPA) to embark on a two-year study of the problem. The study, which began in July 1981, was to determine the extent and severity of the contamination and to develop strategies to control the groundwater contamination problem. Specific objectives of the study included: (1) defining and describing the extent and severity of present groundwater contamination in the San Fernando Valley Groundwater Basin, (2) investigating and examining information relative to potential sources of the contamination, (3) developing and evaluating engineering and regulatory strategies for controlling the contamination problem, and (4) recommending specific programs or actions necessary for protection and usage of the basin, including proposed funding alternatives for the implementation of remedial action.[6] The study's overall objective was to develop a basinwide groundwater quality management plan that included recommendations for implementing strategies to ensure the future protection and safe use of the basin.

Activities of the study included field investigations, industrial site surveys, searches of archives and other records, literature reviews, and water quality analyses of more than 600 samples.[7] The investigation of potential sources of groundwater contamination included: (1) commercial and industrial establishments, (2) accidental spills and unintentional releases of hazardous materials, (3) dry weather urban drainage, (4) landfills, and (5) other commercial waste sources that included private disposal systems and sewer ex-filtration and permitted industrial waste discharges. The approach of the investigation was to examine all potential sources of groundwater contamination and to evaluate current industrial practices for the handling, storage, and disposal of hazardous materials.[8]

The study determined that the contamination, located primarily in the upper zone of the basin, was spreading. About 45 percent of the water supply wells in the eastern portion had contaminant concentrations exceeding the state action levels. The study concluded that "although it was not possible to determine the specific origins of the contaminants or to accurately define contaminant plume patterns, there appeared to be a distinct relationship between groundwater contamination and commercial and industrial developments."[9]

The contamination was believed to be a result of disposal practices used two or three decades ago before priority pollutant designations and adequate hazardous materials regulations became established. The study also pointed out that both TCE and PCE are not subject to significant biodegradation under existing conditions in the basin, and that the only apparent method of reducing the level of contaminant concentration was through removal. Because corrective measures were costly, the report recommended that a maximum effort be mounted to prevent further input of hazardous chemicals to the groundwater in order to assure the continued safe use of the basin in the future.[10]

The problem was one of eliminating the causes of contamination—by controlling and regulating hazardous materials to minimize future contamination of the basin—and reducing or eliminating the contamination already present in order to assure a continued water supply that was safe for drinking. The problem of existing contamination was temporarily dealt with by shutting down highly contaminated wells and by blending water from wells with lower levels of TCE and PCE with untainted water from other wells or from the Los Angeles aqueduct. This blending reduced contamination concentrations enough to meet state action levels.

The long-term solution, however, consisted of a number of recommendations that were part of the San Fernando Valley Groundwater Management Plan. The report recommended eight specific groundwater management strategies, including regulation of private disposal systems; regulation of storage tanks, sumps, and pipelines; a program to deal with small-quantity hazardous waste generators; landfill regulations; a groundwater monitoring program; and aquifer management and groundwater treatment. Also recommended was a public education program to impress upon the public the importance of groundwater protection. It was hoped that the educational effort would gain support for and compliance with the recommended programs. These measures were implemented under the direction of a 12-member Interagency Coordinating Committee. Such coordination was necessary to assure the most efficient and effective arrangement and utilization of manpower.[11]

FURTHER DEVELOPMENTS

Occasionally contamination levels in water from the San Fernando Basin would increase. For example, in October 1985 when a concrete channel bringing water from the Owens Valley broke, investigators had to tap eight to ten extra wells. When these wells were opened for normal monitoring, it was discovered that TCE levels had jumped to 11.97 ppb on average, well above the five-ppb state action level. The highest level of TCE, 12.7 ppb, was reached on October 7, 1985. Also, the DWP had to draw on the wells during warmer weather, which increased TCE concentrations. During May 1984 for example, the average was 8.3 ppb, while the average for the entire period of September 1984 to August 1985 was 3.5 ppb. Similar emergency situations posed a problem for the water department.[12]

In November 1985 the results of a new state study were released showing that contamination of underground wells was a major problem in the San Fernando Valley and other parts of Los Angeles County. Forty percent, or 127 out of the 318 wells in the entire state found to be contaminated with one to thirty industrial or agricultural chemicals, were located in Los Angeles County. Of these 127 wells, sixty-nine had levels of one or more contaminants that exceeded state guidelines or legal limits. The state health director said this result was not unexpected since they were already aware of significant contamination in the San Gabriel and San Fernando valleys. The report was based on a check of more than 2,500 wells operated by 753 large water systems which provided drinking water to about half the state's population.[13]

Then in December 1985 the state Water Resources Control Board designated 150 dumps and landfills for further testing to determine whether they were leaching hazardous wastes into groundwater supplies. Sixteen of these sites were in Los Angeles County and were among the more than 1,800 solid waste sites that had not been included on earlier lists of hazardous waste sites. Legislation enacted in 1984 required the board to rank dump sites on a statewide basis according to potential hazards and to conduct surveys at the rate of 150 per year. This testing would either detect problems or help reassure the public that the site was safe. The legislation was intended to look at dump sites not considered dangerous enough to be on the state Superfund list of the most hazardous sites.[14]

In the early part of 1986 the press began accusing the City of Los Angeles of lagging behind in getting the problem of contaminated wells solved. Even though the problem was discovered in 1980, it was late 1985 before the Los Angeles City Council passed an ordinance forcing valley businesses to abandon septic tanks where sewers were available. It took several more months to mail notices giving business entities with access to sewer systems one more year to hook up to the system.[15]

In 1983 the City Council passed an ordinance to raise construction standards for buried chemical and fuel tanks and to require the thousands of existing tanks already buried to be monitored for leaks on a regular basis. Even though the law required tank owners to begin checking for leaks by January 1, 1985, the city, by 1986, had not yet developed a plan for checking compliance. Another recommendation in the 1983 report involved the creation of a collection service for small generators of hazardous waste that, because of high disposal costs, might be tempted to dump illegally.[16]

The DWP responded that even though the problem of groundwater pollution was discovered in 1980, it wasn't until 1983 that the department believed it had a "fair understanding of even the extent of the contamination."[17] Since that time corrective measures had slowed due to uncertainty over the allowable solvent levels that would be issued by the EPA. Also, the federal government, through the Superfund program, had not provided any money to the city to plan and implement cleanup measures. Without federal assistance, the city did not have enough money to carry out all the recommended measures. However, the DWP and the EPA negotiated a contract that allowed the city to carry out a $2.8 million study of wells in Hollywood, Burbank, Glendale, and Crescenta Valley to pinpoint the location of major plumes of contaminated water.[18]

It was also reported that the DWP and other utilities were taking great interest in the controversy over classifying TCE as a carcinogen. The scientific community was divided on this issue. Direct evidence linking TCE to cancer was limited to a small number of studies that showed increased liver tumors in mice, but some scientists questioned whether this was sufficient to regulate TCE as a human carcinogen. However, in November 1985 the EPA clarified its position, stating that it classified TCE as a possible carcinogen based on a variety of evidence, and that TCE met the agency's requirements as a possible cancer-causing agent in humans.[19]

In March 1986 it was reported that underground toxic contamination had spread significantly through parts of Burbank and North Hollywood during the past four years, contaminating thirteen additional wells and endangering up to thirty-three more.[20] The state's Department of Health Services then released a report which stated that another 101 contaminated drinking water wells had been discovered in Southern California, most of them in Los Angeles County. Out of a total of 291 contaminated wells in Southern California, 221 of them were in the San Fernando, San Gabriel, and central water basins of the county. In the county, 41 percent, or 221 of the 535 wells tested, were found to have some levels of contamination, and 46 percent had concentrations higher than that recommended by the state.[21]

In April 1986 the Department of Health Services announced that it had concluded that DCE, or dichloroethylene, also found in valley wells, is not nearly as toxic to humans as earlier studies suggested. As such, it was raising the standard to six ppb, which would bring approximately thirty wells in the Los Angeles region into compliance. The formerly recommended maximum concentrations had largely been based on a 1984 Italian study involving rats. The study was discounted because of a lack of "quality control" and "good lab analysis." While the study indicated that DCE was a possible cancer-causing agent in animals, it would now be treated as a noncarcinogenic, although still toxic, agent. The new standard meant that if a person were to drink two liters of water a day containing six ppb of DCE for seventy years, there would be no observable adverse health effects.[22]

In May 1986 the EPA announced that the San Fernando Valley Groundwater Basin had been added to the list of sites eligible for federal Superfund money. Four specific areas were designated to receive funds for cleanup of toxic solvents found underground in the vicinity of the North Hollywood wells, Crystal Springs wells, Pollock wells, and wells in the community of Glorietta (see Figure 2-3-1). This action was an important milestone, as no money could be released for the $2.8 million study agreed to earlier unless the sites were placed on the Superfund list. These four sites were selected based on the types of contaminants, underground contaminant movement, and their proximity to population centers.[23]

Figure 2-3-1
EPA Superfund Areas

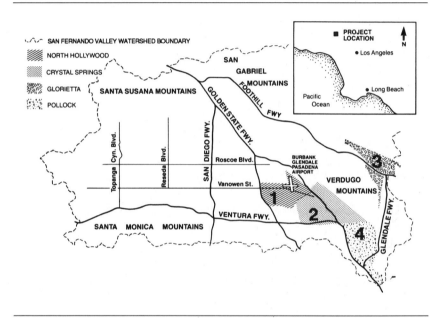

Source: U.S. Environmental Protection Agency, "EPA and DWP Begin Investigating Groundwater Contamination in the San Fernando Valley," Fact Sheet #1, March 1988, p. 2.

The day after the federal assistance announcement, California announced its own plan to clean up contaminated wells throughout the state, including sites in the San Fernando Valley. The money would come from a $100 million bond issue the voters had approved in 1984, some federal Superfund money, and financial contributions required from firms held responsible for the pollution.[24] Regarding the latter, a state investigation turned up five sites that had significant groundwater pollution because of leaking underground tanks in the San Fernando and Glendale areas.

Finally, Citizens for a Better Environment, a Los Angeles–based environmental group, charged that toxic chemicals from landfills in the San Fernando Valley could be contributing to the contamination of the valley's underground water supply. The group urged the regional Water Quality Control Board to take stronger measures to clean up the contamination from the landfills. An official from the board called the charges premature and stated that there were no data to support the group's claims. But a researcher from the environmental group argued that eight of the sixty landfills in the valley, most of which were closed, could be leaking toxic chemicals into the groundwater basin. Much of the contamination could be coming from everyday household waste such as paints, pesticides, solvents, and oil routinely taken to local dumps.[25]

THE TOWER

One method proposed by the DWP was to construct a 45-foot aeration tower to help evaporate contaminants from groundwater. Under this proposal, contaminated groundwater would be extracted from the ground and conveyed through a collector line to the aeration facility where it would flow to the top of the tower (see Figure 2-3-2). The water would then fall through packing material in the tower while an upward airstream would be passed through the water. The water would be aerated, which would transfer the volatile organic compounds into the airstream through evaporation. The airstream would be filtered through granulated activated carbon filters to remove the volatile organic chemicals. This process was expected to bring the water into compliance with state action levels. The treated groundwater would then be conveyed to a pumping station for chlorination and distribution into the public water supply.[26]

Construction would address the immediate problem in the North Hollywood–Burbank area while a more complete investigation of the valley's overall groundwater problem was being accomplished. Prompt implementation would stop the spread of contaminants and reduce the need for a larger-scale project in the future. In October 1985 the DWP notified North Hollywood residents of its intent and requested a permit from the South Coast Air Quality Management District to build the tower. The proposal also needed the approval of Los Angeles zoning officials.[27]

The entire project was expected to cost about $2 million, with $300,000 allocated to the tower itself ($700,000 with the carbon filters) and the rest used to drill wells and install collector lines, pumps, and related equipment. The tower would treat as many as 2,000 gallons of water per minute, or about one billion gallons of water per year. DWP officials said that solvent levels in the air near the tower would be low enough not to create a health hazard. Data submitted by the DWP indicated that the tower would emit about 20 pounds of solvent vapors each day, or about 3.7 tons per year, an amount roughly equivalent to that released from an average-size dry cleaning establishment. While these solvents were present in the water at parts-per-billion concentrations, they would be at parts per trillion in the air around the tower.[28]

Figure 2-3-2
Proposed Aeration Tower

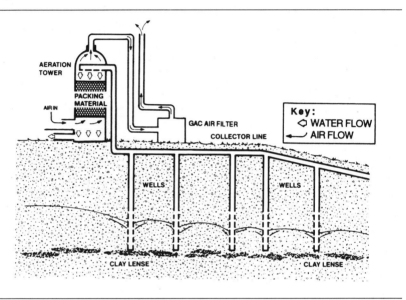

Source: U. S. Environmental Protection Agency, "EPA and DWP Begin Investigating Groundwater Contamination in the San Fernando Valley," Fact Sheet #1, March 1988, p. 6.

Even at this small concentration, however, TCE vapors could react with other chemicals and sunlight to form ozone, the most widespread pollutant in the South Coast Air Basin. While the emissions from the tower could be filtered, the DWP estimated the cost to be about $20,000 per year, not including installation. The DWP asked that its ratepayers be spared this effort, because the use of emissions control equipment was not cost effective and therefore not required under existing guidelines.[29]

In December 1985 the South Coast Air Quality Management District agreed to hold a public hearing on this request. Opposition to the proposal began to mount as local environmental groups and residents of the area questioned the wisdom of transferring the contaminants from one medium to another. They suggested that the DWP consider another method of removing the pollution from the water. The EPA recognized two water treatment techniques as "best-available technologies," meaning that they were proven effective and feasible. Aeration was one approved technology and granulated activated carbon filtration was the other. The latter process was used by bottled water companies and a number of smaller utilities around the country.[30]

In the granulated activated carbon method, carbon is exposed to gas at high temperatures. Thousands of tiny holes are made in each carbon particle, and these particles are placed in tall tanks where water is forced through them. As the water moves downward, the toxic chemicals adhere to the surface of the carbon particles and to the tiny holes so that the water has been purified by the time it leaves the tank. The problem with this method is that it is about three times as expensive as aeration. While this technique would remove about 99 percent of the chemicals in the water, it would cost about $7.5 million per year, or about $1 per month per customer.[31]

At a February meeting the Los Angeles Board of Water and Power Commissioners gave preliminary approval to the DWP's tower project, which had now become a $2.5 million program. Meanwhile, the DWP attempted to soothe opposition to the project, but property owners and citizens continued to voice concerns. A coalition of environmental groups called on the DWP to prepare an environmental impact statement before building the tower. The coalition wanted the DWP to examine the potential health effects of releasing contaminants into the air and to study alternatives to its proposed aeration method.[32] More than 100 people attended the hearing held by the South Coast Air Quality Management District to solicit public testimony before voting on whether to approve construction. The plan received an overwhelmingly negative response as representatives of neighborhood and environmental groups came out swinging.[33]

As a result of this opposition, the DWP decided to filter the chemical vapors that would be emitted by the aeration tower. Officials insisted that this action was only being done to reassure the public, that the amount of uncontrolled emissions was too low to endanger the health of people nearby. Carbon filters trapping about 90 percent of these vapors would make people feel more comfortable about having the tower in their backyard. This decision was said to be a victory of sorts for critics of the proposal, even though it would add about $170,000 to the cost of construction.[34]

The DWP drew praise for this decision, as many people who had opposed the project now gave it their support. Some critics, however, still insisted that a thorough study of the project's safety and effectiveness be conducted, and the results be contrasted with other treatment methods.[35] Finally, in July 1986 the Los Angeles Board of Water and Power

Commissioners gave their approval and rejected requests that the project first be subjected to lengthy environmental studies. Citizens for a Better Environment threatened to sue if the board failed to order the environmental impact statement required by the state. Despite this approval, the DWP still needed a permit from the South Coast Air Quality Management District and the DHS before it could proceed with the project.[36]

In September 1987 the EPA signed a Record of Decision to construct the aeration facility to treat contaminated groundwater in the North Hollywood–Burbank area. The EPA agreed to provide funds through Superfund to the DWP through a cooperative agreement to implement the project. The EPA also joined with the DWP and the DHS in a three-party agreement that defined specific agency responsibilities, cost sharing, and other applicable provisions for the construction, operation, and maintenance of the groundwater treatment system.[37] The facility was dedicated on March 30, 1989, and went into operation to begin cleansing the water.

Discussion Questions

1. Is anyone to be faulted for disposing of hazardous wastes improperly? Was the lack of knowledge about possible contamination of groundwater a fault of the system? Could groundwater contamination have been prevented given the context in which it took place and the state of technology at the time?

2. Who has primary responsibility for assuring that public health is protected? How is this responsibility carried out and what forms does it take? What role can business organizations play in protecting drinking water and safeguarding public health?

3. Why does it take so long to make decisions and get something done in these kinds of situations? How much of a factor is uncertainty, in terms of deciding what to do and when? Can this uncertainty be reduced? What specific questions needed more definitive answers?

4. Describe the political context in which the issue regarding the aeration tower was played out. Who were the major stakeholders and what influence did they have? How was the situation finally resolved? Was the final resolution satisfactory to all parties concerned?

5. Describe the different levels of government involved in this problem. Do the different agencies have overlapping responsi-

bilities? Is there too much bureaucracy with respect to pollution and hazardous waste control? How could more efficiency be introduced into the decision-making process?

6. What role did the media play in this situation? On the whole, did the media play a constructive role? What responsibility do the media have in a complex situation such as groundwater pollution? How can they carry out this responsibility given the media's interest in selling newspapers or promoting viewer interest?

NOTES

1. Los Angeles Department of Water and Power, "Quality on Tap," February 1987, p. 2.
2. Los Angeles Department of Water and Power, "Groundwater Quality Management Plan: San Fernando Valley Basin," July 1, 1983, p. 3.
3. Ibid., p. 1.
4. United States Environmental Protection Agency, "EPA and DWP Begin Investigating Groundwater Contamination in the San Fernando Valley," Fact Sheet #1 March 1988, p. 3.
5. Ibid.
6. L.A. DWP, "Groundwater Quality Management Plan," p. 2.
7. Ibid.
8. Ibid., p. xv.
9. Ibid., p. 12.
10. Ibid., p. 13.
11. Ibid., p. xvii.
12. Jeff Gottlieb, "High Carcinogen Levels in Some L.A. Water," *Los Angeles Herald Examiner,* October 12, 1985, p. A–2.
13. Dirk Werkman, "Polluted Ground Water Examined," *Valley Daily News* (Los Angeles), November 7, 1985, p. 2.
14. "Water Board Boosts List of Hazardous Dumps, Landfills," *Los Angeles Daily Journal,* December 20, 1985, p. 4.
15. Myron Levin, "Plans by L.A. to Clean Up Tainted Wells Lag Behind," *Los Angeles Times,* February 24, 1986, p. II-6.
16. Ibid.
17. Ibid.

18. Ibid.

19. Michael Balter, "Taint Misbehaving: How L.A. Water Officials Learned to Stop Worrying and Love Pollution," *Los Angeles Weekly*, February 28, 1986, p. 3.

20. Dirk Werkman, "Finn: Toxics Poison More Wells," *Valley Daily News* (Los Angeles), March 7, 1986, p. 6.

21. Larry B. Stammer, "101 More Bad Wells Found in Southland," *Los Angeles Times*, March 22, 1986, p. II–1.

22. Larry B. Stammer, "State Increases Level of DCE Acceptable in Water Wells," *Los Angeles Times*, April 11, 1986, p. I–3.

23. Tony Knight, "EPA Cleanup List Adds Valley Basin," *Valley Daily News* (Los Angeles), May 21, 1986, p. 1.

24. Dirk Werkman, "Plan to Clean Valley Toxic Sites Outlined," *Valley Daily News* (Los Angeles), May 22, 1986, p. 3.

25. Karen West, "Group Links Landfill Leakage to Ground-Water Pollution," *Valley Daily News* (Los Angeles), November 25, 1987, p. 5.

26. U.S. EPA, "EPA and DWP Begin Investigating," p. 7.

27. Richard Simon, "Water Tainted: DWP Trying Again to Get OK for Tower," *Los Angeles Times*, October 26, 1985, p. II–7.

28. Myron Levin, "Push on for Tower to Aid Water Cleanup," *Los Angeles Times*, November 25, 1985, p. II–2.

29. Ibid.

30. Michael S. Balter, "The Wrong Way to Remove Toxics in Our Tap Water," *Los Angeles Times*, April 6, 1986, p. II–3.

31. Ibid.

32. "Health Study of DWP Tower Project Urged," *Los Angeles Times*, May 9, 1986, p. II–7.

33. Myron Levin, "Plan to Cleanse Water Draws Fire from Crowd in N. Hollywood," *Los Angeles Times*, May 13, 1986, p. II–6.

34. Myron Levin, "DWP to Filter Tower's Vapors," *Los Angeles Times*, May 23, 1986, p. II–11.

35. Myron Levin, "Air Filters for DWP Tower Praised; More Study Sought," *Los Angeles Times*, June 11, 1986, p. II–6.

36. Myron Levin, "Water Board OKs Aeration Tower," *Los Angeles Times*, July 11, 1986, p. 11–7.

37. U.S. EPA, "EPA and DWP Begin Investigating," p. 6.

APPENDIX A

Glossary

Action Level: Unenforceable water quality standards set by the California Department of Health Services (DHS) at levels to protect public health. For carcinogens in drinking water, state action levels are based upon one-in-one-million cancer risk. This means that a person exposed to that level of contamination throughout his or her lifetime (drinking two liters of water per day for seventy years) has a one-in-one-million chance of contracting cancer as a result of ingesting the contaminant. As an example, the state action levels for trichloroethylene and perchloroethylene are five and four parts per billion, respectively. When contaminant levels rise above the state action level, DHS recommends against consuming the water and requests the water supplier to take measures (such as treatment, discontinued use, or blending) to reduce contaminant concentrations in the water.

Aeration Facility: A treatment system that removes volatile organic compounds from contaminated water by forcing air through the water. The volatile chemicals evaporate upon exposure to the air, leaving the water clean.

Aquifer: An underground rock formation composed of materials such as sand, soil, or gravel that can store and supply groundwater to wells and springs. Most aquifers used in the United States are within a thousand feet of the earth's surface.

Contaminant Plume: A three-dimensional zone within the groundwater aquifer containing contaminants that generally move in the direction of, and with groundwater flow.

Granular Activated Carbon (GAC): An absorptive material which attracts and holds contaminants. GAC has been demonstrated to be especially effective due to its large adsorption surface area.

Groundwater: Underground water that fills pores between particles of soil, sand, and gravel or openings in rocks to the point of saturation. Where groundwater occurs in significant quantity, it can be used as a source of water supply.

Hazardous Substance: Any material that poses a threat to public health and/or the environment. Typical hazardous substances are materials that are toxic, corrosive, ignitable, explosive, or chemically reactive.

Monitoring Wells: Special wells drilled at specific locations on or off a hazardous waste site where groundwater can be sampled at selected depths and studied to determine such things as direction in which groundwater flows and the types and amounts of contaminants present.

National Priorities List (NPL): A list of the top-priority hazardous waste sites in the country that are eligible for investigation and cleanup under the Superfund program.

Parts per Billion (ppb): Units commonly used to express low concentrations of contaminants. For example, one ounce of trichloroethylene (TCE) in one billion ounces of water is one ppb.

Perchloroethylene (PCE): A nonflammable solvent used commonly in dry cleaning and to remove grease from equipment. It is a suspected carcinogen.

Potentially Responsible Party (PRP): Any individual(s) or company(ies) (such as owners, operators, transporters, or generators) potentially responsible for, or contributing to, the contamination problems at a Superfund site. Whenever possible, EPA requires PRPs, through administrative and legal actions, to clean up hazardous waste sites they have contaminated.

Remedial Investigation and Feasibility Study (RI/FS): A two-part study of a hazardous waste site that must be completed before the site remedy is implemented. The first part, or Remedial Investigation, examines the nature and extent of site contamination. The second part, or Feasibility Study, identifies and evaluates alternatives for addressing site contamination.

Risk Assessment: An evaluation performed as part of the remedial investigation to assess conditions at a Superfund site and determine the risk posed to public health and/or the environment.

Superfund: The common name used for the Comprehensive Environmental Response, Compensation, and Liability Act, as amended by the Superfund Amendments and Reauthorization Act (SARA), also referred to as the Trust Fund.

Trichloroethylene (TCE): A nonflammable liquid used commonly as a solvent in dry cleaning and to remove grease from metal. It is a suspected carcinogen.

Source: United States Environmental Protection Agency, "EPA and DWP Begin Investigating Groundwater in the San Fernando Valley," Fact Sheet #1, March 1988, p. 8.

2-4

OCEAN SPRAY CRANBERRIES, INC.

*This case was written by Bert White and Thomas W. Peters
under the editorial guidance of James E. Post, Professor of
Management Policy, Boston University School of Management.*

"Actions have consequences, and criminal actions have criminal consequences," said U.S. District Attorney Frank McNamara, referring to Ocean Spray Cranberries, Inc. at a Boston press conference.[1] Ocean Spray, in a released statement, said, "Our response is that at no time did Ocean Spray endanger the public's health or the environment. We believe that Ocean Spray will be found innocent of the charges."[2] A company spokesperson, Thomas Linehan, said the government was charging Ocean Spray with releasing small amounts of cranberry juice and cranberry skins into the river. According to Linehan, "The government might conceive that one cranberry falling from a truck into a river could constitute a violation of this regulation."[3]

On January 28, 1988, Ocean Spray Cranberries, Inc. was indicted by a federal grand jury on 78 counts of violating the nation's Clean Water Act. The charges were filed in the U.S. District Court. The suit included 6 felony and 72 misdemeanor counts. The felony charges were the first filed against a corporation since Congress toughened the Clean Water Act in 1987.

The indictment stated that between February 1983 and October 1988 Ocean Spray illegally and knowingly discharged untreated wastewater and other pollutants from its plant in Middleboro, Massachusetts, into the Nemasket River. According to Assistant U.S. Attorney Richard Welch, who was named to prosecute the case, the 6 felony counts related to Ocean Spray's intentional dumping of its untreated wastewater from its plant into the town's sewage system. The remaining 72 counts related to Ocean Spray's discharges into the Nemasket River and its adjacent wetlands. If found negligent, the felony counts carry a maximum penalty of $50,000 each, while the misdemeanor counts carry a maximum penalty of $25,000 each. Felonies may also carry a maximum three-year prison sentence per violation for persons who knowingly violate pollution laws.[4]

Under the amended Clean Water Act of 1987, felony charges can be filed if employees know, or should have known, that the firm was breaking the law. According to McNamara, "This is the first case in the country which has utilized the provision."[5] He continued, "This should send a signal to all companies—no matter how large, no matter how powerful—that they cannot pollute the nation's water and hope to pay small fines as a cost of doing business."[6]

THE COMPANY

Ocean Spray was founded in 1930 by independent and competing cranberry farmers from Plymouth and Wareham, Massachusetts, and New Egypt, New Jersey. By pooling their marketing resources, the cranberry growers accumulated financial and managerial resources to enter and expand into the national food production and distribution industry. Ocean Spray Cranberries, Inc.'s purpose is to insulate cranberry farmers from cyclical demand and oversupply patterns by providing ongoing annual income stability to its farmer-owners. This is done by increasing the popularity of cranberry products, balancing supply and demand of cranberries, and increasing growers' total profitability.

Ocean Spray markets fresh and processed cranberries. The corporation neither owns bogs nor grows cranberries; grower-members own their bogs and raise their own crops which are processed and marketed through the Ocean Spray cooperative. Through this ownership structure, cranberry sales grew from $1 million in 1930 to $736 million in 1987. Ocean Spray's goal is to reach $1 billion in sales by the early 1990s. Moreover, the number of member-growers increased from less than 100 in 1930 to 915. Cranberry member-growers range geographically from New England to New Jersey, Wisconsin, Oregon, Washington, and Vancouver, Canada. Citrus fruit growers have also joined the cooperative.

The "Ocean Spray" brand name—inspired by salt spray drifting over Cape Cod cranberry bogs—has been in use since 1912 for canned cranberry products.[7] Recent product development activities at Ocean Spray have led the company into a year-round array of cranberry and citrus products.

Ocean Spray controls 85 percent of the nation's cranberry sales, making it a Fortune 500 company.[8] In April 1988 Ocean Spray registered 385 on the Fortune 500 list, an improvement over 410 in 1987. "We're very pleased," said John Lawlor, Ocean Spray's manager of public relations, of the company's move up the list. "We think it's indicative of the strong relationship that exists between Ocean Spray management and the cranberry growers through southeastern Massachusetts that have made this progress possible."[9]

Recent years at Ocean Spray have been characterized by the development of processing innovations and the marketing of new products. The retrofitting of concentrators, paper box container systems, and bottling operations required large investments. These improvements strained additional capital expenditures.

Ocean Spray has been a major support to the town of Middleboro. Between 1983 and 1986 the company purchased over $12 million in goods and services from local vendors.[10] In 1987 Ocean Spray paid a property tax of $238,000, a sewer bill totaling $152,000, and water bills of $160,000.[11]

THE TOWN OF MIDDLEBORO

Settled in 1660, and located near the Nemasket River, Middleboro now has a population of 17,300. Its industrial base includes cranberries, fire apparatus, shoes, brass goods, lumber, bricks, grain elevators, and novelty items. Developers have recently discovered Middleboro, and cows graze near signs announcing the arrival of national and multinational companies. Yet this small, rural town's principal feature is its location near Boston and several population centers in southeastern Massachusetts, including New Bedford and Taunton, as well as Providence, Rhode Island.

Townspeople are torn between the benefits of economic development and preservation of the town's rural character. Town qualities include a pattern of neighborhood development fostered by several small, neighborhood-based elementary schools; scattered village centers; farms; natural resources such as the Nemasket River; significant wetland and water systems; and historic native American sites. Municipal leaders increasingly discuss the community's dilemma of an escalating rate of land usage which conflicts with resource protection.

Middleboro is extremely proud of being home to Ocean Spray. Nearly everyone is related to or knows of someone directly involved with the company. The title page of the town's 1988 Annual Report carries the heading "Cranberry Capital of the World—319 Years of Progress." Its cover displays the new world headquarters of Ocean Spray on cranberry-colored paper. The town has a long history of manufacturing diverse products, but the cranberry has become king. Ocean Spray's new world headquarters, completed in 1988, straddles the Middleboro-Lakeville town line. In addition, the world's largest cranberry processing plant, operating 24 hours a day and owned by Ocean Spray, is located in Middleboro. Full-time employees number approximately 280, swelling to almost 1,000 during the autumn harvest season.

Middleboro Town Manager John Healey, who initiated the federal indictment process against Ocean Spray, said, "We have a very good relationship with Ocean Spray. While this situation might strain it a bit, I don't think it changes it."[12]

RECURRENT POLLUTION PROBLEMS

The handling and processing of fruit at Ocean Spray is highly mechanized. The process involves: receiving and testing, dumping, temporary holding, destoning, dechaffing, drying, separation, bulking, washing, concentrating, juicing, and bagging the berries. The process objective is to gather bulk berries and prepare them either for storage or for processing into frozen fresh berries, sauce, and juice. These successive operations require extensive water baths, rinsing, and cleaning processes. Middleboro's municipal water and sewer facilities are heavily utilized by Ocean Spray and are critical to the company's operations. Ocean Spray is the town's largest industrial user, discharging approximately 200,000 gallons of wastewater a day into the town's sewage system.

In 1967, when Ocean Spray was expanding its processing plants, Middleboro offered to provide the company with a wastewater pump station located four miles from the town's main wastewater treatment plant. Ocean Spray accepted. By 1971 the state required Middleboro to upgrade its gravity-feed trickling filter plant. Wastewater, including the town's domestic sewage and Ocean Spray's processed waste, was high in acid. Moreover, wastewater was occasionally flowing directly into the Nemasket River damaging fish and wildlife. The contamination of the Nemasket posed far-reaching environmental problems. The Nemasket connects with the Taunton River, which eventually flows into the Atlantic Ocean.

According to Joe Ciagio, Middleboro's wastewater superintendent, "There was a lengthy history in Middleboro of pH fluctuations below the critical level of five, indicating high acidity. This is an inherent aspect of cranberry waste." The high level of acidity appeared to be killing the bacteria necessary to process the wastewater. As a result, viscose bulking, or slime, occasionally flowed into the Nemasket River from 1967 to 1980.

Under the Industrial Coast Recovery (ICR) legislation, the federal government mandated corporate users of public facilities to pay for the capacity which municipalities reserved for their use. Ocean Spray contracted with Middleboro in 1973 to take a major position in the town's wastewater treatment facility. Pollution levels were stipulated and agreed upon by both parties. However, heavy industrial lobbying resulted in Congress voiding the ICR payment requirements in October 1977. In its place, the Clean Water Act was passed. Federal law now required companies to treat their wastewater to limit or remove harmful chemicals, corrosive materials, and excessive acid. The 1973 Middleboro–Ocean Spray contract had become outdated.

The high acidity problem grew between 1980 and 1985. Sludge was not settling and the Middleboro wastewater plant was not meeting its National Pollutant Discharge Elimination System permit level. Consequently, in 1985 Ciagio requested technical assistance from the state's Department of Environmental Quality and Engineering (DEQE). DEQE identified the culprit as a low pH acidity problem and highly variable Biochemical Oxygen Demand (BOD) levels.

Water pollutants are dispersed in two forms: Total Suspended Particles, which are visible, and Biochemical Oxygen Demand (BOD) units, which are invisible. BODs indicate the oxygen required to decompose organic material. Experts agree the accepted rule for "really decent, healthy sludge quality" is 100 BODs to five nitrogen to one phosphorus. Expected presence of urine in wastewater contains sufficient nitrogen to provide the 100–5–1 balance for the bacteria to process normal domestic waste. Ciagio describes the process to eliminate pollutants as "keeping the bugs happy and well fed on a properly balanced 100–5–1 diet." Without this balance, bacteria function improperly and slime occurs.

Seventy-five percent of Middleboro's wastewater volume comes from the town and other non–Ocean Spray sources. However, a significant pH factor and 80 percent of BOD loading comes from Ocean Spray's 25 percent of wastewater volume. Public experts, backed by data, persuaded Ocean Spray into an informal agreement whereby it agreed to add sodium hydroxide to its cranberry wastewater. This would reduce the acidity by increasing the pH level. From Ocean Spray's perspective, however, the pH and slime problem belonged to Middleboro's taxpayers. The company questioned its culpability and pointed to various possibilities for the pH imbalance: deferred and poor maintenance of the treatment facility, mechanical breakdown, improper plant design, or lack of knowledge by the town's employees.

Concurrent with its informal agreement to add sodium hydroxide to its wastewater, Ocean Spray was developing a cranberry–citrus juice product line. Juice production requires frequent process changes which utilize large amounts of water to flush out leftover skins and juices. The procedure increases wastewater input to the Middleboro facilities.

In early 1987 the DEQE announced the Nemasket River and its downstream wetlands were at risk. DEQE tests indicated high acidity in the water. Also the Middleboro waste plant's sludge would not settle, and viscose bulking was consistently exceeding the town's National Pollutant Discharge Elimination System permit level. Consequently, the EPA had to be notified. The town was in violation of the Clean Water Act and risked being fined.

The DEQE immediately convened an on-site technical experts meeting at the Middleboro wastewater treatment facility. Town, EPA, Ocean Spray, and DEQE specialists were invited. "I will never forget how [furious] the DEQE representative was," remembers Ciagio, "when Ocean Spray showed up with both its technical staff *and* its lawyers."

In April 1987 the DEQE ordered Ocean Spray to construct a pretreatment plant to process its wastewater prior to releasing it to the town's system. In August Ocean Spray appealed the agency's order in court. According to attorney Neil Bryson, Ocean Spray pursued an appeal as a means to be heard, otherwise discharge standards would be set only by the state and town.[13] The DEQE was responsible for scheduling an appeals hearing.

On October 8, 1987, thousands of gallons of juice concentrate and cleaning solvents were released into storm drains at the Ocean Spray site. The spill was caused by a faulty pipe at the processing plant. Plant manager Raymond Nolan initially denied that the spill ever occurred. Finally, Ocean Spray's public relations manager, John Lawlor, admitted that the spill happened but claimed it was contained before it reached the river. Middleboro Town Manager Healey and Jeff Gould, chief of DEQE's Water Pollution Control Division, claimed the spill reached the river.

Between 1983 and 1987 the town fined Ocean Spray $14,400 for pretreatment violations. Each violation carried a $200 fine. The untreated Ocean Spray wastewater was also costing the town added expenses at its municipal sewage facility. Additional electricity, for example, was required to treat the wastewater several times before it could be released. From 1985 to 1988 electric consumption at the municipal plant increased by 45 percent.[14]

The biggest problem for the town's treatment facility was the solid loadings that the Ocean Spray processing plant produces. These loadings include cranberry skins, orange and grapefruit rinds, and other high-acid, bulky material. Without adequate pretreatment, the loadings overwhelm the town's sewer system. Healey said the Ocean Spray indictment was the culmination of more than two years of conflict between the town and the company. According to Middleboro selectman Moushah C.

Krikorian, "The town has been after them for a long time to build some kind of pretreatment plant."[15] After extensive and unsuccessful efforts beginning in 1986 to get Ocean Spray to expand its pretreatment activities, Healey forwarded the case to the Environmental Protection Agency's Criminal Investigation Division.

THE SETTLEMENT

At its February 24, 1988, arraignment, Ocean Spray pleaded innocent to all 78 charges. Outside the court, U.S. Attorney Welch said that 65 of the counts referred to 65 separate dates when pollutants with a pH level lower than five were discharged into the town's sewer system.

During the time Ocean Spray was facing arraignment, company officials authorized $25,000 to hire an expert to solve the waste treatment problems at the town's treatment facility. The offer was made to the town of Middleboro. Healey applauded the offer and said that while Ocean Spray will "pay the bills, we'll direct the study."[16] According to Healey, "We need to be able to establish standards for the pretreatment of wastes produced by industry. So we'll direct the study under the watchful eye of the Department of Environmental Quality and Engineering."[17] Ocean Spray also offered to pay its share of the sewage plant's electric bill on a monthly basis, rather than the agreed-upon quarterly basis, to avert cash flow problems for the town.

Dr. Paul Klopping, an environmental expert from Oregon, was hired to study the wastewater problems at the Middleboro municipal treatment plant. In May 1988 Klopping reported nutrient imbalance in the combined industrial and residential wastewater treated at the town's plant. He suggested that adding nitrogen to Ocean Spray's wastewater at its processing facility would eliminate the problem. Ocean Spray implemented Klopping's recommendation.

Ocean Spray also donated $12,500 to allow the town to begin a DEQE-ordered study to identify and set pretreatment standards for industrial sewage users. Both the town and company were under state orders to modify wastewater treatment to meet pollution standards. According to town selectman Stephen D. Morris, Ocean Spray's gift allowed the town to initiate the study without asking voters to a special meeting to appropriate funds.[18]

Under the direction of the DEQE and the EPA, Ocean Spray modified its drainage system and plant operation to help eliminate future discharges into the river and wetlands. Linehan, Ocean Spray's spokesperson, said the company spent more than $1 million at the Middleboro plant to improve wastewater quality. He added, "Though we are dismayed by the severity of the government's charges, as well as the heavy-handed manner in which they were leveled, we are entirely prepared to continue to work with government agencies to meet their concerns."[19]

On December 22, 1988, Ocean Spray Cranberries, Inc. reversed its innocent plea. The company pled guilty to 21 misdemeanor counts of releasing improperly treated wastes from its plant into the town's sewer system and ultimately into the Nemasket River and adjoining wetlands over a five-year period. The company, which had faced as much as $2.1 million in fines, was fined $400,000 for its violations of the federal Clean Water Act. The company also agreed to buy the town a piece of equipment valued between $100,000 and $125,000 that will be used to improve sludge handling at the municipal plant. As part of the plea agreement, 51 other misdemeanor counts and the 6 felony charges were dropped.

U.S. Attorney Welch said the company's willingness to make restitution to the town of Middleboro was a key factor in the avoidance of a lengthy trial. "We wanted to be sure that the town received restitution," Welch said. He noted that the guilty plea marks "one of the first environmental convictions in which a town received restitution." An EPA spokesperson endorsed the view that Middleboro had been a "victim" and that it was more important to get the town the equipment than it was to press the felony charges.

In a press release issued after the change of plea, the cranberry cooperative's president, John Llewellyn, Jr., called the settlement "tough and costly and fair."

Discussion Questions

1. What factors account for Ocean Spray's indictment? Is this a case of unintentional or intentional harm?
2. To what extent does Middleboro bear responsibility for the pollution of these water resources?
3. Why resort to lawsuits? Is this the best way to get business and local government to work together in developing solutions to environmental problems?
4. What management changes should Ocean Spray make to ensure that no future problems arise?

NOTES

1. "Ocean Spray Faces Fines for Pollution," *Middleboro Standard-Times* (Massachusetts), January 29, 1988, pp. 4, 12.
2. Ibid.
3. Ibid.
4. Desiree French, "At Home, a Struggle to Overcome Damage from Federal Indictment," *Boston Globe*, February 16, 1988, p. 25.
5. "Ocean Spray Faces Fines for Pollution," pp. 4, 12.
6. Ibid.
7. "The Ocean Spray Story," Ocean Spray Cranberries, Inc., Plymouth, MA, n.d..
8. French, "At Home, a Struggle to Overcome," p. 25.
9. "Ocean Spray Moves Up," *Middleboro Standard-Times* (Massachusetts), April 10, 1988, p. 1.
10. French, "At Home, a Struggle to Overcome," p. 25.
11. Ibid.
12. Ibid.
13. Meagan Secatore, "Ocean Spray to Finance Study of Sewage Treatment," *Middleboro Standard-Times* (Massachusetts), March 4, 1988, p. 5.
14. Jane Lopes, "Budget Shortfall Related to Ocean Spray," *Middleboro Standard-Times* (Massachusetts), February 4, 1988, p. 1.
15. "Ocean Spray Faces Fines for Pollution," pp. 4, 12.
16. "Ocean Spray Offers to Hire Consultant," *Middleboro Standard-Times* (Massachusetts), February 25, 1988, p. 1.
17. Ibid.
18. Meagan Secatore, "Ocean Spray Gives Middleboro $12,500," *Middleboro Standard-Times* (Massachusetts), April 12, 1988, p. 25.
19. "Ocean Spray Faces Fine for Pollution," pp. 4, 12.

2-5

THE FORGOTTEN DUMPS

This case was written by Rogene A. Buchholz, while Professor of Business and Public Policy at the University of Texas at Dallas, Richardson, Texas. The author acknowledges the assistance of Robert P. Bringer, Staff Vice-President of Environmental Engineering and Pollution Control, Russell H. Susag, Director of Environmental Regulatory Affairs, and Lowell F. Ludford, Public Relations Manager, all of 3M Corporation.

The Pinelands National Reserve covers parts of seven counties in southern New Jersey. This one-million-acre wilderness contains prime forests, cedar swamps, tidal creeks, and cranberry bogs.[1] Beneath the reserve lie the pristine waters of the Cohansey Aquifer, one of the largest on the East Coast. The aquifer contains about 17 trillion gallons of water, which is the equivalent of a 2,000-square-mile lake with a uniform depth of 37 feet.[2] In addition to supplying drinking water for much of South Jersey, the Cohansey Aquifer supports the region's fragile wetlands ecology, blueberry and cranberry industries, and coastal estuaries.[3]

As a remote and sparsely populated area, the Pinelands also served as a popular dumping ground for toxic wastes. In 1984 the region contained at least seven industrial lagoons and forty-three known landfills, seventeen of which have been closed since 1980 per order of the Pinelands Commission of the New Jersey Department of Environmental Protection (NJDEP). From 1976 to 1979, 60,000 gallons of hazardous chemicals were spilled in the Pinelands—either deliberately or accidentally—in forty-one separate incidents. Eventually these wastes began to cause serious groundwater contamination problems and threatened the pristine quality of the aquifer.[4]

Landfills were the greatest threat, producing what is known as leachate, a brew of toxic chemicals and heavy metals formed when rainwater mingles with waste material. In 1979 it was estimated that the ten licensed landfills then operating in the Burlington County portion of the Pinelands were generating 110.5 millions gallons of leachate per year. The actual amount of leachate could be twice as much when illegal dumps were included. State regulations passed in the mid-1970s required that new landfills be lined with clay or plastic to prevent chemicals from entering groundwater. The Pinelands Commission's Comprehensive Management Plan, adopted in 1980, stipulated that by 1990 all the region's dumps were to be closed.[5]

Tests conducted through 1984 concluded that groundwater at more than a dozen Pinelands sites was contaminated but the pollutants had not yet spread beyond the immediate areas of those dumps. However, if not cleaned up soon, the dumps' pollutants were expected to spread to other areas, particularly if large amounts of water were pumped from the aquifer to supply other cities. The groundwater movement caused by the pumping action could disperse the contaminants now concentrated near the dump sites.[6]

Removal of hazardous wastes is a slow and expensive process. The federal government's Superfund program was designed to clean up existing dump sites, but engineering and environmental studies taking up to three years or longer must be completed before actual treatment and removal can begin. New dumps are found every year and new wastes are discovered at licensed landfills that are not authorized to receive them. State and federal governments are racing against time to begin the cleanup process before the water beneath these dumps is irreversibly harmed.[7]

WOODLANDS TOWNSHIP SITES

During 1979 two abandoned chemical dump sites were discovered within the headwaters of the Wading River—at the center of the Pinelands—which is used to irrigate the area's many cranberry bogs. The dumps were located in Woodlands Township, just off route 532 near Chatsworth and near route 72 in the Pinelands' Pygmy Forest section. The route 72 site consisted of 15 acres and the route 532 site, 35 acres. The sites are within a mile of each other. Piles of rusted-out drums were strewn about each of the sites, and puddles of colored liquids were visible. The dumps were closed in the early 1960s, but odors of chemicals lingered, potent enough to give visitors a slight headache.[8]

The nearest home was more than a mile away, so little fear of a public health danger existed. It was initially believed that the dumps' most severe threat was to cranberry production, the area's biggest industry. Cranberries are not particularly sensitive to water quality, but the impact of contaminated water on the bogs was not immediately known. Public reaction to the dumps, however, was extremely sensitive in the aftermath of Love Canal, where a whole neighborhood was evacuated because of toxic wastes seeping into the basements of area homes. Love Canal focused the nation's attention on the toxic waste problem and resulted in federal government appropriating funds to search for abandoned dumps that may contain dangerous chemicals. Before this incident toxic waste dumps were all but forgotten.[9]

Chemical samples taken from the Woodlands Township sites were sent to the NJDEP for analysis. Scattered throughout the route 532 site were patches of an asphaltlike substance containing carcinogens such as benzene, di-methyl-phenol, and similar substances. More than 30 chemicals were found on this site. Groundwater tests indicated that if the contaminants had entered the ground they had not yet spread to adjacent areas. The route 72 site included standing trenches of drum-laden, oddly colored, thickly coated water which contained sticky tar along the trench bottoms. One of the site's wells contained concentrations of several different agents, some known to be toxins and many of which were suspected carcinogens. Groundwater below the route 72 site was believed to be highly contaminated, but the contaminant plume was not detected in off-site wells. The Cohansey Aquifer, while only 30 to 40 feet below the surface in the route 72 area, runs very deep.[10]

The chemicals were believed to have originated at the 3M Company, Rohm and Haas, and the Hercules Company. Worn-out Scotch tape packages were found at the dump sites where defective tape was formerly burned. Fumes and smoke from the tape's burning eventually led to the closing of the route 72 site.[11] The companies neither owned nor operated the sites, but waste materials from the 3M plant in Bristol Township, and a Rohm and Haas plant in Bristol, Pennsylvania, were dumped there. The Philadelphia-based Rohm and Haas later submitted a survey showing that 7,500 tons of chemical waste from its Bristol plant were disposed or burned at the Woodlands dumps. Wastes from the Hercules' Burlington plant may also have been dumped there at one time.[12] The three companies recalled that Rudy Kraus of Industrial Trucking was the hauler and operator of the sites. Mr. Kraus hauled wastes from their plants over a ten-year period in the 1950s and 1960s.

Identifying the companies involved in the dump sites was important to the NJDEP's investigation. The companies were not only in the best position to know what was buried at the sites, they also had the expertise to help neutralize whatever dangers existed.[13] The first step in cleaning up these dumps was to notify the potentially responsible parties and request information on the types and quantities of wastes sent to the Woodlands sites.

THE 3M COMPANY

3M is a worldwide company serving customers with a broad range of innovative, high-quality products and services. Headquartered in St. Paul, Minnesota, the company employs 82,000 people and has operations in forty-nine countries. While perhaps best known for its Scotch tape, it produces a wide range of consumer and industrial products. It is organized into four sectors: Industrial and Consumer, Electronic and Information Technologies, Life Sciences, and Graphic Technologies. Many of its products, particularly in the Industrial and Consumer sector, involve the production of waste materials, some of which are toxic.

Lewis W. Lehr, Chairman of the Board and CEO, received a letter dated July 19, 1983 from John F. Dickinson with the Office of Regulatory Services in the NJDEP. The letter stated that Rudolph Kraus had hauled waste material from 3M's Bristol Township, Pennsylvania, plant to the Woodlands Township dump sites. The letter disclosed that according to tests, the sites' soil and groundwater had been substantially contaminated by hazardous chemical compounds leaching from the disposed material.[14] Also, these sites sat directly on top of the Cohansey Aquifer and at the headwaters of the Wading River, which was the source of irrigation water for the area's cranberry farms. In order to undertake remedial action at the sites, Mr. Dickinson asked 3M for the following information: (1) the types of waste placed with Mr. Kraus for disposal; (2) the quantities of waste; (3) the precise nature of all methods of disposal; and (4) the dates the disposal operations took place.

Several provisions of the New Jersey Spill Compensation and Control Act were mentioned in Dickinson's letter. Enacted in 1976, the law applied to discharges occurring both before and after its enactment. In the case of pre-act discharges, the law empowered the NJDEP to undertake cleanup action where the "discharge poses a substantial risk of imminent damage to the public health or safety, or imminent and severe damage to the environment." The letter cited the joint and several liability for all cleanup and removal costs of any person or corporation that discharged a hazardous substance. The law empowered the NJDEP to direct the discharger to remove or arrange for the removal of the discharge. Failure to obey could result in a liability equal to three times the removal costs. Finally, any person or corporation that may be subject to liability for either a pre- or post-act discharge must notify the NJDEP. Failure to do so is subject to a penalty of up to $25,000.[15]

By mentioning the provisions of the law, the NJDEP affirmed that "3M's failure to cooperate with our efforts to resolve this matter shall subject 3M to liabilities in excess of those resulting from it[s] waste disposal activities. The Department is hopeful that recourse to the above-referenced provisions of law will be unnecessary and looks forward to 3M's full cooperation being proffered in a timely fashion."[16] 3M was effectively put on notice that if it did not cooperate the state could pursue legal action against the company.

On September 1, 1983, the company sent a certified letter to Dickinson. The letter, from Russell H. Susag, Director of Environmental Regulatory Affairs for 3M Company, stated that a review of company records was made regarding operations at the Bristol plant, but none were found pertaining to the disposal sites in Woodlands Township. However, the company was able to compile some information based on recollections of former 3M employees. Also, waste types and quantities were estimated based upon the company's product mix during the time Mr. Kraus hauled wastes from the Bristol plant:[17]

> *Chemicals:* Consisting of resins and adhesives with very small quantities of caustic, sulfides, amines, and laboratory chemicals (probably containerized in 55-gallon drums)—40 tons.
>
> *Organic liquid mixtures:* Mixtures of adhesives, resins, and waste with organic liquids such as acetone, heptane, hexane, methyl ketone, methyl isobutyl ketone, naphtha, and textile spirits (containerized in 55-gallon drums)—4,000 tons.
>
> *Solids contaminated with organic liquids:* Rags, gloves, and filters contaminated with 10 to 15 percent organic liquids (containerized in 55-gallon drums)—4,000 tons.
>
> *Heavy metal contaminated waste:* Materials contaminated with iron, magnesium, manganese, and zinc—200 tons.
>
> *Dry Scrap:* Product-converting waste, paper, cardboard, wood, empty pails and drums (bulk)—50,000 tons.

According to Susag's letter, 3M understood that the organic liquid waste was burned to facilitate recovery of the drums. These drums were sold to junkyards for scrap. The letter also said the company would cooperate with the state of New Jersey regarding this matter. A copy of the letter was sent to Brian Davis, Senior Attorney with the Office of General Counsel for 3M Company. It mentioned a meeting that would be held with Dickinson on September 20.

The NJDEP called a meeting in Trenton for the potentially responsible parties (PRPs), which at that time included three major dischargers, two minor dischargers, one transporter–operator, and two landowners. It expressed its concern and called for the PRPs to conduct an investigation and begin remedial action to clean up the sites, or the NJDEP would carry out the remedial action itself and then seek treble damages from the PRPs under the provisions of the Spill Compensation and Control Act. The PRPs agreed to cooperate with the state and requested time to prepare a response to the state's request.

In October 1983 the three major PRPs—3M, Rohm and Haas, and Hercules—agreed to conduct an investigation of the sites. An outside consultant was hired and directed to develop a work plan in consultation with the staffs of the NJDEP and the U.S. Environmental Protection Agency Region II. From October through December meetings were held between the consultant and the respective state and federal environmental staffs to develop an investigation work plan. The investigation was to determine the extent of the problem at the two sites and gather all necessary data to support the feasibility study. The work plan consisted of a remedial investigation and a feasibility study.[18]

Documentation of a sample's history was referred to as the "chain-of-custody" procedure and was in accordance with EPA requirements relating to field sampling collections and analyses. These procedures ensured the integrity of the sample from collection to data reporting. Thorough documentation was especially important if the data or conclusions based upon the data were used in litigation. The safety plan dealt with the health and safety requirements of personnel involved in the remedial investigation. Finally, a detailed quality assurance plan had to be developed for the sampling, analysis, and data-handling aspects of the remedial investigation.

THE CONTROVERSY BEGINS

In January 1984 several staff changes took place at NJDEP, including the director. Soon after, the NJDEP proclaimed that the Woodlands PRPs would not conduct the investigation but that the NJDEP itself would do so and that the PRPs were to provide the necessary funds upfront. Initially, NJDEP staff were disposed toward working with industry, but the change in staff resulted in a more hard-line or adverse posture, that "industry could not be trusted to direct a cleanup program because industry caused the problem." Based on its new position, the NJDEP proceeded to develop its own remedial investigation and feasibility study work plan.[19]

At a February 1984 meeting held in Trenton NJDEP staff reaffirmed their desire to direct the investigation, and unless the PRPs provided the funds to support the investigation in escrow, the state would send a request to the EPA for federal Superfund money. The only participation in this process that the NJDEP proposed was for the PRPs to select two representatives on a panel of five (the other three being NJDEP staff) that would in turn select the consultant to carry out the investigation. As majority rule prevailed, the state maintained control. The PRPs asked for time to consider this proposal and to suggest modifications that would give them more meaningful participation.

In April 1984 the industry group offered to provide the escrow funds for the Remedial Investigation and Feasibility Study if they were given equal representation with the NJDEP on the management committee that directed the study. The PRPs further proposed that the chairman of the committee be a person independent of either industry or the NJDEP, someone with an irreproachable reputation who could bring objectivity to the situation. The NJDEP rejected the proposal and indicated it would not accept any modification that gave it less than a majority vote on any project management committee. As a justification, the NJDEP stated that "industry could not be trusted to direct a remedial investigation and the NJDEP could not give up the requirement it has as the responsible state agency to direct such investigations." The NJDEP adopted Administrative Order 69 (AO69), which states that disposal site investigations will be directed by the NJDEP with input from PRPs on an investigation management committee on which the state agency has the majority vote (provided that the PRPs pay in advance for the cost of the investigation).

The relationship between the state and industry was now cast in adversarial terms. Even though the PRPs notified the NJDEP that they would proceed with an investigation in accordance with the NJDEP work plan, little productive activity was accomplished throughout the remainder of the year. Both the industry group and the NJDEP spent their time evaluating alternatives. One the industry group pursued was funding and directing the investigation under the auspices of the EPA's Region II, since the NJDEP had indicated it intended to seek federal Superfund money. Upon learning of the discussions between the industry group and the EPA's Region II, the NJDEP withdrew its notice of intent to seek federal Superfund assistance so as to retain total control of the Woodlands project.

To speed the cleanup of toxic dumps on the national priority list, the EPA allowed the responsible firms to directly control the study on how to best remediate the situation. The EPA's policy was at odds with the NJDEP's, which insisted that the state retain control over who did the study as well as the scope and direction of the study. Without this control, state officials believed that firms would negotiate with the federal government for a better deal, and feared that if private firms controlled the study cleanup would be limited to the bare minimums required by the federal government. The state wanted to ensure that the DEP was involved in all aspects of the study process, and that permanent solutions (e.g., waste removal or detoxification) were considered.[20]

In January 1985 the PRPs decided to initiate their own remedial investigation of the Woodlands sites based on the NJDEP work plan. Subsequently the NJDEP ordered the group to pay $880,000 within seven days for the funding of the NJDEP-directed remedial investigation, citing as its authority AO69 and threatening treble damages. After this action the Hercules Company reached an agreement with the NJDEP and paid $275,000 as its portion of the costs for the remedial investigation. The other major PRPs, 3M and Rohm and Haas, sought to have the order set aside. Failing in this attempt they then filed suits in state court challenging the legality of the adoption of AO69, and in federal court citing a denial of civil rights through the treble damages threat.

The NJDEP then hired a consultant, Camp, Dresser, and McKee (CDM), to conduct the state's version of the Remedial Investigation and Feasibility Study. The first phase of CDM's investigation was estimated to cost $1.4 million, which was considerably higher than the earlier $880,000 estimate. After mid-year CDM began the first phase of the NJDEP's investigation. The industry group's directed investigation, however, was hampered by delays in the issuances of necessary permits by the NJDEP, and was relegated to the role of observer so as not to interfere with the NJDEP-directed study. Toward the end of the year, the civil rights portion of the PRP suit in federal court was denied.

In January 1986, 3M and Rohm and Haas paid $610,000 to the NJDEP, which fulfilled the terms of the NJDEP order issued a year earlier. The federal court's decision concerning the civil rights violations was appealed by the industry group. In April 1986, 3M and Rohm and Haas met with the NJDEP. Agreement was reached allowing for regular technical communications and data sharing, provided the industry group contributed to the cost of the study. The first phase of the study was now estimated to cost $1.76 million, not including approximately $300,000 in NJDEP administrative costs.

In April 1986 the state court rendered a decision in the industry group's favor, setting aside AO69 as not having been properly promulgated. The NJDEP appealed, and in September 1986 the first technical meeting between the NJDEP and industry group representatives was held to review the data from the first phase of the study. The industry-directed investigation as a separate parallel study changed to a review and supplement of the NJDEP-directed investigation. In December 1986 a second technical meeting reviewed the proposed second phase of the program, to begin in early 1987. The study's estimated cost was now $2.4 million, excluding NJDEP administrative costs.

The remedial study was expected to be completed by fall 1987, and actual remediation would begin no earlier than mid-year 1988. However, administrative delays in a contract change order between the NJDEP and its consultant delayed the feasibility study completion to nearly mid-year 1989. The earliest date for the record of decision (ROD), which specifies which remedial action is to be conducted, was expected to be September 30, 1989. It would be spring 1990 or later before remedial action could be initiated.

Technical meetings between the NJDEP and industry staffs continued monthly throughout 1987, 1988, and 1989. Relationships had been good, resulting in productive critiques of both the remedial investigation and the feasibility study. On September 1, 1988, the Woodlands Private Study Group (consisting of 3M and Rohm and Haas) proposed a preferred remedial action program to the NJDEP and formally offered to conduct this remedial action. The offer was respectfully received by the NJDEP, subject to completion of the formal process.

The cost of the study was now $2.5 million, with another million or more spent by the PRPs in their independent studies and overseeing the NJDEP consultant. These costs are not out of line with other Superfund projects, and the time involved is not untypical for other Superfund sites. For Woodlands Township, six years had passed from the date of NJDEP's first notification letter. It would be at least one more year before remediation began, and two to six years before complete remediation. The exception was the site's groundwater, which would need to be pumped and treated for the next thirty years.

Discussion Questions

1. What threats do toxic waste dumps pose for the environment and human health? Why were these threats not apparent when the dumps were first created? What happened to change perceptions regarding the disposal of toxic waste material?

2. What is joint and several liability? What is the intent of this kind of provision? Is this a fair method of apportioning the

costs of cleanup between the responsible parties? What are some alternative methods of dealing with liability?

3. Why did the state adopt a hard-line attitude toward business? Comment on the position that "industry could not be trusted to direct a cleanup program because industry caused the problem." Is this a realistic viewpoint? What did the state agency have to gain by maintaining control of the project?

4. The residents of Woodlands Township were denied a role in the decision-making process and investigative study. Is this fair to these residents? Is it adequate in these cases to just keep local residents informed? Explain.

5. Why did the costs continue to escalate? What was actually accomplished with the money that was spent? Was the delay in getting started a major factor in this escalation? What can be done to control these costs in the future? How can more of the money be directed to actual cleanup efforts?

6. Why does it take so long to get started with a cleanup effort? What are the various incentives of the major stakeholders in this situation? Is the lack of appropriate incentives a problem? What can be done to design a better management system that is results oriented?

7. Given the lack of trust, how can industry participate meaningfully in this kind of cleanup effort? What role should the state and federal governments play? Is there a need for a third party who is neutral to oversee the investigation of environmental damage and selection of remedial actions?

8. Did the companies involved act responsibly in this case? If you were the head of one of the firms, what would you have done differently after being notified of the problem? How would you have seen your firm's responsibility in this situation?

NOTES

1. Marc Duvoisin, "The Tainting of the Pinelands' Most Precious Resource," *Philadelphia Inquirer,* January 16, 1984, p. 4–B.

2. Brett Skakun, "Chemical Dumps Found in Pines," *Atlantic City News,* April 29, 1979, p. 1.

3. Duvoisin, "The Tainting of the Pinelands," p. 4–B.

4. Ibid.

5. Ibid.

6. Ibid.

7. Ibid.

8. Skakun, "Chemical Dumps Found in Pines," p. 1.

9. Tony Muldoon, "Pine Barrens' Breeze Could Be Lethal," *Camden Courier-Post* (New Jersey), April 27, 1979, p. 3.

10. Ralph Siegel, "Two Dumps in Woodland Pushed for Superfund Aid," *Burlington County Times* (New Jersey), November 19, 1982, p. 1.

11. Skakun, "Chemical Dumps Found in Pines," p. 1.

12. Siegel, "Two Dumps in Woodland," p. 1.

13. Muldoon, "Pine Barrens' Breeze Could Be Lethal," p. 3.

14. Letter from John F. Dickinson, Office of Regulatory Services, Department of Environmental Protection, State of New Jersey, July 19, 1983.

15. Ibid.

16. Ibid.

17. Letter from Russell H. Susag, Director, Environmental Regulatory Affairs, 3M Company, St. Paul, MN, September 1, 1983.

18. Draft of PRPs' consultants' work plan.

19. Draft of NJDEP work plan.

20. Tom Johnson, "Quarrel over Toxic Cleanup Control Begins to Imperil Jersey Program," *Star Ledger,* (New Jersey) October 21, 1984, p. 33.

2-6

THE POLITICS OF RECYCLING IN RHODE ISLAND

This case was written by Robin F. Ingenthron with the assistance of Thomas W. Peters, under the editorial guidance of James E. Post, Professor of Management Policy, Boston University School of Management.

The nation's cities, counties, and states are facing an enormous task—the relocation of landfills. In 1988 the Environmental Protection Agency (EPA) announced that the average life span of a landfill was less than five years. Waste haulers in New York, who planned to ship garbage to lesser-developed countries for burial, were shocked when the "Mobro 2000" garbage barge returned to Staten Island still loaded with refuse after being turned away from every Atlantic port during a six-week voyage between New Jersey and Panama. (The barge was finally emptied at New York's Fresh Kills landfill.) As landfills become more scarce, tipping fees (the per-ton fee paid by garbage trucks which "tip" their loads at the dumps) become higher. And as tipping fees increase, illegal dumping proliferates.

New England faces the worst landfill shortages in the country. In Massachusetts and Connecticut two thirds of them will be closed before 1992. Many municipally owned landfills have begun refusing commercial wastes in an attempt to control the cost of waste disposal. States with larger landfills and small populations, such as New Hampshire and Maine, are less willing to accept waste from out of state. While courts ruled the "Interstate Commerce Clause" makes it unconstitutional for a state to prevent a private landfill from accepting out-of-state wastes, government-managed landfills are generally free to do so. Prices and politics demand that states develop their own solutions.

In Rhode Island, most residential, institutional, and commercial garbage goes to the Central Landfill in Johnston, opened in 1955. By the late 1980s the Central Landfill was 265 feet high and buried over 4,000 tons of garbage per day at an operating cost of $13 million per year. The

Central Landfill occupies 121 acres and serves thirty-one communities. Eight smaller landfills, serving specific Rhode Island. communities, were scheduled to close by the early 1990s. In 1987 Rhode Islanders spent $200 million to collect and dispose of their trash. This cost was expected to increase annually by as much as $300,000.

Up to half of Central Landfill's rubbish tonnage comes from commercial and institutional sources, the rest from residential waste. The quantity and content of wastes vary with the time of year. Forty-one percent is paper, and approximately 10 percent each for food waste; yard waste; rubber, leather, and textiles; and metals. Eight percent is glass and 7 percent plastics. Central Landfill, scheduled to close in 2003, will at its current rate of waste growth reach capacity by the early 1990s. In 1989 Governor Edward D. Diprete agreed with Johnston's mayor to close the landfill no later than 1997. It is estimated that at least $20 million will be required to cap, close, and monitor the landfill.

RHODE ISLAND'S RECYCLING LEGISLATION

Rhode Island has a long history of grappling with solid waste dilemmas. The state's first major solid waste disposal legislation was the 1974 act creating the Rhode Island Solid Waste Management Corporation. In the 1980s two other main pieces of legislation were passed—the OSCAR program and the 1986 Flow Control Law.

The Rhode Island Solid Waste Management Corporation

Created in 1974, the Solid Waste Management Corporation (SWMC) is "a public corporation of the state, having a distinct legal existence from the state and not constituting a department of the state government . . . ." The act that created the SWMC was amended between 1986 and 1988, thus providing a vehicle for a number of new solid waste statutes. In its 1987 Annual Report, the SWMC's purpose is described as follows:

> [SWMC] was created in order to provide and/or coordinate solid waste management services to municipalities and persons within Rhode Island. It is intended that the [SWMC] will receive sufficient revenue through resource recovery and sales of its services to be financially self-sufficient. The [SWMC] has the power to issue negotiable notes and bonds to achieve its corporate purpose. The [SWMC] is exempt from federal and state income taxes.

The SWMC serves as manager of Rhode Island's state-owned landfill. Through tipping fees it funds recycling, resource recovery, and landfill replacement efforts. Under the 1986 Flow Control Law, SWMC's

Central Landfill was recognized as the primary solid waste disposal site in Rhode Island.

OSCAR

In 1984 the Rhode Island legislature created the Ocean State Cleanup and Recycling program (OSCAR). OSCAR legislation specifically regulated littering and was not intended to act as a vehicle for the creation of new forms of waste management. Consequently, the program was put under the control of the Rhode Island Department of Environmental Management (DEM).

OSCAR was funded by a $.05 tax on every case of twenty beverages sold in the state. The program, however, had no money for state or local recycling programs. In the words of a DEM employee, OSCAR "was basically a litter bill, with the word 'recycling' tagged onto the end of it as an afterthought. The bill neither funded or mandated recycling." Unlike other states' bottle bills, the OSCAR program did not significantly affect the recycling or trash hauling economies. (See box for a discussion of state "bottle bills.")

Deposit "bottle bills" have already been enacted in a number of states. In a bottle bill state, each bottle or can bears a deposit of five or ten cents redeemable upon return of the bottle to the vendor. The vendor is repaid a higher fee by the bottling company to account for handling costs. The bills are opposed by both the bottling companies, who maintain that the deposits dampen demand for their products, and by aluminum and glass recycling brokers, who see a 90 percent reduction in scale. All of the aluminum can buyers in Massachusetts, for example, closed shortly after passage of the bottle bill and were replaced by one large company, New England Crinc, which collects and redeems deposits, essentially getting the aluminum and glass materials free.

Glass industries and recyclers feel that bottle bills speed up the move away from recyclable glass to nonrecyclable plastic containers (requested by grocers who have to accept containers for deposit because they are lighter and easier to handle). The collection of the plastic deposit bottles is nevertheless leading to experimentation with plastics recycling; a plastics recycling plant was being planned in Billerica, Massachusetts, to take advantage of the secondary plastic feedstock available from returned plastic deposit bottles.

Bottle bills are being promoted by environmental groups as a recycling measure in response to the increasing prevalence of disposable containers. Bottle bills have led to a reduction in litter and an increase in recovery of aluminum.

1985 Flow Control Bill

In 1985 the SWMC submitted a bill on solid waste disposal. The bill requested permission to fund the creation of waste-to-energy facilities and proposed an expansion of the Central Landfill. The bill would close or freeze operations of the state's smaller landfills, making the Central Landfill the "official" state dump. This allowed the SWMC to guarantee the tonnage necessary to generate tip fee income and to avoid additional fees to the new waste-to-energy incinerator. Waste-to-energy plants (or "Resource Recovery Facilities") must burn garbage (fuel) at capacity to generate enough electricity to break even. This leads to contracted tonnages—the government must either supply a minimum threshold of garbage or must pay the incinerator operator a fee for each ton below that threshold. This "put-or-pay" fee is usually higher than the tip fee charged at the incinerator, and RRF companies consequently negotiate for large plants and high-tonnage thresholds.

Victor Bell, director of the DEM, explained the 1985 Flow Control Bill as follows:

> The major purpose of the Flow Control Bill—99 percent to 100 percent of its purpose—was to route garbage for disposal to the SWMC's landfill and allow the SWMC the guaranteed tonnage [and related tip fees] necessary to float bonds for the construction of incinerators. In fact, it was because recycling was not addressed at all in the 1985 bill that it failed to pass the committee.

The bill had several opponents, namely communities abutting the proposed site and environmental organizations opposed to incineration. A commission was formed to study the waste disposal bill more closely. Once it was sent to the commission for study, Bell used it to promote recycling. That summer, OSCAR provided funds to Brown University's Center for Environmental Studies to devise plans for integrated solid waste management. When the bill failed, Brown student Adam Marks's senior thesis was sent to the review commission. According to Marks:

> We designed a statewide recycling strategy and showed the commission how it would pay for itself in avoided disposal cost. The commission added money to the Flow Control Bill for recycling and approved resource recovery facilities [waste-to-energy incinerators] with smaller capacity than SWMC originally requested.

Flow Control Act of 1986

The 1986 version of the Flow Control Bill contained mandatory recycling regulations for both municipal and commercial waste. The law set a minimum goal of 15 percent recycling of all solid waste generated in Rhode Island. Unlike other state and local recycling bills, the Rhode Island laws affected commercial businesses as well as curbside residential collections. For years environmentalists had claimed that recycling and waste reduction were the best methods for conserving scarce resources. With the passage of the Flow Control Act in 1986, Rhode Island became an environmental pacesetter.

A document prepared by the DEM summarized the legislation as follows:

> The Flow Control Law has three major components. First, it strengthens the control of the Solid Waste Management Corporation over the final disposal of all solid waste generated in Rhode Island, with minor exceptions. Second, it sets a fixed dollar amount and escalator to be paid by Rhode Island municipalities for municipal solid waste delivered to a RISWMC facility. Third, it requires separation of solid waste either at the source or at collection/transfer points and requires the construction of recycling facilities at or near all resource recovery facilities.

The law mandated all municipalities, with the exception of those that use their own landfills, to dispose of their wastes at SWMC facilities. Low rates were set ($10 per ton in 1988, $11 per ton in 1989, etc.), not to rise above 1.075 times the previous year after 1991. However, to qualify, municipalities had to separate the waste, and the DEM had the authority to determine what was recyclable. Recyclable components could be tipped free of charge at the SWMC's Materials Recovery Facility (MRF). When the MRF (New England's first) opened in 1989, some questioned whether it would sell enough loads of recyclables to make a profit, or would operate solely on the basis of avoided landfill costs. Recyclers and haulers wondered about the competition—the traditional scrap dealers for industrial clients. The key was market demand. To increase both market demand and supply of recyclables, the law ordered the state Department of Administration to purchase recycled paper products "wherever the price is reasonably competitive" defined as "a comparable recycled product with a cost premium of no greater than 5 percent over the lowest bid or price quoted by suppliers offering nonrecycled paper products."

The Flow Control Law was popular within the SWMC and the DEM. However, the agencies had to design a system of implementation. Recycling and waste hauling were old industries and managers had years of experience. Some believed that the laws would succeed only to the degree that the two industries would cooperate.

Stakeholders: Winners and Losers

SWMC

The Flow Control Law gave the SWMC permission to build a waste-to-energy plant and a recycling facility with the tip fees earned at the landfill and the bonds those fees helped support. Both were designed to reduce the amount of waste going into the Central Landfill, thus prolonging the life of the site. While construction of the waste-to-energy plant would take several years, the SWMC began operations of the MRF in 1989. MRF (pronounced "murf") is the primary receiving station for separated recyclable residential, institutional, and commercial wastes, including commingled recyclable trash of different colored glass, metals, some plastics, and various grades of paper. MRF does not remanufacture new products but brokers the secondary materials to end-user industries. Beginning with MRF's 1989 opening, the SWMC intended to make its commitment to recycling visible and profitable. New England Crinc, founded as Mass Crinc in 1985 to collect Massachusetts deposit beverage containers, won the bid to build and operate the Rhode Island MRF.

The SWMC's tip fees were also the funding source for the DEM's antilitter and recycling promotion program. Before the opening of MRF the DEM program aided communities in developing recycling collection plans. These plans were then reviewed by the SWMC. The SWMC in turn provided the equipment necessary for a curbside recycling program (e.g., segregated department trucks, colored "recycling" boxes).

DEM

The DEM is a major player in the government's solid waste management scheme. In charge of regulating all types of environmental pollutants, including air emissions, water pollution and treatment, and solid and hazardous waste, the agency is one of the fastest growing departments in Rhode Island government. The DEM became involved with recycling in 1984 with the passage of OSCAR. While OSCAR had no money attached for the implementation of recycling programs, Victor Bell, director of the DEM, was committed to making recycling a state policy. The 1986 Flow Control Law gave the DEM several responsibilities, including the "definition of recyclables" and "coordinating municipal recycling efforts and administering a program of financial and technical assistance to participating cities and towns."

Traditional Recyclers

The term *recycler* usually refers to the parties who collect and broker secondary raw materials, which they send free of contaminants to manufacturers of new products, or "end-users" (e.g., glass, paper, and steel mills). Most recyclers service large commercial waste generators, such as printers or machine toolers, that regularly generate large quantities of scrap. The recycler requires the generator to keep the recyclables separate from the normal waste stream in separate waste containers. A minimum is normally required for collection; the quantity depends on the value and the mass of the material. Dense, valuable computer paper can be collected and paid for in quantities under 500 pounds. Bulky, less-valuable cardboard has to be baled and compacted before collection, usually in amounts approaching 5 to 10 tons. Mixed paper is suitable only for making paperboard (movie tickets, cereal boxes, etc.), and is usually collected for a fee.

To solicit recyclable waste, paper and aluminum can recyclers do not always approach managers. Many prefer to meet employees or custodians after hours; in these cases, the custodian salvages valuable scrap for some set fee per pound. Other recyclers set up more-visible programs with middle-level employees. With the exception of cardboard from large retail businesses and metal cuttings from heavy industry, recyclers have not been able to capitalize on avoided waste disposal costs at commercial sites.

Most scrap dealers express alarm when government discusses recycling as a waste disposal alternative. Brokers fear that government, driven by avoided disposal costs, will try to get rid of more recyclables than the industrial market can absorb. Many blamed such "dumping" for the precipitous drop in price for newspaper in 1988. (In New England, prices dropped from an average of $40 per ton to just $2 per ton.) Criticism of state bottle bills and collection programs by recycling experts is straightforward: "When the government suddenly drops large quantities of scrap onto the market, the very people who know the most about recycling will be hurt."

In Rhode Island steps were being taken to safeguard the interests of these recyclers. The MRF was only allowed to serve commercial accounts "as a recycler of last resort." Theoretically, businesses would be allowed to tip clean loads of DEM-defined recyclables at the MRF only after they had been refused by area recyclers; these businesses and their contracted haulers would be charged a fee of 25 percent of the Central Landfill tip fee—about $12.25 when the MRF opened in 1989.

In spite of their distrust of government, some recyclers voiced support of Rhode Island's commercial recycling law. One recycler who collected inside Rhode Island said,

> I don't know why businesses are belly-aching about this law. I'm normally against any government involvement in recycling, but maybe it's time someone made them consider it. Last week I made a presentation to managers at [a large manufacturing plant] and offered to pay them for their waste paper. I spent 45 minutes showing them how they could save money from avoided disposal costs. I guess they don't feel it's worth their time.

Other recyclers fear the waste hauling industry even more than government. Most recycling collectors—those who set up programs, collect the materials, and transport them to brokers—are smaller than the hauling companies and pick up smaller amounts of waste at each generator site. However, the SWMC's paper recycling consultant felt that the big waste haulers would only take interest in the largest accounts. Said the SWMC consultant,

> We get half our income from the top 15 percent of our clients. We depend on the large accounts, but we pick up smaller amounts of paper to defray our trucking costs between stops. When the haulers get involved, all it will take is a clause in the waste hauling contract—that they will have the right to the recyclables in the garbage they collect—and our best clients will be gone.

Some experts have been skeptical of the effectiveness of recyclers. "They only want the cream," said one critic. "To get the largest percentage of recyclables out of the waste stream—cardboard and mixed paper—the state has to get the haulers involved."

Solid Waste Haulers

The solid waste hauling industry, having merely dabbled in the recycling market, became more involved after the passage of mandatory recycling bills in New Jersey, Connecticut, and some West Coast communities. Garbage collection had in fact become big business. In the mid-1970s the first national, publicly owned, solid waste hauling corporations were created: Waste Management, Inc. (WMI); Browning-Ferris Industries (BFI); and Laidlaw. (A fourth was forced to break up after losing a series of lawsuits involving illegal activity.) These three had found niches in communities where landfill and tipping space were scarce, and local "Mom-and-Pop" haulers had to use their landfills, incinerators, and waste transfer stations (where waste is recompacted in large trailers for trips to more distant landfills).

Many small haulers still operated in Providence, however. But they had difficulty competing with the national firms for curbside residential waste collection and continued to service commercial waste generators (factories, office buildings, and institutions). The larger commercial waste generators are billed according to two criteria: (1) volume, based on the size of the rubbish container at the building and the estimated tonnage contained, and (2) the number of times the container is collected each month. Office complexes sometimes pay annual rubbish fees over $100,000 per year. Competition for municipal and commercial accounts is intense, and Rhode Island's waste hauling industry has a reputation for playing hardball to secure contracts. Most small haulers were unaffected by the state's first recycling statutes. However, when the commercial recycling components went into effect in 1989, they became much more involved.

CREATING RECYCLING GUIDELINES

The Flow Control Law mandated that recycling be conducted at commercial businesses. As of January 1989 businesses of 100 employees or more were required to file a waste reduction plan with the Rhode Island DEM.

In 1988 the DEM and the SWMC came together to develop protocols and policies needed to implement the commercial applications of the recycling law. The regulations would be based upon waste audits and an analysis of the commercial waste hauling contracts. A waste audit, which traced the flow of materials through a company and documented the processes that produced waste by-products, was already a common way to trace the flow of highly regulated toxic wastes. At the end of the day, product composition plus waste had to equal the amount of chemicals taken from inventory in an accounting procedure known as "mass balance." Chemical, petroleum, and metal companies had already developed elaborate methods of tracing hazardous waste production. In addition to federal and state enforcement of hazardous waste auditing, there were natural incentives for companies to do so. Unidentified chemical wastes were up to 20 times more costly to dispose of, and it did not pay to have barrels of methyl alcohol taken away at the same price as cyanide. Although the largest part of hazardous waste is treated on-site at the manufacturing plant, professional waste treatment services had grown dramatically in recent years. In addition, some audit mechanisms were in place to begin audits of nonhazardous waste. Other businesses and institutions, however, did not know what was expected of them. The DEM and the SWMC needed to formulate separate regulations for municipal and commercial recycling. The municipal recycling mandate was clearly defined and affected relatively fewer stakeholders. Conversely, the law's commercial waste-related segments were less specific, yet affected many more stakeholders.

Commercial waste generators are very numerous. Similarly, the numbers of waste haulers servicing commercial accounts is greater than the number of haulers serving municipalities. The SWMC could refuse to let municipal haulers tip at the Central Landfill but had no way of determining how many buildings a commercial waste hauler had visited or who the violating commercial generators were. Enforcement was even more complicated when haulers stopped at a waste transfer station and mixed their garbage with that from several other trucks. Despite these difficulties, the SWMC and the DEM were able to agree on what the legislation should require of businesses. In the spring and summer of 1988, the DEM created the official *Regulations for Reduction and Recycling of Commercial and Non-Municipal Solid Waste*. The key provision was that if the waste stream consisted of more than 30 percent recyclables, then businesses would begin a recycling program, preferably with an existing recycler, although they could tip their recyclables in clean loads at the MRF "as a market of last resort."

In order to track and determine the recyclability of wastes, a detailed description of the components making up the waste stream (the percent of high grade paper, corrugated cardboard, aluminum, plastic, etc.) was required. Four methods of waste audit protocols were developed and tested. These were as follows.

1. Inventory receipts are used as a way of predicting the amount of materials entering the waste stream. For example, if the business ordered 25 boxes of computer paper per month, and the cardboard boxes weighed 4 pounds each, 100 pounds of cardboard should be in the waste stream each month. Paper, however, was more complicated. Some percentage stayed in the office as reference material, some was circulated in reports outside of the building, some might already be collected and sold for recycling (often by custodians, who could receive over $100 per ton for computer printouts), and some was often destroyed to protect company secrets.

2. The contents of the trash receptacles could be sampled in separate areas of the building and at each operation, to give the manager and the waste auditor a picture of where the problem areas are, and to indicate where to put recycling containers.

This would also help identify the levels of document destruction and unreported recycling.

3. A simpler method of sampling placed the auditor at the mouth of the dumpster, segregating wastes and weighing them for a period of time. This was sufficient for a business wishing to comply with the law, and for a recycler who wants to know over the phone what is available for recycling.

4. A fourth method, already offered as a service by some recyclers and solid waste haulers, was an actual audit of the contents of the dumpster. The dumpster had to be emptied and the contents raked aside and weighed separately. This process made collection unpleasant and required the full cooperation of the waste hauler, who might not disclose the fact that the dumpster was not completely full. The fill level of the dumpster could be extrapolated from the sampling; the typical density of compacted wastes was made available from studies by the SWMC.

The DEM's waste audit required operations managers to walk through their building and document the production of waste starting from the beginning inventory. Because wastes going into the dumpster could simply be measured at the "port of exit," a more comprehensive audit system was adopted. According to Dr. Ward at Brown University's Environmental Studies Center,

> First, we want the actual practice to educate the manager exactly as to where waste is occurring. That will help to set up the program in-house. Second, we want DEM to have the information from the various SIC codes available to track wastes in the future. Third, since we have few enforcement provisions in the law, we hope that this will at least lead the company to take some action. If we leave it at the dumpster, no one will do anything.

Regarding the auditing method, one expert said, "I've had to survey business people before, and I think they are going to hate this thing. Even with the mandatory recycling law, I'm not sure the state has any business with half of this information. I just hope the whole thing doesn't give recycling a bad name."

To assist businesses in their waste audits, the DEM created a *Guide to Preparing Commercial Solid Waste Reduction and Recycling Plans.* Self-audits and recycling plans had to be filed with the DEM by June or December, 1989, depending on the size of the company. Also during this time the DEM and the SWMC compiled a recycling directory which served as a form of market research. Businesses needed to know whom to call to collect what type of recyclable material. From a manager's perspective, it would be a mistake to set up an internal recycling program without first having called for prices and investigated the mechanisms used to collect the material.

In July 1988 the waste hauling industry and commercial businesses testified before the DEM. A spokesperson for the National Solid Waste Management Association described the legislation as an unfortunate necessity and complimented the DEM and the SWMC on what he said was a "well thought out, workable program." His testimony was followed by that of representatives of several small haulers, all of whom said that the law was unfair, impractical, and anti–small business.

TECHNICAL ASSISTANCE PROGRAM

In response to the impending regulations, both the DEM and the SWMC received requests for assistance from businesses in setting up recycling programs and performing solid waste audits. As a result, each agency saw the value of a technical assistance program (TAP) and were working independently on one to provide businesses with professional waste audits and recycling referrals. Bell described the cooperation of the two agencies as follows:

> The relationship between DEM and SWMC is extremely cooperative. We are holding workshops, visiting waste generators, and publishing material together. The solid waste crisis is everyone's problem, and we'll have to continue working together to solve it. DEM will continue to present workshops (as we did for the municipal technical assistance), and the SWMC will have a strong role to play in the enforcement of the regulations.

Bell further explained:

> At DEM, we have a very good technical assistance program established. We now have a handbook on recycling, a handbook on solid waste audits, and an auditing staff which will go to the business to assist with the audit. We've also held about 50 workshops (including residential and apartment manager workshops).

When asked about the SWMC's role in technical assistance, Bell said:

> We've jointly sponsored several workshops. We're cooperating on an enforcement plan—SWMC is going to enact enforcement provisions at the landfill, and they'll send out warnings or fines. I haven't seen their own version of the Technical Assistance Program. I think

their program is aimed more at the waste haulers who are bringing the waste to the landfill and shows them how to separate and recycle and find markets. DEM will concentrate on the waste generators.

The SWMC's plan for a commercial technical assistance program was described in OSCAR's *Commercial Waste Recycling Handbook* as follows:

> Responsibilities:
> It is the policy of [SWMC] to undertake various responsibilities in the areas relating to reduction and recycling of commercial . . . solid waste including:

a. *technical assistance* to commercial waste generators, commercial waste haulers, and to others whom [DEM's] commercial regulations apply.
b. *enforcement* of commercial regulations at [SWMC] facilities.
c. financial and staff resources to support and carry out secondary *market development* efforts in conjunction with [DEM] and [state and local governments].
d. service as a *back-up market* for recyclable materials at one quarter of the commercial tip fee, when those materials are not being handled by Rhode Island private recycling brokers.

While each agency offered to walk through the building with affected managers, neither agency's staff had an expert on recyclable markets, the necessary equipment, or preparation specifications. The SWMC hired a paper recycling consultant to design the outline of its TAP, which would be used to solicit funding from both political sources and foundations. If funded, the SWMC's TAP offered to do the following:

1. Provide a telephone hotline and recycling referral service.
2. Perform waste audits of the dumpsters to see what they contained, or sample the waste stream before it entered the container.
3. Compare the results with the beginning inventory, if desired by the company.
4. Supply the company with a list of recyclable collectors.
5. Offer low-interest loans if storage and packing equipment were necessary.
6. Offer workshops to affected business people.

The yearly budget for the SWMC's proposed TAP was well over $100,000, not including a fund for low-interest loans for recycling and waste-reduction equipment.

The SWMC's proposed audit differed from the DEM's. It did not require the auditor to sample waste at every stage of the production process. When the SWMC decided to offer its services as a consultant, it envisioned a program similar to "Rhode Islanders Saving Energy" (RISE), a TAP aimed at energy conservation. The RISE program sent auditors into businesses to examine energy consumption and recommend measures which would pay for themselves. According to the SWMC's recycled paper consultant,

> If I'm collecting paper from your building, I only need to know how much you can store, and how often you need it collected. Internally, it's pretty much the same in every building: a paper bin in the copy room, collect cans by the pop machine, etc. I don't normally need to see an inventory sheet. If it's not going into the dumpster, then it's none of the state's business, anyway. The goals of the Technical Assistance Program are to make recycling as simple and efficient as possible. If the SWMC decides at some point that it should do mass balance of inventory for cardboard, aluminum cans, white paper, etc., and document each production process, it can always add that service.

UNRESOLVED ISSUES

It was originally thought that market demand would create a private corps of recycling and waste production auditors and consultants. However, it was becoming apparent that the audit which DEM regulations required could be bypassed. If neither the SWMC's nor the DEM's technical assistance programs offered to track the waste flow within the company, how would they audit compliance? Waste container audits were extremely difficult and unpleasant; if the regulators had all the necessary information in hand, they merely had to check to see whether the figures balanced and audit the hauler collection contract against the receipts from incoming inventory.

Meanwhile a new issue was developing. Many waste recycling plans filed with the DEM were incomplete, except for the statement, "our waste hauler is taking care of it." The larger waste haulers with transfer stations had evidently convinced many waste generators that they could mix wastes at the transfer station in such a way as to guarantee that less than 30 percent of the contents would contain recyclables. DEM officials were furious. An OSCAR staff person said, "What they are doing is sabotaging the entire recycling program. They knew all along what we intended, and we did our best to cooperate. This is terrible. . . ."

The SWMC's commercial TAP did not stray significantly from the outline which the DEM had published in the handbook. But questions of duplication of services were surfacing. Should recycling assistance be offered by the DEM, the SWMC, recyclers, haulers, or private consultants?

Finally, Rhode Island's Flow Control Law, lauded by environmentalists and waste hauling lobbies, was receiving national attention, and many groups and political leaders were watching Rhode Island to assess the workability of the new laws.

Discussion Questions

1. Identify the various stakeholders affected by the Rhode Island Flow Control Law. What is at stake for each of these groups? Should concessions be made to the small recyclers over the waste hauling industry? Why? What do the smaller recyclers have to offer that the waste hauling industry does not? Is this important to the success of the law?

2. Do you think this law can be successfully implemented? What incentives are there for commercial businesses to comply? What incentives would you suggest be included in the legislation?

3. Under the Flow Control Law, Rhode Island places the onus of waste reduction on commercial businesses. Should manufacturers of consumer products also be regulated in terms of waste reduction (e.g., packaging)? How could this be implemented?

4. Assess the working relationship of the SWMC and the DEM. Are they working together effectively? How does this affect other stakeholders?

5. What problems are inherent in setting up a recycling campaign? Compare recycling with other methods of waste control such as incineration, landfilling, ocean dumping, and reduction. As a lawmaker in Rhode Island, which method would you favor? Why?

APPENDIX

Waste Composition Study: Rhode Island Central Landfill

Waste audits performed at the Central Landfill in May 1987 led to an estimate of the following waste composition of daily tonnage dumped at the landfill (open 6 a.m.–4 p.m.):

3,336,000 lbs. of paper	41.7%
850,000 lbs. of food waste	10.6
791,200 lbs. of yard wastes	9.9
756,000 lbs. of rubber, leather, and textiles	9.4
723,200 lbs. of metal and aluminum	9.0
637,600 lbs. of glass	8.0
607,200 lbs. of plastics	7.6
298,400 lbs. of wood	3.7
8,003,000 lbs. or 4001.5 tons of waste	

(0.1% error due to rounding)

The Central Landfill does not accept for burial: motor vehicle batteries, aerosol and industrial containers, free liquids, dead animals, untreated storage tanks and infectious waste, oil-contaminated materials, out-of-state wastes, odorous waste, sludge, industrial, and liquid wastes which do not meet lab tests and standards, hazardous industrial and household waste, uncured materials, asbestos, dusty materials except as delivered between 6 and 7 a.m., dredged muck or sediment, speed-dry or other sundries.

————PART III————

BUSINESS AND THE
"NEW ENVIRONMENTALISM"

This background note was written by Alfred A. Marcus and Gordon P. Rands, both of the Curtis L. Carlson School of Management, University of Minnesota, and by Professor Rogene Buchholz of Loyola University, New Orleans.

The "new environmentalism" poses numerous challenges to business. In Part III we offer specific guidelines in the areas of strategy and organization, public affairs, law, operations, marketing, accounting, and finance, all drawn from the experiences of several companies that have had some success in dealing with environmental problems. While the public sector is never totally out of the picture, often it is the private sector that must take the initiative. As in Parts I and II, the cases in Part III illustrate the issues.

Case 3-1 concerns the cleanup of a Minnesota dump site. It provides an interesting contrast to case 2-5 in Part II in that now a private corporation, 3M, takes the lead. It also shows how major problems with dump site cleanup are not always technical ones; they can be political and organizational as well. Case 3-2 tells the story of a private effort to solve the nation's hazardous waste problem through recycling and the difficulties the small company encountered. Cases 3-3 and 3-4 concern waste minimization as a strategy by two large corporations, Polaroid and Dow Chemical, to solve the problem of hazardous waste. Case 3-5, about ARCO Solar, Inc., shows how difficult it can be for a private enterprise to develop new technology and make it economically feasible. Case 3-6 describes the collapse of an oil tank in Pennsylvania, and shows one company's "crisis management" efforts. Finally, case 3-7 discusses Du Pont's Freon® Products Division strategy in light of evidence that the production of CFCs is hazardous to the earth's stratospheric ozone layer.

Clearly, as the cases illustrate, the "new environmentalism" poses numerous challenges to business. Companies are expected to make environmental considerations part of their decision making from the very beginning, not an afterthought. The philosophy of the "new environmentalism" calls for going beyond mere compliance with regulations. Imaginative solutions are sought that save a firm's money and at the same time improve the environment, preserve natural resources, and enhance the company's reputation. Major profit making opportunities in the 1990s and beyond lie in the realm of creating and marketing environmentally sound products. They include developing the capabilities for cleaner manufacturing and for manufacturing products that generate less waste. Safer pest control strategies and cleanup methods that help eliminate past environmental harm also provide opportunities for profit (Shea 1989).

Various companies have carried out creative programs that respond to environmental expectations. Their responses may have relevance for other companies as they face the same challenges. Based on these creative responses, a comprehensive list of actions that companies may wish to take has been developed. The prescriptions are organized along functional lines to show how environmental management penetrates into every aspect of a business. First, the area of strategy and organization is examined; next, staff functions such as public affairs and legal are reviewed; then, traditional functional areas such as operations, marketing, accounting, and finance are considered. Finally, an elaboration of some of the philosophies behind business' response to the "new environmentalism" is presented.

STRATEGY AND ORGANIZATION

Guidance in this area consists of the following:

Cut Back on Environmentally Unsafe Operations. Du Pont, the leading producer of chlorofluorocarbons (CFCs), has announced that it will voluntarily pull out of this $750 million business by the year 2000, if not sooner. AEG, a West German appliance manufacturer, has announced a line of energy-efficient kitchen appliances to replace the energy-intensive appliances now commonly in use (Shea 1989).

Carry Out Research and Development on Environmentally Safe Activities. Du Pont has announced that it is spending up to $1 billion on the best replacements for CFCs. General Motors has been conducting research on an electric car. Called Impact, this car can accelerate nearly as well as cars powered by conventional internal combustion engines.

Extension of battery life would make the cars more cost competitive, because current operating costs are estimated to be twice that of conventional cars (McKee 1990). ARCO has spent more than $2 billion on a reformulated gasoline product that can prevent 350 tons of pollutants a day from entering the smog-filled skies of Southern California (*U.S. News & World Report* 1990). Other companies have been working on chemical-free pesticides that can be used in a safe way in underdeveloped countries. In Nigeria aerial crop sprayers are dispensing parasitic wasps instead of chemical pesticides to assault pests naturally. The parasites have been manufactured by biotech firms such as Mycogen Corporation, Ecogen, and Crop Genetics International, which are developing and marketing the natural pest control products (Shea 1989).

Develop and Expand Environmental Cleanup Services. Building on the expertise gained from cleaning up its own plants, Du Pont has formed a safety and environmental resources division to help industrial customers clean up their toxic wastes. The projected future revenues are $1 billion by 2000 (Kirkpatrick 1990). Based on a recycling program that it began internally, Weyerhaeuser has started an office recycling program called WOW (Wecycle Office Waste) which it offers to other businesses (*Conservation Exchange* 1989). Opportunities abound for companies that can develop innovative products in the solid waste area. A-1 Products of Ontario, Canada, has made a simple box homeowners use to carry recyclables to the curb, which has proven to be very profitable. Opportunities exist for companies that can create new uses for old newspapers, magazines, plastics, and food wastes. Innovative waste management products needed include crushers, paper balers, plastic pelletizers, containers for holding glass, paper, metal, and lawn clippings, and specialized trucks for hauling curbside collectibles (Shea 1989).

Compensate for Environmentally Risky Endeavors. To compensate for a coal-fired plant it was building in Connecticut, Applied Energy Services agreed to donate $2 million in 1988 for tree planting in Guatemala. The trees are meant to offset the utility plant's emissions that might lead to global warming.

Purchase Environmentally Safe Businesses. Anheuser-Busch Companies bought Sea World, a chain of four theme parks dedicated to aquatic life. At the Orlando site, Sea World scientists have been rescuing turtles damaged by boat propellers. They are also playing an important role in trying to save the Guam kingfisher, an endangered bird species (McKee 1990). With the price of energy increasing, businesses that manufacture turbines for wind power and photovoltaic cells that convert sunlight to electricity (see case 3-5) should be very attractive. Businesses that produce electricity from biomass fuels such as rice husks, orchard prunings, pulp, and sugar cane residue also should be attractive.

Make Changes in Structure, Compensation, and Other Systems. The Valdez principles suggest that companies appoint an environmentalist to the corporate board and that they conduct an annual audit of the company's environmental progress. The Coalition for Environmentally Responsible Economies, a group of institutional investors who control $150 billion in pension funds and other assets, suggests that it may not extend funds to companies that refuse to adopt the Valdez principles (*U.S. News & World Report* 1990). Du Pont has made environmental criteria a part of determining a manager's compensation. Another step the management can take is to encourage the development internally of environmentalists, something that Pacific Gas and Electric (PG&E) has attempted.

PUBLIC AFFAIRS

Here, guidance to management consists of the following:

Try to Avoid Losses through Appearing Insensitive to Environmental Issues. One cost to Exxon of appearing to be unconcerned after the Valdez accident was that 41 percent of Americans said they would consider boycotting the company (Kirkpatrick 1990).

Attempt to Gain Environmental Legitimacy and Credibility. The cosponsors of Earth Day 1990 included Apple Computer, Hewlett-Packard, Shaklee, and the Chemical Manufacturers Association. McDonald's has made efforts to show it is a proponent of recycling and has tried to become a corporate environmental "educator." Edgar Woolard, CEO of Du Pont, has delivered speeches on corporate environmentalism. Employees of the Combustion Engineering Company have spent time in Tunisia inspecting cement plants and recommending pollution control solutions. Employees of Wolverine World Wide, a manufacturer of Hush Puppies, have visited tanneries in Tunisia, Thailand, and Turkey to give advice about treating waste and recovering chemicals. AT&T and Northern Telecom have decided to share technology about producing circuit boards without using chlorofluorocarbon-containing solvents with third-world nations (*Conservation Exchange* 1989).

Collaborate with Environmentalists. PG&E's executives claim they seek discussions and joint projects with any willing environmental group. Woolard of Du Pont regularly meets with environmentalists. PG&E has teamed up with environmental groups to study energy efficiency, and the company is now renting a computer model from the Environmental Defense Fund that shows the relationship between conservation and electricity costs. McDonald's Corporation has worked with staff members of the Environmental Defense Fund to learn more about composting and recycling (Jacobs 1990). It established a joint task force with the environmentalists to identify alternatives for reducing and recycling waste at McDonald's 11,000 restaurants and has launched an ambitious recycling program (*U.S. News & World Report* 1990). H.B. Fuller has collaborated with the Sierra Club to rejuvenate a dying pond (*Conservation Exchange* 1990).

LEGAL

This area is closely related to public affairs. Here, guidance to management involves the following:

Try to Prevent Confrontation with State and Federal Pollution Control Agencies. W.R. Grace faces expensive and time-consuming lawsuits from its toxic dumps, and Browning-Ferris, Waste Management, and Louisiana-Pacific confront violations which have damaged their reputations. Union Carbide faced years of litigation from the explosion of its facility in Bhopal, India, which killed an estimated 3,000 people.

Comply Early. Since compliance costs increase over time, companies that act early have lower costs. This enables them to increase their market share and profits, and win competitive advantage. Thus, 3M's goal is to meet government requirements to replace or improve underground storage tanks by 1993 instead of 1998. The company tries to meet or surpass federal requirements by changing products and processes and by redesigning equipment and reusing materials (McKee 1990). The new vice president for Union Carbide's community and employee health, safety, and environmental protection, Cornelius C. Smith, Jr., maintains that corporate environmental programs evolve naturally from reaction and damage control to compliance with laws and regulation, to prevention ("compliance plus") and leadership ("prevention plus"). Companies at the highest level have both environmental training and audit programs and try to minimize the amount of wastes they generate through comprehensive programs (*Environmental Manager* 1990).

Take Advantage of Innovative Compliance Programs. Instead of source-by-source reduction, the EPA's bubble policy allows a factory to reduce pollution at different sources by different amounts provided that the overall reduction meets EPA standards. 3M therefore has been able to install equipment on some production lines and not on others at its tape manufacturing facility in Pennsylvania (Brunner et al. 1981), which has lowered its overall compliance costs.

Rely on Self-Regulation Rather Than Government Requirements. The Chemical Manufacturers Association has a program called "Responsible Care" which has industrywide safety codes. Companies that do not sign an agreement saying they will comply with the codes cannot join the association. The Institute for Nuclear Power Operations (INPO), formed after the Three Mile Island nuclear power accident, evaluates plant safety and presents recommendations to plant management for change. These recommendations complement those made by the Nuclear Regulatory Commission.

OPERATIONS

Here, companies can take many steps toward environmental improvement.

Promote New Manufacturing Technologies. Louisville Gas and Electric has taken the lead in installing smokestack scrubbers, Consolidated Natural Gas the lead in using clean burning technologies, and Nucor the lead in developing state-of-the-art steel mills. Dow Chemical, Scott Paper, and other companies have taken the lead in the area of cogeneration (Shea 1989). They generate their own electricity and use the heat to warm their factories. PG&E has agreed to rely on a combination of smaller-scale generating facilities, for example, windmills and cogeneration plants, alongside aggressive conservation efforts. PG&E's management has canceled plans to build large coal and nuclear power plants. H.B. Fuller has built a passive solar facility that requires no fossil fuels for heating or cooling (*Conservation Exchange* 1989).

Encourage Technological Advances That Reduce Pollution from Products and Manufacturing Processes. 3M's "Pollution Prevention Pays" program (Brunner et al. 1981) is based on the premise that add-on technologies are too costly. Instead, management should try to eliminate pollution at the source. Add-on equipment is expensive because it not only requires resources to remove pollution, it also generates pollution, thereby requiring even more resources to control wastes. The 3M program tries to involve employees throughout the company in making suggestions to reduce emissions. Since the program began, 3M has undertaken more than 2,500 projects (McKee 1990). Other companies have similar programs. Chevron has one called SMART (Save Money and Reduce Toxics) which began in 1987. In two years it has reduced hazardous wastes by 60 percent and saved the company $3.8 million (*Environmental Manager* 1990).

Develop New Product Formulations. One way to accomplish source reduction is by developing new product formulations. 3M's rapid fire-extinguishing agent for petroleum fires did not meet EPA requirements. Thus, the company had sought to develop a new formulation. The new formulation was one fortieth as toxic but more effective and less expensive to produce.

Modify Production Equipment and Change Manufacturing Operations. Another way to accomplish source reduction is to modify equipment and operations. For example, 3M's new Kenlevel metal plating process does not require the use of cyanide. This process is up to 50 percent more energy efficient and creates a competitive advantage for the company.

Eliminate Manufacturing Wastes. With fewer wastes, add-on equipment becomes less necessary. 3M's philosophy is to invest in reducing the number of materials that can trigger regulation. For example, it has replaced volatile solvents with water-based solvents thereby eliminating the need for costly air pollution equipment. IBM's Endicott, New York, facility in 1990 cut toxic emissions 75 percent compared to the previous year by replacing water-based chemicals for the solvent-based chemicals that had been used in the high-volume circuit panel manufacturing process (*Environmental Manager* 1990). Amoco and Polaroid (see case 3-3) have similar programs. Dow's program, called WRAP (Waste Reduction Always Pays), was started in 1986. It estimates that its 1988-1989 projects will reduce the waste stream by 88 million pounds per year (*Conservation Exchange* 1990).

Try to Find Alternative Uses for Wastes. When Du Pont halted ocean dumping of acid iron salts, it discovered it could sell these salts to water treatment plants at a profit. Anheuser-Busch Company, at its breweries in Fort Collins, Colorado, and Jacksonville, Florida, employs a waste treatment process to reuse the agricultural by-products created in the brewing process (McKee 1990). The company turns the leftover substance into a nutrient liquid that is applied directly to farmland. Amoco Chemical Company has found that it can sell the aluminum chloride its Texas City plant had been generating. Ideally, Amoco claims that it tries not to generate a waste product, but if it does, it attempts to discover "what's the inherent value" of the waste product so that it can sell it to someone else (*Environmental Manager* 1990).

Recycle Wastes. Anheuser-Busch has been a leader in recycling aluminum cans (McKee 1990). It buys back aluminum from consumers at hundreds of collection centers throughout the country and sells it to aluminum fabricators for a profit. Weyerhaeuser recycles yearly 1.5 million tons of paper through 16 resource recovery stations throughout the country (*Conservation Exchange* 1989). AT&T recycles 25 truckloads of scrap—metals from solder, circuit boards, wires and switch hooks, and plastics from telephone and computer housings—every day (Shea 1989). Many small companies have active paper recycling programs. Local recycling companies provide and pay the companies for regularly filling the bins. In one of the country's most ambitious recycling efforts, Unocal Corporation has been buying back pre-1971 autos in the Los Angeles area at a price of $700 per car for scrap and recycle. The reason for this program is that the new cars emit fifteen to thirty times less pollution than the old models. Other firms with active recycling programs are Safety-Kleen (solvents and motor oil), Wellman (plastic), Jefferson Smurfit (paper), and Nucor (steel). 3M is recycling and reusing solvents it once emitted to the atmosphere. Dow and Huntsman Chemical Company have established model recycling programs for the federal government in some of the national parks. They have put recycling bins in the parks and have supervised the collection and transportation of the waste (McKee 1990).

MARKETING

Another area where the "new environmentalism" poses challenges is marketing. Among the actions to be taken are the following:

Try to Cast Products in an Environmentally Friendly Light. The *Green Consumer Guide* was England's best-selling book in 1989. A 1989 Michael Peters Group survey found that 77 percent of Americans said that a company's environmental reputation influences what they buy. Companies such as Procter & Gamble, ARCO, Colgate-Palmolive, Lever Brothers, 3M, and Sunoco have tried to act on the basis of this finding. Anheuser-Busch is tying its campaign to eliminate pollution from Chesapeake Bay to its Budweiser commercials that air in that region (McKee 1990). Wal-Mart has made efforts to provide customers with recycled or recyclable products. The Body Shop, a London-based chain of skin and hair care stores, provides literature on ozone depletion and global warming to its customers and has collected customer signatures on a petition asking the Brazilian president to save the rain forest. Its cosmetic products are not tested on animals and are packaged in cheap refillable containers. Loblaw, a Canadian grocery chain, has introduced a "Green-Line" of environmentally friendly products. These include re-refined motor oil, recycled toilet paper, biodegradable soaps and cleansers, and phosphate-free laundry and dishwashing detergent. Loblaw has sold more than twice the amount of these products than it projected (Shea 1989). Numerous mail order companies (Seventh Generation in South Burlington, Vermont, Earth Care Paper in Madison,

Wisconsin, and Livos in Santa Fe, New Mexico) have thrived by selling environmentally safe products.

Avoid Being Attacked by Environmentalists for Unsubstantiated or Inappropriate Claims. British Petroleum claimed that a new brand of unleaded gasoline caused no pollution, a claim it had to withdraw after suffering much embarrassment. The degradable plastics controversy provides companies with another warning about the perils of unsubstantiated or inappropriate claims. Companies have to be honest with their customers and have to educate them incessantly.

ACCOUNTING

Accounting, too, can have a role in the response to environmental expectations. Here, guidance consists of the following:

Make Sure to Demonstrate that Antipollution Programs Pay. 3M's "Pollution Prevention Pays" program is based on the premise that only if the program pays will there be the necessary motivation to successfully carry it out. Because of environmental pressures, U.S. companies have to spend large sums of money that otherwise could have been used for capital formation, new product research and development, and process improvements which could raise productivity. Thus, every company owes it to itself and society to use a minimum of resources in achieving pollution reduction. Companies should develop approaches that not only reduce pollution but encourage innovation at the same time.

Show the Overall Impact of the Pollution Reduction Program. Companies have an obligation to account for the costs and benefits of their pollution reduction programs. 3M's 1980 status report lists 394 projects in 3M operations worldwide that have generated savings of $56.5 million in five years: $13 million for pollution control equipment and facilities which were delayed or eliminated, $16.8 million for reduced pollution control costs, $1.8 million for energy savings, and $9.7 million for sales of products that might otherwise have been removed from the market. By 1989 3M reported that it had reduced wastes by 50 percent and had saved the company over $4 million (*Conservation Exchange* 1989). In 1989 3M's pollution prevention program added almost 6 cents a share or $13 million to the company's profits. This figure does not include the value of reused material or savings coming from reduced disposal costs. Other companies are doing equally careful accounting of the money they are saving from pollution reduction. Amoco claims it has saved $50 million since 1983 through its waste reduction efforts (*Environmental Manager* 1990).

This number does not account for recycling credits or less liability for environmental damage.

FINANCE

This is the final functional area where environmental challenges are important. Here, guidance consists of the following:

Gain the Respect of the Socially Responsible Investment Community. Socially responsible rating services and investment funds try to help people invest with a "clean conscience" (Irwin 1985). Their motto is that people should be able to "do well" while they are "doing good." The theory is that socially responsible investments are likely to be profitable because if the companies can deal creatively with pollution, safety, and employment problems, they will tend to be innovative in other areas as well. The problem is there is no consensus on what constitutes socially responsible investing. Definitions may be more or less restrictive. Comparisons may be made within an industry or between industries. The socially responsible funds only have government enforcement data and interviews with corporate officials upon which to rely. They may have trouble reconciling inconsistent company behavior; for example, Fort Howard Paper Company has played a leading role in recycling paper but it also has played "hardball politics" with regard to the Wisconsin Clean Air Act, using "job blackmail," the threat that it may lay off workers, to get its way (Irwin 1985). It is also the largest papermill source of PCBs.

Some of the funds emphasize "positives"—demonstrated commitment to the environment or efforts to go beyond legal requirements. They also tend to include corporations that sell systems to analyze, clean up, or protect the environment. Other funds emphasize "negatives." They identify companies with records where investors should refuse to put their money.

Franklin Research and Development of Boston, a socially responsible investment firm, evaluates corporate environmental activities. In 1989 it listed Polaroid, Digital Equipment, Stanley Works, Consolidated Paper, Apple Computer, and H.B. Fuller as companies that socially responsible investors might want to consider (*Conservation Exchange* 1990). The Dreyfus Third Century Fund ranks companies on the basis of social criteria and then selects the most profitable ones for its investments. Its four areas of special concern are the environment and natural resources, occupational health and safety, consumer protection, and equal employment. In addition, it invests up to one third of its assets in companies that contribute to the quality of life in America by developing products, services, or technology related to health, housing, education, and transportation. The Calvert Managed Growth Portfolio assesses companies' financial performance first and then compares them against others in the industry on social issues. It looks for products and services that sustain the natural environment, invite worker participation, provide equal opportunity, and foster a commitment to human goals. The Calvert Fund contains no investments in nuclear power, weapons, or South Africa. The New Alternatives Fund is the smallest of social investment funds. It focuses on natural resource investments in solar and alternative energy companies. A favorite of almost all the funds is Ben and Jerry's ice cream, which uses ingredients from tropical rain forests in its ice creams as a way to help save these forests. Nut brittle ice cream contains pine nuts and Brazil nuts harvested from the Amazon rain forest. (*U.S. News & World Report* 1990).

Recognize True Liability. Since environmental liabilities can affect financial health, the Securities and Exchange Commission has mandated that corporations list these liabilities in annual reports (*U.S. News & World Report* 1990). Smith Barney, Kidder Peabody, and other investment houses have environmental analysts who search for true environmental liabilities in evaluating a company's performance (Crudele 1990). These analysts have, for instance, looked closely at ITT Corporation's $30 million charge against earnings for a plant in Georgia that made creosote-soaked railroad ties and telephone poles. The land on the plant site had been damaged and would have to be cleaned up. Indeed, a 1986 Maryland court ruling holds banks responsible for cleanup costs on foreclosed property, thus necessitating that banks do environmental assessments before making loans (*U.S. News & World Report* 1990). Even such mundane transactions as those involving restaurants and hotels are subject to careful analysis because of the potential environmental liabilities that may be involved.

Recognize Business Opportunities. Smith Barney's Index of Stocks in solid waste businesses rose 59 percent in 1989, and its index of hazardous waste stocks rose more than 42 percent, while the overall stock market rose just 27 percent. The prospects for solid waste companies (e.g., Waste Management, Laidlaw Industries, and Browning-Ferris) is reportedly very good because of a scarcity of landfills in parts of the country, and because cities like New York have no alternative ways to dispose of their garbage. The prospects of hazardous waste companies may be good because the Departments of Defense and Energy will have to clean up the toxic wastes they created in various parts of the country.

In sum, there are numerous things a firm can do that cover all aspects of its business to meet the challenge from the "new environmentalism." To meet these challenges, firms need motivating philosophies.

PHILOSOPHIES MOTIVATING THE RESPONSE

Philosophies are important in motivating firms to meet the challenges of the "new environmentalism." They include:

Sustainable Growth. Generally defined as development that meets the needs of the present without compromising the ability of future generations to meet their own needs, the notion of sustainable growth is much more acceptable than limits to growth which were discussed in the late 1970s. No one wants to hear about limits unless they already have what they want, especially when the limits apply to someone else or some other country that has yet to develop its resources. Sustainable growth makes sense, at a theoretical level, but needs to be operationalized in concrete situations where resource usage is involved.

Waste Minimization. This strategy involves reduction of waste rather than end-of-pipe thinking. The idea here is reducing waste by designing products that involve less waste and designing production processes that produce less waste to dispose of later. Waste minimization also involves thinking of waste as a resource that has uses beyond what people ordinarily consider. The greatest success story has been the recycling of aluminum cans because of the high cost of processing new aluminum. The incentives for paper and glass and other resources are not as good, and may have to be provided by state and local governments. As the cost of disposing of solid waste mounts across the country, more reliance will have to be put on recycling.

Design for Disassembly. This is a new concept that some companies are beginning to incorporate in their thinking and their products. With pressures growing to recycle metals and plastics, being able to take things apart efficiently may soon become as important as putting them together right. Design for disassembly involves simplifying parts and materials to make them easy and inexpensive to snap apart, sort, and recycle. Implementation of this concept will make it cost-effective to segregate materials in durable goods for recycling. This concept requires new technology and skills in manufacturing. Composites, for example, are enemies of recycling. They combine glass, metals, plastics, and other fibers, making coding and separation of materials nearly impossible and certainly uneconomical. Glues and screws are also enemies of design for disassembly. The concept involves the use of fewer kinds of plastics and composite materials and new ways of fastening things together.

Good Old Efficiency. The final philosophy is simply the promotion of good old efficiency. We are a wasteful society, but when multiplied across the entire country, a few simple changes in wasteful habits can make quite a difference. More fuel-efficient automobiles and a few extra miles per gallon, for example, could preclude the need for imports and the need to risk opening up new oil fields in environmentally sensitive areas. Use of more efficient light bulbs throughout the country could make a real impact on usage of electricity. Americans have to get over the idea that more is better and begin to think in terms of efficiency. The throw-away society and the out-of-sight, out-of-mind type of thinking with respect to waste has to change.

REFERENCES

"Amoco Chemical Saves $50 Million through Waste Reduction," *Environmental Manager,* Vol. 1, No. 12, July 1990, pp. 5–6

David Brunner and Nan Stockholm, "3M Company: Creating Incentives within the Individual Firm," in D. Brunner et al. (eds.), *Corporations and the Environment: How Should Decisions Be Made* (Palo Alto, CA: Stanford Business School, 1981), pp. 97–110.

"Business's Green Revolution," *U.S. News & World Report,* February 19, 1990, pp. 45–48.

"Chevron Gets SMART on Waste Reduction," *Environmental Manager,* Vol. 1, No. 10, May 1990, pp. 3–4.

John Crudele, "Environmental Issues Could Be Hot Item of '90s," *Minneapolis Star and Tribune,* March 18, 1990, p. 2–D.

"Growing Greener: Corporations Coming Around to the Environmental Cause," *Conservation Exchange,* Vol. 7, No. 3, Fall 1989, pp. 1, 6–8.

"IBM Plant Nixes 75% of Toxic Emissions,"*Environmental Manager,* Vol. 1, No. 12, July 1990, pp. 1-2.

Robin Irwin, "Clean and Green," *Sierra,* November–December 1985, pp. 50–56.

Deborah L. Jacobs, "Business Takes on a Green Hue," *New York Times,* September 2, 1990, p. F–25.

David Kirkpatrick, "Environmentalism: The New Crusade," *Fortune,* February 12, 1990, pp. 44–55.

Bradford A. McKee, "Environmental Activists Inc.," *Nation's Business,* August 1990, pp. 27–29.

Synthia Pollock Shea, "Doing Well by Doing Good," *World Watch,* November–December 1989, pp. 24–30.

3-1

OAKDALE: A SUCCESS STORY

*This case was written by Rogene A. Buchholz, while Professor of
Business and Public Policy at the University of Texas at Dallas,
Richardson, Texas. However, most of the material was excerpted
from a paper titled "Remedial Actions to Alleviate Groundwater
Pollution from a Former Industrial Waste Disposal Site" prepared by
Robert A. Paschke, Michael A. Santoro, and Allan G. Gebhard for
the 57th Annual Conference of the Water Pollution Control
Federation held September 30 to October 4, 1984, at New Orleans,
Louisiana. Information from this paper was supplemented by a per-
sonal interview with Robert A. Paschke, Manager, Environmental
Engineering and Pollution Control, 3M Corporation, St. Paul,
Minnesota. Thanks are due to these people and the 3M Corporation
for permission to use this material.*

Throughout the 1940s and 1950s several companies near the city of
Oakdale, Minnesota—using the accepted waste disposal method of the
period—hired a contractor to haul their wastes away. One of these companies was 3M Corporation. The Oakdale contractor disposed of the generated materials on a 60-acre site in undeveloped lowlands about 10 miles from
St. Paul. The site consisted of areas for burning material, a drum recycling
operation, and disposing both organic and inorganic residues. When open
burning was outlawed, the contractor used trenches and low-lying areas on
the site to keep up with disposal. By 1960 most of the disposal areas were
filled and the contractor ceased operations. The site then became covered
with foliage and eventually the property changed hands, helping to obscure
past usage. In 1978 the state pollution control agency, having heard about
this site from some of the area's residents, conducted a preliminary investigation. In early 1980 the agency notified the potentially responsible parties,
including present and past land owners, transporters, and waste generators.

REMEDIAL INVESTIGATION

Later that year the potentially responsible parties, including 3M, were
called to a meeting at the state pollution control agency to discuss a
course of action. 3M pointed out the need for an immediate investigation

and offered to fund it, with the approval of the agency. Barr Engineering, a Minneapolis-based independent consulting firm, was hired to conduct the investigation, designed to attain the following objectives:

1. Obtain a definition of the disposal site limits, including the locations of areas that were used to dispose the wastes.
2. Define the site hydrogeology, including directions of groundwater movement and characterization of the underlying soils and bedrock in the vicinity of the site.
3. Determine the concentration and extent of contamination both in the soil and groundwater beneath the disposal site and in the surface water.
4. Recommend any further studies or remedial measures that are warranted by the results of the investigation.

To thoroughly understand the site hydrogeology and determine the extent of contamination, the investigation was conducted in three phases. The first phase consisted of obtaining deep bedrock and soil borings and creating a number of shallow monitoring wells around the contaminated site. From these locations, samples of soil and groundwater were analyzed to determine the extent of chemical migration into the site's shallow groundwater. Several groundwater measurements were also taken to define the direction of groundwater movement in the aquifers under the site.

The second phase further defined the waste disposal area, the site geology, and the extent of horizontal and vertical migration of contaminants through the bedrock aquifers. The first two phases were designed to gain an understanding of the mechanisms of contaminant migration from the shallow groundwater to the deep aquifers underlying the site. Based on this knowledge, a remedial action plan could be developed that would remove the primary sources of contamination and control the movement of the shallow contamination that could potentially contaminate the deep aquifers. These two phases were completed in April 1983 and showed that there were three separate disposal areas. These three sites were named the Abresch, Brockman, and Eberle sites after the owners of the property at the time of disposal activity.

The Abresch site, the largest of the three, consisted of about fifty acres. Initially, disposal was limited to the most southerly portion where wastes were buried in shallow trenches and burned on a regular basis. Sometime after 1955 surface waste disposal was carried out in low-lying areas and in several trenches located on higher ground. During that time the burial of waste in trenches occurred principally in the northern portion of the site where a highway was eventually constructed. In the last years of site use it appeared that most of the disposal took place just south of the highway where it was placed on the ground's surface and partially covered with soil.

Waste disposal at the Brockman site took place during the 1940s and 1950s. The site was often used when trucks could not access the low-lying areas of the Abresch site. The total area affected was about five acres. The Eberle site was used for open burning of waste, primarily off-spec products and solid waste. There was no evidence of surface disposal or waste burial in trenches at this site. The land area involved in waste disposal was about two acres.

The third phase of the investigation consisted of a final definition of the contaminant plume and a determination of the extensiveness and depth of contamination. To determine the direction of groundwater movement and to characterize the underlying soils and bedrock in the vicinity of the site, several shallow soil and deep bedrock borings were placed in and near the disposal sites. Measurements from these borings were used to determine the direction of groundwater movement in both the shallow and deeper site aquifers. This phase was completed in July 1983.

REMEDIAL ACTION

Based on the data collected during the investigations, Barr Engineering recommended a remedial action plan consisting of the following four major programs. The primary objective was to remove the major sources of contaminants and prevent any future movement of contaminants into the deeper aquifers.

1. *Reconstruct multiaquifer wells.* An aggressive program should be implemented to locate and plug multiaquifer wells where volatile organic compounds have reached deeper geological formations. The goal of this program would be to prevent the migration of contaminants into the deeper site aquifers.

2. *Remove concentrated deposits of waste.* Concentrated deposits of waste in the Abresch and Brockman sites should be removed or otherwise isolated so that they do not leach into the groundwater system beneath the disposal sites.

3. *Remove shallow groundwater.* If feasible, a shallow groundwater pump-out system should be used at the Abresch site to remove shallow groundwater which has been impacted by the waste and

to contain the migration of waste that cannot be removed from the disposal sites.

4. A network of monitoring wells should be used to assess the effectiveness of the previously described remedial measures. The wells should be sampled on a semiannual basis.

The investigation showed that the deeper groundwater formations had not been impacted by the disposal sites, and 3M saw the need to act quickly before the contamination spread. Based on the recommendations of Barr Engineering, 3M developed a more detailed remedial action plan and in December 1982 proposed this plan to the Minnesota Pollution Control Agency, the EPA, and the local government. This proposed plan was revised and amended during a series of meetings with consultants and the involved government agencies.

In July 1983 a revised and detailed remedial action plan, consisting of the four recommended programs proposed by Barr Engineering, was approved by 3M, the state pollution control agency, and the EPA. The plan focused only on the Abresch and Brockman sites. Historical evidence showed that waste burial did not occur on the Eberle site, and monitoring data collected during the remedial investigation showed insignificant levels of contaminants at and near that site.

The key to its acceptance was that the plan allowed the involved government agencies some flexibility in modifying portions of the program. As work and knowledge progressed, the agencies believed it might be necessary to adjust the plan, and under the terms of the agreement they were free to do so. The basic philosophy of 3M in the agreement was to cooperate with the regulatory agencies and local government units and resolve issues on the basis of actual data and the operating history of the system. The company tried to keep politics to a minimum.

IMPLEMENTATION

The first program involved the abandonment of multiaquifer wells. The goal was to abandon and seal all contaminated wells located in the contaminant plume. 3M assumed all costs, and, if the well was inactive, compensated the owner for the loss of the property asset. If the well was active, compensation included the value of the future water that would be lost because of the well abandonment program. The company also compensated the well owner for the inconvenience caused by the abandonment procedure.

The second program involved the removal of concentrated waste. In some cases, all materials in the disposal area were removed, and in other cases, only excavation of individual or groups of drums was accomplished. In addition, soils and waste materials that contained high levels of solvents were removed and the land was either treated or properly handled. All excavated wastes were tested by an on-site laboratory and if compatible, were incinerated at the 3M hazardous waste incinerator located about 17 miles from the sites. As a result of the burning process, the waste material volume was reduced by 80 to 90 percent. Other wastes were disposed of in the EPA's permitted disposal facilities. Procedures were developed for air quality monitoring, site security, safety and health of on-site personnel, sampling and analytical testing, transportation, and waste staging and storage.

The third program consisted of a shallow well pump-out system to contain and in the long run remove highly contaminated shallow groundwater beneath the disposal sites, preventing its movement into deeper site aquifers. Based on the types and concentration of the contaminants, several alternatives for disposing the shallow groundwater were considered. Negotiations with the Metropolitan Waste Control Commission—the local sewer authority—resulted in an agreement that allowed untreated direct discharge into the sewer system provided that mechanical ventilation and a continuous lower explosive limit meter were installed in the first discharge manhole. To assess the effectiveness of this system and the need for continued operation, samples were taken semiannually from shallow monitoring wells near the pump wells and reviewed annually with the state pollution control agency.

The fourth and last program involved establishing a monitoring well network. The network was to assess the effectiveness of the remedial programs and to detect any future contaminant migration. It consisted of several deep and shallow wells which were to be sampled every six months. The samples are analyzed for a list of indication parameters agreed to by the state pollution control agency. This monitoring process is scheduled to continue for thirty years. Results are reviewed by the state agency annually to determine if changes to the program are necessary.

Since the disposal sites were located fairly close to new community developments, it was essential to maintain positive and assertive community relations during the entire cleanup program. This was accomplished with regularly scheduled town meetings involving local residents and by maintaining a positive rapport with elected officials of the community. In addition, 3M produced a monthly newsletter to inform the residents of cleanup progress and changes in the program. A local citizen group was encouraged to comment on various technical plans submitted to the state pollution agency. And finally, a 24-hour hotline was established at the site so that concerned citizens could contact key project personnel during the cleanup. This line was intended as a direct communication link for local residents in the event that anything unusual occurred at the site, such as odors or vandalism, as well as a way for residents to express more general concerns about the cleanup.

The entire cleanup effort, from first notification to final remediation procedures, was completed in just five years. The success of this effort indicates that under certain conditions a waste dump can be cleaned up effectively and rather quickly, compared with other cleanup efforts.

Discussion Questions

1. What are the factors that contributed to the success of Oakdale's waste site cleanup? What lessons can be learned from these factors? Compare Oakdale with Woodlands Township (case 2-5). How did 3M's role change in the two cases?

2. What were the key management factors that made this cleanup a success story? Can the lessons learned from this situation be transferred to other waste sites? Are there some unique factors about Oakdale that make any generalizations suspect?

3. What was the accepted practice in the 1940s and 1950s regarding disposal of hazardous waste material? What problems has this practice caused? Is there any way these problems could have been avoided given the state of our knowledge at the time? Was it possible at that time to take more precautions?

4. What are the specific steps involved in investigating a hazardous waste disposal problem? What are the objectives of this phase of dealing with the problem? How well were these objectives attained in this case situation?

5. What remedial actions were taken? What specific problems did each of these actions address? How well were these actions implemented?

6. What kind of a monitoring network was developed to check for problems in the future? What was its purpose? How long will this monitoring program have to be continued?

3-2

MARINE SHALE PROCESSORS, INC.

This case was written by Rogene A. Buccholz, College of Business Administration, Loyola University of New Orleans. Research assistance was provided by Carol Zajicek, an M.B.A. student at Loyola University.

THE PROBLEM

Every American household generates more than a ton of rubbish per year on average. Sixty million tons from commercial activities and 90 million tons from industry make a total of around 250 million tons of solid waste produced each year in the United States. On top of this, 250 million tons of hazardous waste requiring special treatment are generated each year. Until the mid-1970s, this rubbish was handled largely by small firms or local government. Most of it was trucked to out-of-town sites and dumped. The dangerous waste was simply buried. Nobody really cared what happened to all this waste material as long as it was out of sight.[1]

Disposal of hazardous wastes is costly and time-consuming, requiring complex measures to control. Uncontrolled waste presents environmental and health risks, and action must be taken to prevent degradation of water, soil, and air and to protect human health. Initial concerns focused on fire hazards and the particulates generated by open burning. In the mid-1960s, for example, legislation was enacted to restrict open burning of garbage.

In the latter half of the 1970s, attention focused on negligent hazardous waste disposal which was causing leaching, contamination, corrosion, and poisoning of land, water, vegetation, and animals as well as human beings by toxic chemicals and heavy metals. Investigations disclosed that between 1950 and 1979 over 1.5 trillion pounds of hazardous wastes had been dumped in about 3,300 sites around the country. In 1978 alone chemical companies had dumped 132 billion pounds of industrial waste. Incidents such as Love Canal heightened public apprehension about the hazardous waste problem.[2]

Hazardous wastes have been defined as wastes that (1) cause or significantly contribute to an increase in mortality or an increase in serious irreversible or incapacitating reversible illness, or (2) pose a substantial present or potential hazard to human health or the environment when improperly treated, stored, transported, or disposed of or otherwise managed.[3] They are wastes that cannot be managed by routine procedures, because improper management threatens public health and the environment. Hazardous wastes are ignitable, corrosive, reactive, and toxic, and contain hundreds of potentially dangerous substances. Most of the 14,000 regulated producers of hazardous waste are chemical manufacturers and allied industries.

Dealing with hazardous waste is a complex, expensive, and continuing problem. The EPA won't estimate what portion of the estimated 264 metric tons generated annually is disposed of improperly. Some estimates, however, state that one out of every seven companies producing hazardous wastes may have dumped illegally in recent years. Many of these wastes found their way into streams, pastures, or vacant lots, where the risk of human contamination is high and the chance of detection slim.[4]

HAZARDOUS WASTE DISPOSAL REGULATIONS

Responsibility for control and eradication of waste disposal problems is lodged in the EPA's Office of Solid Waste and Emergency Response. This office implements two federal laws related to waste disposal, the Resource Conservation and Recovery Act (RCRA), which regulates current and future waste practices, and the Comprehensive Environmental Response, Compensation, and Liability Act (CERCLA), commonly called Superfund, which provides for cleaning up old waste sites.

RCRA controls the generation, transportation, storage, and disposal of wastes at existing or future waste facilities. Specifically, the law provides for (1) federal classification of hazardous waste, (2) a "cradle-to-grave" manifest (tracking) system for waste material, (3) federal safeguard standards for generators and transporters and facilities that treat, store, or dispose of hazardous wastes, (4) enforcement of standards for facilities through a permitting system, and (5) authorization of state programs to replace federal programs.[5]

The basic purpose of the RCRA is to regulate the management of hazardous wastes. The law provides control from point of production through point of disposal. Those who produce wastes have to obtain a permit to manage them on their own property. When shipping them to a treatment, storage, or disposal facility, they have to provide a manifest containing basic information about the waste material. All treatment, storage, and disposal operations are required to meet minimum standards to protect public health and the environment.[6]

Regulations to implement the RCRA were developed in phases. The first phase included identification of solid wastes considered to be hazardous and the establishment of reporting and record keeping for the three categories of hazardous waste handlers: generators, transporters, and owners or operators of treatment, storage, and disposal (TSD) facilities. In November 1980 these regulations became effective. By July 31, 1985, the EPA had identified 52,864 major generators of hazardous wastes, 12,343 transporters, and 4,961 TSD facilities.[7]

The second phase involved the development of technical standards related to the design and safe operation of the various types of treatment, storage, and disposal facilities. These standards serve as the basis for issuing permits to such facilities. Technical standards have been issued for incinerators, and for new and existing land disposal facilities, along with financial responsibility and liability insurance requirements for all facilities.

Congress intended the states to eventually assume responsibility for the RCRA hazardous waste program. The EPA is authorized to approve qualified state plans for hazardous waste management. To receive final authorization to operate the entire RCRA program, states must adopt regulations fully "equivalent to" and "consistent with" federal standards. Delaware became the first state to receive full authorization to operate its own program. States can be granted interim authorization by setting regulations that are "substantially equivalent to" EPA's regulations. All fifty states were expected to seek final authorization to manage their own hazardous waste programs.

Congress reauthorized the RCRA in late 1984, imposing new and far-reaching requirements on the 175,000 enterprises that generate small amounts of waste per month (between 220 and 2,200 pounds) and those that own or operate underground storage tanks. These are called small quantity generators (SQGs), and rules implemented in 1985 and modified in 1986 require any business producing or using hazardous materials or chemicals to register with the agency, and to be able to prove that the wastes from these materials are being disposed of properly. The new RCRA also bans the land disposal of hazardous wastes unless the EPA finds they will not endanger human health and the environment.[8]

THE HAZARDOUS WASTE DISPOSAL INDUSTRY

Federal and state governments have passed strict environmental standards related to disposal of hazardous waste. This action led to the formation of waste disposal companies with the capability of meeting the new environmental standards requiring safer and costlier methods of disposal.[9] These companies generally use the following four methods to dispose of hazardous waste safely:

1. *Landfills.* These burial sites for waste are high-tech operations lined with impermeable materials and constantly monitored. Trenches are built into the base of the landfills to collect noxious fluids that could leak out and contaminate drinking water. These are then pumped to the surface and made inert. Landfills that do not meet such stringent standards are being closed all over the country.

2. *Incineration.* There are over 100 incinerators in the United States today that burn waste material and in some cases generate energy from this burning. Hazardous waste is burned at very high temperatures in special incinerators. These incinerators must have the technology to capture noxious fumes that are generated in the process of burning. Some of these incinerators have been in operation for several years and may need to be modernized.

3. *Recycling.* Some hazardous waste is recycled, but the problems with respect to recycling hazardous waste are even greater than the problems involved with recycling solid waste. The EPA wants to build a nationwide waste exchange to facilitate the exchange of both solid and hazardous waste and promote recycling.[10]

4. *Storage.* Some hazardous waste is simply stored in covered facilities that are not in close proximity to populated areas. Proper protection must be provided for leaking drums that might threaten groundwater supplies, and the stored material must be constantly monitored for leakage and other potential problems.

The costs of disposing of waste materials has increased dramatically over the past several years. In 1978, for example, it cost about $2.50 to have a ton of hazardous waste dropped into a safe hole in the ground. In 1987 the cost of disposing of hazardous waste in this fashion ranged from $200 a ton upwards. Burning the waste cost $50 a ton in 1978, while in

1987 fees ran at over $200 a ton and $2,000 a ton for really nasty waste. Garbage companies a decade ago charged only $3 a ton to get rid of common or garden rubbish. Today a community like Long Island, which ships out nearly all of its household rubbish, will pay $130 a ton to have the stuff removed.[11]

Even though operating margins of the garbage companies have increased, making them quite profitable, the industry has problems with regulators and the public. The laws regulating disposal are inconsistent, laxly monitored, and seldom enforced, which creates distortions in the market. Definitions of hazardous waste differ and national laws on air, water, and soil pollution are seldom mutually coherent. Companies find it difficult to get permits for landfill sites and incinerators because of the "not-in-my-backyard" syndrome. Nations and communities alike object to the importation of waste from elsewhere.[12]

A SOLUTION

Anyone who can promise to eliminate hazardous waste is bound to attract attention. In 1984 Jack Kent, a high school dropout and native of Tangipahoa Parish in Louisiana, took a rather simple idea about toxic waste material, combined it with an abandoned lime kiln, and built a different kind of recycling plant near Morgan City, Louisiana. While others continued to talk about waste management and control and treatment of hazardous waste, Kent was talking about hazardous waste elimination.[13]

Kent had worked for more than 15 years in the aggregate abrasives and barite (oil-drilling muds) business in southern Louisiana. These wastes contain high levels of heavy metals and various toxic organics. His experience with handling these wastes apparently gave him some hope that these materials could be processed and recycled to make them into nonhazardous and reusable materials. What he had in mind was to completely burn away the chemical poisons and recycle the shale rock, the barite drilling muds, the drill-bit metals, and anything else useful that could be found in those marine sludges.[14]

Thus was founded Marine Shale Processors (MSP). The word *Marine* referred to the receipt of drilling cuttings by water, *Shale* referred to the drilling cuttings, and the word *Processing* represented the process which changed the shale from a hazardous substance to a nonhazardous product. Kent adapted a 275-by-12-foot rotary kiln that was once used to produce lime to process hazardous waste. The kiln could generate very high temperatures which made it possible to treat a much wider variety of wastes than the oil field material. It was discovered that the "little cooker" could oxidize just about anything and reduce it to an inert, nontoxic aggregate that could be used as construction filler in road building or dock filling.[15]

MSP received state and federal permits to operate as a recycler rather than as a commercial incinerator of hazardous wastes and became the largest hazardous waste recycler in the country. Daily capacity was estimated at five times that of typical incinerator facilities elsewhere in the country, and in 1987 and 1988 volume totaled in excess of 120,000 tons annually. In early 1985 the company employed only thirty people; by 1988 MSP had 300 employees. The company boasted of being just short of having seventy Fortune 500 companies as clients, and was adding one more major company each week to its list.[16] Sales bounded from $5.5 million in 1986 to $39 million in 1988, and in 1989 revenues were expected to reach between $60 and $80 million. In 1988 MSP ranked 43rd among Louisiana's top 100 private companies.[17]

Some experts were skeptical about claims that MSP had discovered a revolutionary new recycling process for solving the country's toxic waste problem. There had been other claims made about the disposal of toxic waste that had proved to be unworkable or unsafe. When signing on as clients, companies sent in their best chemists, engineers, consultants, and lawyers to make sure that their wastes would be eliminated in a manner that is environmentally safe. MSP also tried to improve its image by claiming to have relied on the technical expertise of such highly regarded environmental consulting and testing firms as Woodward-Clyde Consultants, West-Paine Laboratories, York Environmental Services, and Wadsworth-Alert.[18] The following is a quote from Woodward-Clyde as to the safety of MSP's operations:

> Based on our knowledge of the Marine Shale Processors, Inc. (MSP) Amelia, Louisiana facility, it is our opinion that his facility is very beneficial to the protection of our environment. MSP used certain recyclable materials, some of which would be otherwise classified as hazardous waste, to produce an environmentally safe aggregate product. The recyclable materials are totally consumed by the process. Except for the aggregate and scrap metal products, and the discharge of flue gases under its stringent air permits, no other streams, water or otherwise, are discharged from the process. MSP's process is a net consumer of water. Consequently, MSP utilizes contaminated rainwater to supplement its process water needs. It is our opinion that the MSP operation is environmentally safe and that it is not a threat to public health and the environment.[19]

MSP claimed to be offering its clients the best available technology in all three (solids, water, and air) of the major components of hazardous waste elimination. In addition, MSP delivered these services with two other major advantages over incinerators. Its prices were about half those of other companies. And its final product was clean enough to be sold for commercial use and did not need to go into a toxic landfill. This reduced exposure of waste generators to future lawsuits that might be filed should the landfill prove to be unsafe and a source of future environmental damage through leakage or spillage.[20] According to a booklet prepared by MSP,

> Marine Shale Processors, Inc. (MSP) has developed a technology that enables it to do what no other company in the world can do: it uses hazardous materials as ingredients and fuel to produce a safe aggregate product. This recycling technology renders incinerators obsolete. We're different from waste disposal companies, partial recyclers, and incinerators because we use 100 percent of the materials we receive to manufacture and produce a safe product. This means nothing goes into a landfill or a RCRA deep well that would increase your liability, an important consideration to any manager with his eye on the bottom line.[21]

The major competitors of MSP operate as incinerators and other industrial furnaces similar to MSP's technology (cement kilns) under federal and state laws and have had to go through a permitting process. They have accused MSP of being a sham recycler and a renegade operating under a loophole in the law. They have been trying in the state legislature and in Congress to have MSP reclassified as an incinerator, which would put the company in regulatory limbo, forcing it to close down at least temporarily while it applied for the necessary permits. The Louisiana State Legislature resisted this reclassification and unanimously passed a bill that recognized, verified, certified, and regulated MSP as a manufacturing facility which legitimately recycles hazardous wastes into commercially valuable aggregates. The company also hoped to convince national lawmakers that MSP's technology is a real solution to the nation's hazardous waste problem.[22]

THE PROCESS

MSP utilizes a vitrification process which it claims is unique in the industry. It initially received a Notice of Allowance from the U.S. Patent Office on its patent application for this unique process, and a U.S. patent was eventually issued in the name of John M. Kent, the inventor of the process (see box). The process effectively removes organics from the feedstock and seals heavy metals at the molecular level to prevent them from leaching into the environment. Vitrification is a thermal process of tightly fusing silica and metallic oxide materials together in a slagged or glasslike matrix by heating the materials to molten temperature of at least 2500 degrees F and then cooling to ambient temperatures. It has been found that molten glass or slag can dissolve or capture most heavy metals and be highly resistant to leaching when cooled to a solid state. Various forms of these glasslike materials are stable and an excellent medium for sealing hazardous waste.[23]

Hazardous waste is formed into non-hazardous non-leaching aggregate by introducing the material to a rotary kiln where the large solids are at least partially combusted to form a primary aggregate. Gaseous combustion by-products and waste fines from the waste materials are introduced into at least one oxidizer operating at a temperature in the range of from about 1800 degrees to 2500 degrees F. Under such conditions, some of the waste fines are melted to form a slag-like material that is cooled to form the non-hazardous aggregate. The portion of the material in the oxidizer that is not melted, is cooled, neutralized and subjected to a solid gas separation. The solid is reintroduced to the oxidizer with the primary aggregate where they are either melted or entrained within the molten material and become an integral part of the non-hazardous aggregate.

Source: United States Patent number 4,922,841 dated May 8, 1990 entitled "Method and Apparatus for Using Hazardous Waste to Form Non-Hazardous Aggregate."

MSP recycles hazardous and industrial solid materials as raw ingredients to produce a usable aggregate product that is free from any hazardous characteristics. The primary elements of the processing system are a 275-foot counter-current rotary kiln, a puddling furnace, two oxidizers, an alkaline dry spray reactor, and baghouses for particulate control. Sludges and solids are fed into the elevated end of the kiln and move toward the lower end with a residence time of 120 to 150 minutes. The lower end of the kiln, where temperatures are maintained at approximately 1200 degrees C, is fired with natural gas and liquid fuels. Oxygen and makeup air are also introduced to support oxidation. Solids coming out of the lower end of the kiln are separated, with fine materials sent to be vitrified in the puddling furnace, and large materials such as gravels and ferrous materials stored for testing before being sold.[24]

THE CONTROVERSY

In 1989 the Hazardous Waste Treatment Council (HWTC) (a lobbying group for the treatment, storage, and disposal industry) and Greenpeace began to warn manufacturers that generate hazardous waste to beware of facilities that claim to "recycle" and produce environmentally safe solids from commercially produced hazardous waste. Greenpeace targeted MSP in particular because, as the largest hazardous waste recycler in the nation, it recycled more than 100,000 tons of hazardous waste a year from all forty-eight contiguous states, and thus offered a way out for companies to dispose of their waste safely. Greenpeace wanted to eliminate the generation of waste in the first place.

These groups challenged MSP's claim to be a recycler, which exempted it from some regulatory standards that apply to hazardous waste incinerators. The groups raised an issue with regard to MSP's operations by charging that few aggregate sales had been documented and that 99 percent of MSP's revenue ($40 million in 1988) came from charging customers to recycle their wastes. Greenpeace warned that generators who send their waste to MSP could possibly be held liable for any resulting pollution and cleanup.[25] Actually, such liability is possible no matter where companies send their waste. But since MSP is producing an end-product that is not subject to regulation, an argument can be made that the liability is gone. The executive director of the HWTC, Richard Fortuna, charged that MSP is "a renegade company that should have been regulated as an incinerator years ago but has masqueraded as a recycler to evade regulation" under the Resource Conservation and Recovery Act (RCRA). Mr. Fortuna noted that MSP hurt the 65 hazardous waste incinerator firms he represents because they put the firms that spend the money and time to comply with RCRA regulations at a competitive disadvantage. He warned Congress that there is a growing trend for hazardous waste burners to redefine themselves out of RCRA regulations by claiming that their own wastes are useful products.[26]

By mid-1989 MSP had been issued proposed penalty notices totaling $4.5 million for more than 50 alleged violations of Louisiana's hazardous waste and air quality regulations. These notices were suspended pending hearing on appeal, but no hearings were held. Some of these alleged violations involved leachate being discharged into a bayou.[27] In 1986 the Coast Guard found that the company had been storing hazardous materials in barges on nearby Bayou Boeuf, and at least one of them was tilted over at a 40-degree angle so that the material could wash into the bayou. The Louisiana Department of Environmental Quality (LADEQ) alleged that MSP had been emitting pollutants into the air, ground, and water since it had opened for business.[28] The LADEQ alleged that the recycler did not have proper waste storage facilities, certain permits, environmental safeguards, waste control, personnel training, sampling procedures, security, or paperwork.[29]

The company was also under investigation by the U.S. Department of Justice and the EPA. However, on January 13, 1989, a federal grand jury in Lafayette ended its 22-month investigation without returning any indictments against the company.[30] There were no allegations of damage to the environment and no charges against any officer or employee connected with the company. The investigation included two criminal search warrants, nine subpoenas for MSP documents, the testimony of over 40 MSP employees, vendors, and consultants, and hundreds of other interviews. The government took and analyzed hundreds of samples at MSP's facility and from Bayou Boeuf, plus dozens of samples of the company's aggregate products both on and off the plant site.[31]

But several months later, the Justice Department announced that MSP had agreed to pay a $1 million fine as part of plea bargain, ending a two-and-one-half-year investigation. The company pleaded guilty to a felony count involving violations of the RCRA for storing creosote sludges in an uncovered pile on a concrete pad for five months. The company also pleaded guilty to two misdemeanors, one involving a violation of the Rivers and Harbors Act of 1899 by discharging into Bayou Boeuf wash water from the outside cleaning of a barge, and the other a violation of the same act for refloating a sunken barge and turning it into a bulkhead. A spokesperson for the company said that MSP believed it could defend itself against the allegations, but decided the plea bargain was in the best interests of the company and its customers.[32] As a result of the settlement, all unfounded allegations including those concerning the company's operating permits, patent-pending process, and aggregate products were dropped by the government.[33]

The state temporarily halted its investigation into MSP's status as a recycler, but a spokesperson for the LADEQ said it would continue to seek information about the aggregate. Some of the violations, orders, and proposed penalty notices were directed at MSP's storage practices, which have the potential for fire, heat, and explosion hazards and may release chemicals into the air and water. But the state also claimed that some of the aggregate produced as a product of the recycling process might be a hazardous waste itself. The state alleged that the aggregate might be contaminated with lead and other heavy metals that may leach into the environment and threaten public health.[34] However, all testing by the LADEQ and the federal EPA failed to prove the substance harmful.[35] (See box.)

"We have not seen evidence of a hazard that would rise to the level of imminent and substantial endangerment to public health and the environment." James O. Neet, Regional Counsel, U.S. Environmental Protection Agency, Region VI, March 29, 1988.

"Based on the best technical advice that we could get from our regional officials, we felt and continue to feel that there is and was no imminent and substantial endangerment. Samples on the aggregate were taken from the MSP site during the execution of the November, 1986, and June, 1988, search warrants. Additional aggregate samples were taken from six off-site locations during a September 16, 1987, inspection. Analysis of those samples did not reveal any health risks." Edward Reich, Acting Assistant Administrator for Enforcement and Compliance Monitoring, U.S. Environmental Protection Agency, September 21, 1989.

"There have been numerous meetings between the Department and EPA, and scrutiny of the factual data EPA has gathered, but never have we been able to conclude that the facility posed an imminent and substantial endangerment to human health or the environment. I have been apprised by the attorneys, by the investigators, that in fact, during the course of the investigation, that there were substantial steps taken to correct problems as they were brought to the attention of Marine Shale." Myles E. Flint. Deputy Assistant Attorney General, Lands and Natural Resources Division, U.S. Department of Justice.

Greenpeace also charged that MSP's incinerator ash, which is what they call the aggregate product, was not safe to use for any purpose. An article in its magazine claimed that the LADEQ identified some of its aggregate piles as hazardous (which was not the case) and directed the company to remove these piles to "an approved off-site facility." The article challenged MSP's commercials saying that the company turns toxic nightmares into harmless materials. In addition to producing "aggregate," the article stated that MSP's so-called recycling process releases a host of toxic by-products into the environment.[36]

A Morgan City citizens group called South Louisiana Against Pollution, which was formed and funded by the HWTC, claimed that toxic discharges from MSP's kiln contributed to an outbreak of rare childhood cancer called neuroblastoma. Two children had died from this cancer. The connection between MSP's emissions and the children's deaths in 1988 has never been proven scientifically, and evidence indicates that the problem is not MSP's.[37] An LSU Medical Center study found no common factor between the five cases of neuroblastoma and two control groups to establish a local cause for the disease. And there was not sufficient evidence to prove that a link exists between the five cases in this area and Marine Shale Processors Inc. of Amelia, which a group of residents had targeted for blame. The incident turned some public sentiment for a time against Jack Kent, the president of MSP, and caused them to question some of the charitable contributions he had made to the city.[38] Some doctors on the staff of Lakewood Hospital in Morgan City signed a resolution asking the government to rescind MSP's permits and shut the company down until investigations involving MSP are finished. This resolution was replied to by the president of the company.

Then in May 1989 the company received a proposed penalty notice of $1 million for illegally accepting waste from a foreign country. The importation charge involved nineteen shipments of waste from two companies based in Ontario, Canada, between July 1988 and January 1989. This action effectively removed all authority for the plant to continue receiving, storing, and burning hazardous waste, but MSP had twenty days to appeal the actions and request a hearing. The company could continue to operate during the appeal process. Even if the LADEQ's actions were upheld in the hearing, the company indicated it would sue to continue operating.[39] Eventually, the state received a court order in July 1989 to announce that MSP's permits were not rescinded.

The state agency also said it was continuing to investigate the aggregate and had issued an order prohibiting MSP from moving the substance off its Amelia site until the state and MSP can agree to a sampling testing program. The aggregate test results are significant because they could mean that waste generators who shipped their waste to MSP were liable for any environmental damages caused by the aggregate. These shippers included federal agencies and many Fortune 500 companies. State officials also won a court order to investigate MSP's records for proof of illegal shipments of dioxins or PCBs from Illinois.[40] No evidence was found that this was occurring.

Jack Kent alleged that the LADEQ was a pawn of competing incinerator companies such as Rollins Environmental Services located in Baton Rouge. Kent wrote in a letter that "[I] . . . have been accused of everything in the world, burning PCBs and dioxins, killing children, causing untold dangers to the environment. . . . When anybody fools with me, I'm going to react. It's just that simple. I'm not going to sit back and let someone slap me." Kent asked that the governor appoint an arbitrator because he believed the LADEQ could not be fair. Kent said he would abide by any decision the arbitrator would make, including shutting down the plant.[41]

In August 1989 a plan submitted by MSP at the request of the LADEQ to sample the sediments in Bayou Boeuf was rejected by state officials. In 1988 the state had issued an order to the company to stop storing hazardous wastes on barges and to sample and clean sediment in Bayou Boeuf. A state official said the plan fails to adequately address the problem and improperly combined a program for soil sampling with a plan to fill a barge slip with aggregate made by the company. The agency would be receptive if the company wanted to resubmit a proposal. Its sediment sampling proposal would have to adequately address the concerns of the department.[42] The company eventually submitted such a sampling plan that was accepted by the state, so the issue is resolved.

Then in September 1989 Governor Buddy Roemer rejected the advice of the State Senate Natural Resources Committee and upheld new environmental rules regulating MSP. The House Natural Resources Committee had accepted the rules unanimously. Roemer stated that the regulations were in keeping with laws passed in 1988 that ordered the LADEQ to draft rules requiring recycling facilities to obtain a permit and meet certain operating standards to limit air emissions. The rules also required recyclers to conduct a trial burn and to meet other requirements. These regulations put recyclers under the same technical and emission requirements as those in the business of hazardous waste incineration.[43]

CONCLUSION

The controversy about MSP thus continued, becoming more and more complicated. It seemed as if most of the allegations were technical and procedural rather than environmental, based on complicated arguments about the applicability of the hazardous waste regulations to the MSP recycling operations. Throughout, two points of view seemed to emerge. On the one hand, MSP was accused of exploiting a loophole in RCRA and getting itself classified as a recycler when in fact it was an incinerator. This classification gave MSP a competitive advantage in charging what it regarded as a fair market value for its services and in advertising that the company produced a harmless product thereby eliminating the threat of any future liabilities for generators. On the other hand, MSP could be a legitimate recycling operation, with competitors pressuring the LADEQ and the EPA to keep on raising questions about its operations as well as its product. When the EPA and the Justice Department investigated the issue over a two-year period, Justice Department officials under sworn testimony concluded in September 1989 that MSP was not a sham recycler.

As for the future of the company, MSP has submitted applications to the Department of Environmental Quality for modification of its existing permits to activate a second rotary kiln on the site and install a puddling furnace for metals recovery in the one that is operational. This latter addition would allow MSP to recycle and recapture high-grade iron ingots from up to 150 tons a week of contaminated iron and steel. The puddling furnace would allow MSP to process enough steel to sustain a small steel mill on adjacent property.[44]

Within the last year, two new baghouses have been installed. A new continuous emissions monitoring system has also been installed and patents have been applied for this system. Plans were also underway to implement improvements to the process control computer, and build a 70,000-square-foot building to contain the process.[45] A Marine Shale Processors research and development team is making history. The world's first continuous real-time speciated organic emissions monitoring system (CEMS) is now being tested at the Amelia company. A complementary ambient air system is already on-line. When testing is complete and the systems are fully operable, MSP will be the first such manufacturer in the world with the ability to monitor air quality for safety on a 24-hour basis. These capital spending projects are expected to cost the company more than $7.5 million and would "further cement the firm's reputation as the nation's foremost innovator of hazardous waste recycling technology" and "ensure that MSP's manufacturing plant is among the nation's most environmentally safe industrial facilities."[46]

Discussion Questions

1. What are hazardous wastes? What problems do they pose for society? What regulations exist with respect to the disposal of hazardous waste? In general, how has the private sector responded to this problem?

2. What was Marine Shale's response to the problem of hazardous wastes? How did the company get started? What was the nature of the technology employed? Was this technology

tested and proven safe and effective? What questions were eventually raised about the technological process MSP employed?

3. What competitive advantages did MSP have over incineration? What claims did it make to try and attract customers? Were these claims legitimate, in your opinion? If you were the CEO of a company producing waste material, would you sent it to MSP for processing?

4. In your opinion, is MSP a legitimate or sham recycler? What evidence can you bring to bear on either side of this question? What was the controversy about? What motives did competitors have to put MSP out of business? Is there any clear resolution to this controversy that has emerged?

5. What about the future of MSP? Is further capital investment a good idea at this point? If you were an investor, should you sell your stock or stick with the company believing in its potential? What political strategies should MSP adopt?

NOTES

1. "The Garbage Industry: Where There's Muck There's High Technology," *The Economist*, April 8, 1989, p. 23.

2. Samuel Epstein et al., *Hazardous Wastes In America* (San Francisco: Sierra, 1982), p. 303.

3. Office of Research and Development, *Controlling Hazardous Waste Research Summary* (Washington, D.C.: Environmental Protection Agency, 1980), p. 4.

4. Barry Meier, "Dirty Job: Against Heavy Odds, EPA Tries to Convict Polluters and Dumpers," *Wall Street Journal*, January 7, 1985, p. 1.

5. Ronald J. Penoyer, *Reforming Regulation of Hazardous Waste* (St. Louis, MO: Washington University Center for the Study of American Business, 1985), p. 1.

6. Environmental Protection Agency, *Better Health and Regulatory Reform* (Washington, D.C., 1987) p. 16.

7. Environmental Protection Agency, *The Resource Conservation and Recovery Act: What It Is; How It Works*, SW-967 (Washington, D.C.), 1983, p. 5; Environmental Protection

Agency, *The New RCRA: A Fact Book* (Washington, D.C.), 1985, p. 4.

8. Environmental Protection Agency, *The New RCRA: A Fact Book,* pp. 1–2.

9. "The Garbage Industry," p. 23.

10. Ibid., pp. 23–24. See also Evan I. Schwartz, "A Data Base That Truly Is Garbage In, Garbage Out," *Business Week,* September 17, 1990, p. 92.

11. Ibid., p. 24.

12. Ibid., pp. 24–26.

13. Maxine Domino, "Louisiana Lava: Marine Shale's Solution to the Hazardous Waste Crisis," *Business & Industry Coordinator,* Vol. 5, No. 4 (August–September 1988), p. 17.

14. Ibid.

15. Ibid.

16. Ibid., pp. 17–18.

17. Jeffery Meitrodt, "The Top 100," *City Business,* January 16, 1989, p. 20.

18. Domino, "Louisiana Lava," p. 18.

19. Marine Shale Processors, Inc., *MSP: Hazardous Waste RECY-CLED to Safe Aggregate!,* booklet, n.d., p. 4.

20. Domino, "Louisiana Lava," p. 24.

21. Marine Shale Processors, Inc., "Chairman's Message," booklet, n.d., p. 1.

22. Domino, "Louisiana Lava," p. 39.

23. C.A. Whitehurst, et al., *The MSP Vitrification Process: A Technology Ready for Transfer,* n.d., pp. 1–2.

24. Ibid., p. 4.

25. Joani Nelson-Horchler, "Beware of Sham Recyclers," *Industry Week,* April 17, 1989, p. 85.

26. Ibid.

27. Ibid.

28. Judy Christrup, "Nasty Business: The Marine Shale Masquerade," Greenpeace, May–June 1989, p. 14.

29. Zack Nauth, "Marine Shale Fined $1.75 Million More," *Times-Picayune* (New Orleans), January 14, 1989, p. A–1.

30. "Waste Company Avoids Indictments," *Times-Picayune* (New

Orleans), January 13, 1989, p. B–6.

31. MSP press release, July 24, 1989.

32. "Marine Shale Agrees to $1 Million Fine," *Times-Picayune* (New Orleans), January 25, 1989, p. B–6.

33. MSP press release, July 24, 1989.

34. Nauth, "Marine Shale Fined $1.75 Million More," p. A–1.

35. James O'Byrne, "State: Marine Shale Failed Air Pollution Permit Test," *Times-Picayune* (New Orleans), March 16, 1989, p. A–28.

36. Christrup, "Nasty Business," p. 15.

37. "LSU Study Finds No Link in Child Cancer Cases," *The Daily Review*, April 28, 1989, pp. 1, 12.

38. Christrup, "Nasty Business," p. 14.

39. Zack Nauth, "La. Seizes Permits of Toxic Waste Plant," *Times-Picayune* (New Orleans), May 27, 1989, p. A–1.

40. Ibid.

41. Ibid.

42. "DEQ Rejects Recycler's Waste Plan," *Times-Picayune* (New Orleans), August 18, 1989, p. B–12.

43. Bill McMahon, "Roemer OKs MSP Waste Regulations," *Morning Advocate*, September 9, 1989, p. 25. See also Jack Wardlaw and Ed Anderson, "Roemer Clears Way for DEQ to Regulate Toxic Waste Recycler," *Times-Picayune* (New Orleans), September 19, 1989, p. B–5.

44. Domino, "Louisiana Lava," p. 41.

45. "Continuous Monitoring System Brings MSP Worldwide Acclaim," *The Daily Review*, June 9, 1989, p. 5.

46. *Hazardous Waste Update*, a quarterly publication of Marine Shale Processors, Inc., Spring 1989, p. 1.

3-3

POLAROID'S TOXIC USE AND WASTE REDUCTION PROGRAM

This case was written by Catherine Frisch with the assistance of Thomas Peters, under the editorial guidance of James E. Post, Professor of Management Policy, Boston University School of Management. The authors are grateful for the cooperation of Polaroid executives and staff. © 1989, Public Affairs Research Program, Boston University, 621 Commonwealth Avenue, Boston, MA 02215.

TOXIC USE AND WASTE REDUCTION AT POLAROID

Late in 1987 Harry Fatkin, director of Corporate Health, Safety and Environmental Affairs, leaned back in his chair, deep in thought. At its spring 1987 stockholders meeting Polaroid announced a plan to reduce the company's total waste by 10 percent per year over the next five years. But it was clear that Polaroid's Toxic Use and Waste Reduction model (TUWR), adapted from Congress' Office of Technology and Assessment's (OTA) model, had some problems. The essence of the OTA model was a ratio of waste generated to product produced. It gave no credit for recycling waste, nor did it differentiate between the levels of waste toxicity. At Polaroid, there was internal resistance to the TUWR program. Fatkin knew he would have to resolve the problems of model shortcomings and internal dissatisfaction before TUWR could effectively work.

Fatkin also wondered how Polaroid should respond to the Toxic Use Reduction bill that MassPIRG, a public interest group, was planning to introduce to the Massachusetts General Assembly. Because Polaroid had endorsed toxic use reduction by adapting the OTA model, Fatkin believed that if Polaroid did not respond favorably to the bill, the company would appear hypocritical to the public. However, to applaud the bill might make Polaroid look "Pollyanna-ish" in the eyes of the industry. Top management held high expectations for the TUWR program. Fatkin, too, was deeply invested in it; he sat on the OTA panel that developed the model and was responsible for implementing TUWR at Polaroid.

METHODS OF WASTE REDUCTION

In-process Recycling

Example: separating and recovering cleaning solvents from wastewater to be used again within the closed loop of the process.

Plant Operations

Example: managing the rinse cycle more efficiently. For instance, to save on the amount of waste rinse water in the nickel plating process, the operator should preheat the rinse water, allow metals to dry in optimal position and optimal time between rinses, and use a fine spray for rinsing.

Process Technology and Equipment

Example: for paint removal, replacing the use of acidic methylene chloride with a modified sandblasting technique which uses recoverable plastic beads instead of sand.

Process Inputs

Example: substituting water-based inks for organic solvent-based inks in printing, and substituting less hazardous solvents for the carcinogen benzene which is used to dissolve chemicals in preparation for blending.

End-Products

Example: changing from oil-base to water-base consumer house paints.

POLLUTION CONTROL VERSUS WASTE REDUCTION

Pollution control focuses on end-of-pipe emissions and therefore generally does not require major disruptions to the production process. Waste reduction seeks to reduce or eliminate pollution at the source, requiring research and development efforts and changes in raw materials, processes, or products. Each approach can be costly but in different ways.

Pollution control devices represent extra costs in production, not additional productive capacity. Many require large initial capital outlays and are costly to operate. The control-oriented system causes the costs of producing, treating, and legally disposing of hazardous waste to increase. Furthermore, even if a waste generator disposes of its waste legally, it can still be named liable under Superfund laws if that waste ends up at a site. (See Appendix for a description of the legal environment.) For example, Polaroid was assessed $400,000 for the actions of one of its vendors who falsified incinerator records and engaged in illegal dumping.[1]

The decision to implement the technology depends partially on the economics of a product and often includes production, finance, and marketing considerations. Waste reduction can alter the raw materials required for production. This can alter the product itself, so a market analysis is critical. The waste generator should perform an audit on where it uses chemicals, what quantity it uses, and where waste, leakage, worker exposure, and production of unsafe products occur.

All generators of toxic waste bear the increasing costs of worker health and disability insurance. Pollution control costs, however, include as well facilities that have to be built, operating costs, increased manufacturing costs, and retained sales of products that may be taken off the market because they are found environmentally unacceptable. Waste reduction costs, on the other hand, are included under capitalization costs and are therefore more difficult to isolate. Production costs may even be decreased due to increased efficiency and safety.

COMPANY BACKGROUND AND ORGANIZATION

Headquartered in Cambridge, Massachusetts, and operating since 1937, Polaroid designs, manufactures, and markets cameras, film, light polarizing filters, lenses, and chemical, optical, and industrial products. In 1987, at fifteen plants worldwide, Polaroid's operations "produced thousands of tons of waste, much of it from a thousand chemicals created or converted as part of the company's manufacturing processes."[2] Polaroid is organized in a divisional matrix along functional and manufacturing lines. Each division is autonomous, with one person responsible for corporate functions. Said Fatkin, "You need to have people who are linked with the structure and development of policy . . . but who are also part of the divisional team because they need to be influential there."

The Health, Safety and Environmental Affairs Division is separated into five areas: safety, toxicology and industrial hygiene, environment, government relations, and the matrix. Polaroid's matrix system requires every division to assign someone to handle safety and someone to handle the environment. These individuals report to a division manager and to Fatkin. As Fatkin explained, a Divisional Safety Engineer would be "taking policy direction in this area from me, but also working in support of the director . . . to help them develop waste reduction plans and do things that make less waste."

Fatkin reports to a vice president whose duties also include product introduction. Fatkin also meets monthly with the Health, Safety and

Environmental Steering Committee. MacAllister Booth, president and CEO of Polaroid, is a member of the steering committee, as are the vice presidents of manufacturing, research and engineering, and human resources, the secretary, and the chief legal officer. The director of public relations and a director of research also sit on the committee. This group makes environmental policy. Booth and Polaroid's senior officers make up the Management Executive Committee, responsible for setting corporatewide goals and policies.

WASTE REDUCTION BEFORE TUWR: POLAROID'S CHEMICAL OPERATIONS DIVISION

Since 1980 Polaroid's Chemical Operations Division thought of itself as waste reduction–conscious. The division, which produces sixty to seventy synthesized dyes used primarily to develop instant photographs, had undertaken projects to reduce costs, which, it was found, reduced wastes. The division is Polaroid's largest waste generator, accounting for two thirds of the company's total waste. Because there was no formal system of waste reduction, the division looked at changes that were easy to make and that provided quick payback. One Polaroid division environmental engineer said of the TUWR announcement,

> For [Chemical Operations], it wasn't a big deal. The big deal was that before [TUWR] we could work at a leisurely pace. We didn't look at categories and say we'll go after some of the more toxic ones first. We looked at the ones that had the best economic payback or were easiest to do. The corporate program formalized [waste reduction efforts]. It made us work a little faster and put our efforts into it. And the implementation was a little faster, a little more formal.

Waste generated at Chemical Operations was of three types: emissions to the air, waste included with water, and solids and liquids collected in the chemical process. Collected wastes comprised the majority of waste handled, and there were various options for disposing of them. Ideally, collected wastes would be managed at the facility that generated them. If this option was unfeasible, the waste would be transferred and recovered at another Polaroid facility. A final option was to send it off-site for treatment by another company. This was the least preferable because Polaroid had less control over what ultimately happened to it. The division initiated informal waste generation and waste management reports, both of which were reviewed at various levels. However, no formal process reports were generated, and no chemical-specific reporting had been done except at the end of each year.

WASTE REDUCTION POLICY AT POLAROID

In 1984 Fatkin joined the OTA Advisory Panel which composed the study, "Serious Reduction of Hazardous Waste: For Pollution Prevention and Industrial Efficiency." Fatkin explored the issue of waste reduction at the panel meetings. In 1985, based on what he learned at the OTA, he began advocating waste reduction strategies at Polaroid. Fatkin remembered,

> I learned a lot about the issue of waste reduction, the definitional problems, the national data base, the charges and counter-charges. As that experience went on in 1984-1985, I and others were working with the divisions on strategies they could develop around waste reduction. I would say from 1985, we were trying to get some joining and some consensus.

During an 18-month period Fatkin put the topic of waste reduction on the agenda of the Health, Safety and Environmental Affairs Steering Committee meetings. Fatkin recalled,

> It was on the agenda six or seven times that year, initiating dialogue around the issue of waste reduction. That set the groundwork for it. We had discussions with all kinds of people in the company just to make sure that we felt good about the commitment, the direction, and the follow through. There was controversy; waste reduction is not self-evident to everybody until you get into it. Mac [Booth] basically bought, as did the Steering Committee, the concept of what gets generated by our processes as the focal point for our reduction program.

Despite the ongoing waste reduction dialogue, no program had been formulated. Then, in 1986, two events caused Polaroid to bring waste reduction to the forefront. First, the EPA changed its definition of volatile organic compounds. Polaroid, under the new definition, was out of compliance. Second, Greenpeace generated bad publicity about Polaroid. A Greenpeace report stated, "Polaroid discharges more toxic chemicals into Boston Harbor each day than General Electric, Honeywell, Monsanto, Gillette, Mobil, Digital Equipment, General Motors, and Hewlett-Packard combined." Bill Schwalm, Polaroid's Senior Manager for Environmental Programs in Manufacturing, remembered how Greenpeace hung sheets by the company's Waltham, Massachusetts, facility that proclaimed Polaroid as the state's biggest polluter. "They hung it over the bridge, right outside the facility on Route 128 so that the cars going under could see it. It certainly didn't help our image." In response to these developments, Polaroid decided to implement the pieces Fatkin had informally promoted among Polaroid's divisions.

Polaroid had based its waste reduction program on the OTA model. This model suggests that companies account for generated materials before end-of-pipe treatment and that programs not be limited by current regulatory status of materials. The OTA model reflects the belief that firms operate under regulations that change quickly, and that these changes often leave companies out of compliance. Fatkin said, "What we really wanted to do was nail down our waste reduction program in some way that would anticipate the future so we wouldn't get jerked around by regulatory definitions."

The OTA model suggests that waste reduction be based on per unit of production. This definition ensures true waste reduction. The OTA stated, "Any statistical system that does not relate waste generated to units produced can distort reality. For example, a slowdown in production may generate less toxic waste *by total volume*, even though waste *per unit of production* remains the same, or even increases."[3]

The OTA goal of 10 percent waste reduction per year over the next five years was also adopted by Polaroid. Fatkin said,

> We decided to put together in one clear, publicly stated, and committed way all those pieces that we had been filling in the previous two years. It seemed to me that there were opportunities for waste reduction, significant waste reduction. The OTA offered this 10 percent a year for the next five years so we looked at that and said . . . let's just go for that.

The OTA program implies that waste reduction saves money because less waste means less costs in hauling, treating, and so on. Jim Ahearn, director of Chemical Process Research and Development, stated,

> You use less substances, throw less stuff away. Most materials now cost less to buy than they do to throw away. You can buy a gallon of methanol for about $.85, and it costs you $1.20 to throw it away. Even if you don't do anything with it, and just take it and put it in the waste drum, you more than double the costs.

Still, Polaroid officials claimed their TUWR program was not economically based but environmentally based. Fatkin said,

> What we did was an environmental initiative. If you only focus on the economics, you may in the short run be doing something that's economically good. But in the long run, you might not be doing something that is economically good. If you only track issues like liability, then you are only dealing with those things that are currently regulated. But if in two or five years the ground rules change, you could be in trouble. Implicit in the thinking about waste reduction is that you can save money; yields are going to go

up, efficiency is going to go up. Generally, you are buying fewer problems, you have fewer issues.

Ahearn offered a different perspective:

> One of the points [of contention] I had with Harry [Fatkin] is that he wants this to be a program uncontaminated by the specter of money changing hands. I expect [TUWR] will save a lot of money and we will reduce our liability. We will have people thinking about the environmental consequences of new programs, and that will lead them to do things they might not otherwise have done.

THE ANNOUNCEMENT

At the May 1987 annual stockholders' meeting, Booth announced Polaroid's TUWR program. He stated the goal of TUWR was to nearly eliminate toxic emissions to the environment, whether to land, water, or air, in the next five years. In addition, Booth committed Polaroid to reducing its volume of all chemical wastes generated per unit of product by 10 percent per year for the next five years. He promised to hire an independent auditor to report on how the company was meeting its goals. Community groups were present at the stockholders meeting. Marco Kaltofen of Greenpeace spoke and criticized Polaroid for its generation of waste, particularly that going into Boston Harbor. Kaltofen publicly charged Polaroid as being the worst polluter in the state. "It's about time you did something to take care of society," Kaltofen said. The press focused either on the business aspects of the meeting or on the Greenpeace pickets. Polaroid's TUWR program received little attention.

IMPLEMENTATION

Polaroid's matrix organization allowed the company's divisions to decide how and what wastes to reduce in meeting the 10 percent waste reduction target of TUWR. To ensure reduction, however, division managers were held accountable to a corporate bottom-line report card. The report card categorically listed the amounts of chemicals used and rated them in terms of toxicity.

In November 1987 Polaroid began to formulate waste categories—based on toxicity definitions—which were prepared by its Health, Safety and Environmental Affairs Division. In addition, Polaroid completed a toxicity review sheet on each new chemical it used. A Material Safety Data Sheet (MSDS) was required for all chemicals used in production and was kept on each chemical covered by the Superfund Amendment and Reauthorization Act (SARA) (see Appendix). The MSDS detailed each chemical's physical properties, its potential health hazards, and proper handling and disposal methods. Categories were assigned based on a variety of information sources—government, academic, and research.

To track and account for chemicals, a three-tier categorization scheme was developed. The first tier consisted of chemicals whose actual use was to be reduced; the second, chemicals for which credit for on-site recycling would be given; the third chemicals for which managers got credit for off-site recovery. Ahearn said,

> The original proposal was that we would have a category of chemicals that we absolutely wouldn't use. That's O.K., but unfortunately one of the chemicals that was to be put in there was Freon®. I've got air conditioning that has Freon® in it. The company cafeteria has refrigerators that have Freon® in them. The film division has freezers to keep film good that have Freon® in them. And the substitutes for Freon® are terrible. There were other examples of materials which the company is so completely dependent on that banning them would not permit us to function. We would reduce our waste precisely to zero because we would go out of business.

There were many different opinions on how to reduce waste. As Fatkin explained, "The categorization scheme gives management everywhere in the company signals to where they ought to be putting their waste reduction efforts first, how they ought to be directing their substitution and reformulation strategies, and where recycling fits into the picture."

Other Polaroid managers were skeptical:

> When Harry first proposed the program, it was essentially a good idea, but not very much else. And the detail was extremely naive. The program made sense, . . . but not to the guys who were doing the process development work. This program, as originally structured, would have been a . . . failure.

MODEL PROBLEMS

Polaroid's TUWR program was based on the OTA study. The OTA model concentrated on the amount of waste produced, regardless of toxicity and whether waste materials are recycled. This focus stemmed from the OTA's per unit concept of waste reduction. Per unit is defined as the ratio of waste generated (numerator) to the number of units of production (denominator). The per unit concept did not account for a reduction in toxicity of materials used. The numerator remained the same whether the waste was high-toxic, low-toxic, or nontoxic. Moreover, the numerator remained the same when waste was recycled. This model deficiency created a negative incentive for Polaroid management: Because the model exclusively emphasized the amount of waste generated, managers would not be credited for, and would therefore be disinclined toward using less-toxic materials or recycling.

Polaroid chemists, researchers, and engineers were troubled by the idea that some chemicals would be banned under TUWR. Ahearn explained how this problem in TUWR was overcome:

> We got a bunch of people together, chemists and chemical engineers, who were especially interested in this program. They formed themselves into a sort of ad hoc committee which made suggestions to Harry and had arguments with him. I would say most of what they suggested was in fact adopted, in one form or another.

In response to their concerns, chemicals were reformulated into five categories ranging from highest toxicity (one) to nonchemical (e.g., plastic, paper, trash) (five), and credit was selectively given for recycling. The new categorization retained the per unit concept. As one manager explained:

> Suppose category three waste in the Chemicals Division is 10 pounds per kilogram of dye manufactured. If we are going to reduce 10 percent, next year I'm going to try and get down to at least 9 pounds of waste per unit of production. And what might happen is that production might change; it might even go up so that the total actual tons of waste go up, but as long as the per unit ratio goes down it will be a real reduction. So it doesn't penalize us when we expand or grow.

Because Booth had promised to reduce the company's overall waste by 10 percent a year, some staff foresaw tensions developing among departments. One said,

> Each of the operating divisions will have their own goals, which will add up to that 10 percent. It's conceivable that as we dig into this year and start to get some progress reports, we may find that one division is going to have a tough time making its 10 percent, but another division can make 15 percent to make up for it, then the corporate goal will still be met. I can just see division managers on the phone with each other: "You turkey, you're having a tough time meeting your goals so I'm getting pressure because I'm doing a good job."

INTERNAL RESISTANCE

Several groups within Polaroid were troubled by the TUWR program. Polaroid chemists were concerned that vital chemicals would be placed in categories prohibiting their use. They felt categorization was used only to placate public opinion. Ahearn recalled:

> The initial run at classification resulted in a lot of disputes among working chemists and Harry and his people. Harry was categorizing chemicals based on public perception, which is good. A lot of the categorization, in fact, remains that way. There are a lot of chemicals in category two that are not going to hurt anybody or the environment. However, it's a matter of public perception, and this is a program that's dealing mainly with public perception.

Ahearn explained the chemists' perspective:

> Chemists and chemical engineers in this day and age are not terrified of chemicals, and most people today have a view of chemicals that makes chemists rather annoyed. Most chemicals are not particularly harmful. Did you know that industries in the United States spewed out into the air 100,000 tons of methanol last year? Most chemists would say, "so what?" Chemists know what the methanol health risks are and that 100,000 tons over a year over the area of the United States is a lot less than is produced by bacteriological decomposition of wood in the forest.

Chemists who worked with materials which were now to be curtailed under TUWR felt the program restricted their research and creativity. Ahearn noted the trade-off between safety for the workers and safety for the environment. Some chemicals are easier and safer to handle than others, but these same chemicals may be more toxic. He said,

> I set the tone for the research division by saying we will never use TUWR as a substitute for our own technical judgment. There are cases where we looked at the materials and would say we ought to use this material in category three because it does the same things as this material in category two. But chemists would say you're crazy, because this one in category three is somewhat less toxic but it is a gas and much harder to handle. This one in category two is liquid with a low vapor pressure and easier to handle but more toxic. Why would I use the gas when I could use the liquid? Especially when they are both going to be destroyed in the process? There are some things that we're going to do, perfectly sound and responsible technical decisions that will fly in the face of this program.

Schwalm, of Polaroid's Manufacturing Division, was concerned about implementing TUWR and not being able to carry out long-standing priorities, such as EPA compliance. He commented:

> While Harry champions the Toxic Use and Waste Reduction program, those of us in the plants, in the operating areas, have to worry with the specifics of the day-to-day compliance and regulations. They are competing priorities. We determined that to meet our compliance goals for the next five years we need a capital program over $40 million. And Toxic Use and Waste Reduction would be another $10 million. We have a corporate view that is a wonderful vision. We can set nice goals, but we have to make sure we have the resources to do it. Long term, Harry is right on, that's where we've got to get. In the meantime, we've got to keep our head above water.

Exacerbating the situation were monitoring agencies which were taking a harder line with companies out of compliance. The Massachusetts Water Resources Authority (MWRA), an agency created by court order to clean up Boston Harbor, was responsible for monitoring emissions to the state's sewer system and its waters. Schwalm stated:

> The operating divisions are responsible not only for meeting their cost–quality schedule codes but all the legal aspects around their division. If you are the plant manager, it is your responsibility to make sure the company complies. The MWRA said they were going to start fining people. They said Polaroid had a pattern of noncompliance and MWRA was going to take some action against it. There was a lot of management energy spent on sitting down with the MWRA people and telling them about implementing TUWR.

Other TUWR conflicts revolved around the program's production process focus. TUWR focused on how much waste was generated during the process, including treated or recycled waste. Some managers felt the focus should be on emissions or waste that leaves Polaroid either for treatment or for release into the environment. Their reasoning was, "Why hold us accountable for waste which we treat on site or recycle? Isn't it waste that leaves Polaroid that matters?" Fatkin believed, "If you only look at the waste end, you are missing an opportunity to encourage substitution or reformulation, to have less worker exposure and less handling."

Quality control managers also took issue with the TUWR program. They believed when less toxic chemicals were substituted for the more toxic and preferable materials, the quality of Polaroid's products could be sacrificed. Polaroid's researchers and engineers felt that top management's objectives were difficult to obtain. Production processes would have to be modified annually to glean the 10 percent per year waste reduction. This would take time away from other research. Managers also believed the initial 10 percent reduction would be easy to obtain due to obvious changes. However, waste reduction would slow until the new process design benefits showed up, potentially in the fourth and fifth years.

CREATING A DATA BASE

In creating a data base, Polaroid originally wanted to use 1986 as the baseline year against which to compare waste generated in subsequent years. However, it could not reconstruct 1986's data with accuracy. When, in late 1987, a decision was made to use categories, more months of data collection were missed. It was decided that 1988 would be the baseline year with which managers would be compared for their waste reduction efforts. Some managers advocated waiting until the TUWR program went into effect to reduce waste. This would allow them time to gain credit for all reductions. Other managers wanted to act in the spirit of the program and begin reducing waste immediately. Moreover, some managers were concerned that Booth's promise to reveal waste levels to the public would give away proprietary information. Ahearn said: "The idea of the categories is that you can lump a whole bunch of things together and not give away confidential business information. But one could make the assumption as to what we throw away and what we use."

Fatkin was assigned to design a data base that would be regulatory-neutral and would contain all chemicals. He felt that all materials should be tracked, and believed that an information auditing system would simplify and add credibility to any reforms Polaroid might make. As he checked into environmental accounting and reporting systems, he found there were no criteria. Disagreement existed over the framework for the data and the degree of accuracy and detail that should be reported. Because methodologies to accumulate data differed, the value and utility to Polaroid of auditing such information would be limited. Fatkin felt data standards and criteria would have to be developed if Polaroid was to publish reports that would be used within the company and believed by the public.

Polaroid's effort to develop a data base of all chemicals used proved to be a mammoth undertaking. Tim Hawes commented, "The big part of the system that has changed is all the records we keep. Because in my mind we developed the most comprehensive environmental accounting and reporting system in the whole world."

The Environmental Accounting and Reporting System (EARS) required a great deal of time to collect data on quantities of waste used, how much released into the environment, and so forth. The effort prompted one manager to note: "We have put far more hours into EARS than we have probably into waste reduction itself." Another manager said of the program: "We can walk around this building, and you would find two things. One is you would find people who didn't know what the program was about, except in the most general terms. Then there are people who know the program, but they think it's silly for various reasons having to do with the bureaucracy, the paperwork, and the accounting."

THE MASSPIRG BILL

State legislation was on the horizon as Polaroid acted. The Toxic Use Reduction bill was being developed in the summer of 1987, and MassPIRG planned to introduce it to the Massachusetts legislature in early 1988. The bill would create a program to motivate businesses in the Commonwealth to use fewer toxins and establish reporting and planning requirements such that firms will report the amount, type, and ultimate destinations of toxics they use. The bill would also formulate plans to reduce the use of these chemicals.

A Toxic Use Reduction Institute and technical assistance program would also be created within the Department of Environmental Management. The institute would help businesses in making technical decisions about use reduction. Loans and tax deductions would also provide businesses with the technical and financial help they need to practice use reduction. In addition, state regulators would be mandated to develop more comprehensive inspection procedures and to get violators to practice use reduction. A task force at the Attorney General's Office would help these regulators with enforcement. The bill would extend right-to-know laws so citizens could review the required reports and plans, except where trade secret protection exists. Citizens could request inspections of facilities and petition to have substances added to the phase-out list.

Fatkin wondered how the company should consider the bill and its problems in implementing its own TUWR program. He favored the bill, but felt it did not contain enough state supports or deal with waste management issues such as siting. Fatkin also recognized that there were factions within Polaroid that still questioned the TUWR program. But the public interest groups were expecting Polaroid to respond favorably to the bill, and Polaroid did not want to attract any more negative press around the waste issue.

Discussion Questions

1. What factors account for Polaroid's commitment to toxic waste reduction?
2. What problems does Harry Fatkin face in trying to achieve waste reduction goals? What "assets" does he have to work with?
3. How can Polaroid develop a data base that will provide accurate and useful information for its managers?
4. What position should Polaroid take on state-level toxics legislation?

NOTES

1. Polaroid Corporation, *Impact*, newsletter, fall 1988.
2. Polaroid Corporation, Special Report, Fall 1988.
3. Polaroid Corporation, *A Report on the Environment*, May 1989, p. 5.

APPENDIX

Hazardous Waste Regulation

Between 1970 and 1986 the federal government enacted several pieces of legislation to guide and control hazardous waste materials. These laws set statutory restrictions on the release of toxics into the air, water, land, and workplaces. In addition, Superfund laws mandated cleanup of sites where toxics have accumulated to dangerous levels. Under Superfund, waste generators are held liable for the cleanup. The OTA estimates that to comply with these regulations, government and industry spend $70 billion a year.

Resource Conservation and Recovery Act (RCRA), 1976

Aiming at pollution control, the RCRA regulated the land disposal of waste. The RCRA required documentation of processes and movements of hazardous waste and created operating standards for generators and transporters of hazardous waste and its treatment. The RCRA also created toxic storage disposal facilities (TSDF) and issued permits for them. The RCRA differed fundamentally from the Clean Air Act (CAA) of 1970 (see below). The RCRA mandated that hazardous wastes be treated, stored, and disposed of properly regardless of the amount of waste. The CAA established limits for specified substances which waste generators met with pollution control technologies. These technological devices captured and removed enough of the substances from the waste stream to bring generators into compliance.

The RCRA was fraught with inadequacies. Under the RCRA, many wastes, generators, and facilities were exempt from regulation and some toxics were not placed on the hazardous substances list. Furthermore, the RCRA's definition of recycling virtually excluded reuse of hazardous waste. The RCRA placed no restrictions on what was disposed at landfills and inadequately controlled discharges to publicly operated treatment works. Finally, hazardous waste management firms attempted to shift leaking sites to Superfund's auspices.

RCRA Amendments, 1984

In 1984 Congress passed amendments to the RCRA which were an attempt to improve it. In the section "Objectives and National Policy" of the Hazardous and Solid Waste Amendments of 1984, national legislators wrote:

> The Congress hereby declares it to be the national policy of the United States that, wherever feasible, the generation of hazardous

waste is to be reduced or eliminated as expeditiously as possible. Waste that is nevertheless generated should be treated, stored, or disposed of so as to minimize the present and future threat to human health and the environment.

The 1984 amendments to RCRA accomplished their primary goal, namely to establish a sense of certainty in the market for and transition to alternative technology in hazardous waste management. The 1984 Amendments act with specificity to provide this program with the direction and backing it needs to institute and maintain the transition towards treatment technology.

Results of the amendments were mixed. Land disposal bans, enacted by the amendments, caused land disposal and surface impoundment units to close. This created a demand for incineration and stabilization services. The permit application period for TSDF was time-consuming. Moreover, the permits were not equipped to handle mobile waste management units.

There was confusion over what constituted waste reduction and what constituted pollution control. Congress considered redefining hazardous waste. One alternative definition was a health-based, permissible concentration level. This definition implied that by lowering the concentration of a hazardous chemical in a waste stream, a generator could eliminate the hazardous waste. Further, in its Hazardous and Solid Waste Amendments of 1984, Congress set up a waste minimization strategy. Waste generators were required to include a description of reduction efforts and results of these efforts. But there was no consistent definition of waste minimization, and it was often interpreted to mean the reduction of hazardous waste after generation. Moreover, no waste minimization entity was established in the EPA, nor did waste minimization become a budget item. Rather, "the determination of what actions constitute waste minimization has been left up to the regulated community [businesses]."[1]

Comprehensive Environmental Response, Compensation and Liability Act (CERCLA—Superfund), 1980

This law was created to address the problems caused by abandoned hazardous waste sites. The Superfund law provided a potentially strong incentive for firms to practice safe management of hazardous waste; liability for a Superfund site could be assessed to a waste generator who could be named responsible, wholly or partially, for creating the site. In addition to fining the generator for disposed waste, Superfund gave the government authority to convict the generator for illegal discharges.

Superfund Amendment and Reauthorization Act (SARA), 1986

The SARA amendments were enacted in 1986 and demanded estimates of certain chemicals which were released to the air, water, land, off-site recycling, and other off-site transfers. The SARA also includes a Community Right-to-Know provision known as Title III. Section 313 of Title III required companies using hazardous chemicals to report use, on-site recycling, and the percentage of material in the product. Only 328 chemicals used in commerce were covered by the SARA. Firms that had to report under the SARA were those that had over ten employees in manufacturing sectors and produced or processed over 25,000 pounds, or otherwise used over 10,000 pounds of a covered substance.

Toxic Substance Control Act (TSCA), 1976

The TSCA authorized the EPA to gather information on a wide range of chemicals and to prohibit or limit the manufacture, process, or distribution of any new chemical. The TSCA also required manufacturers to clearly mark a chemical's hazards. As of 1984, 4 percent of premanufacturing notices were subject to some kind of restriction by the EPA. In the TSCA's first seven years the EPA issued regulations for only four substances. This lack of action was partially due to the enormous task of studying tens of thousands of chemicals.

Clean Air Act (CAA), 1970

The CAA of 1970 designated specific substances to be regulated by establishing maximum emissions levels. The act promoted prevention and control of air pollution in three ways: First, it established the National Ambient Air Quality Standards, which regulated six conventional pollutants. These substances are carbon, ozone, sulphur dioxide, nitrogen oxide, lead, hydrocarbon and particulate matter; second, CAA established the National Emissions Standards for Hazardous Air Pollutants, another set of guidelines for substances classified as hazardous; and third, the CAA required the EPA to set standards for new stationary sources of pollution based on the "application of the best technological system of continuous emission reduction."

Under the CAA, waste generators were regulated on the amounts of pollutants released into the environment. Through the use of technology, waste generators removed specified quantities of substances from their waste streams. This would bring them into compliance. Unlike a modification in the production process resulting in less waste produced, pollution control devices do not necessarily discourage the generation of waste. Waste is often merely shifted from one medium to another.

Clean Water Act (CWA), 1972

The CWA, passed in 1972, provided comprehensive federal regulation on all sources of water pollution and aimed to eliminate the discharge of pollutants into navigable waters by 1985. The CWA set discharge limits on 129 pollutants. Because end-of-pipe methods often resulted in waste being shifted to another medium, critics felt elimination must be defined as elimination from source (waste reduction). According to the OTA, "Air and water pollution control devices typically generate solid, hazardous waste that goes to landfills and too often leaches from there into groundwater."[2] Waste that appears eliminated by pollution control devices still exists, albeit in a different form, and is not eliminated in the true sense of the word. Therefore, the only way to eliminate waste would be to use less hazardous material in the production process.

The CWA established that the only legal discharges were those that were regulated. There were two groups of legal discharges. The first pertained to discharges made directly into surface waters. To ensure water quality, the CWA required a permit for facilities which discharged pollutants into U.S. waters. This permit was called the National Pollutant Discharge Elimination System. The second group pertained to discharges emitted into publicly owned treatment works. Direct discharges were limited by maximum quantity or quality for toxic and conventional pollutants. These discharges had pretreatment standards.

Under the CWA, direct discharge limits were phased in. The first phase, which was to be completed by 1977, mandated dischargers to make use of "the best practicable control technology currently available." The second phase, which was to be completed by 1984, required companies to use the "best available technology economically achievable" for conventional pollutants and the "best conventional pollution control technology" for toxic pollutants.

NOTES

1. Office of Technology Assessment, *Serious Reduction of Hazardous Waste: For Pollution Prevention and Industry Efficiency,* report, p. 161, n.d..
2. Ibid., p. 8.

3-4

DOW CHEMICAL: ENVIRONMENTAL POLICY AND PRACTICE

This case was written by William Wubbenhorst under the editorial guidance of James E. Post, Professor of Management Policy, Boston University School of Management. The authors are grateful to Robert Dostal, Corporate Director of Safety, Environmental Affairs, Security, and Loss Prevention, Dow Chemical, for making this case possible.

In 1989 the Dow Chemical Company received the World Environment Center's Gold Medal for International Corporate Environmental Achievement. In its award citation, which praised Dow's leadership in waste reduction and community involvement, the panel noted that Dow serves as a model for industry in protecting "the global environment for future generations." Dow also ranked high in the eyes of executives; it rated tops among chemical manufacturers on *Fortune*'s 1989 list of most admired corporations.

THE GROWTH OF DOW CHEMICAL COMPANY

Dow Chemical was founded in 1897 in Midland, Michigan, by Herbert Henry Dow.[1] The first product Dow sold was bleach. By 1918 Dow had expanded its product line, and virtually all the chemicals it produced went to the war effort. From 1920 to 1930 Herbert Dow devoted his efforts toward developing the use of a magnesium alloy in the manufacture of steel for automobiles. Throughout the decade, sales grew from $4 to $15 million, mostly from bulk chemicals sold to makers of rubber, drugs, paint, and so forth. The company also began to make inroads in sales of agricultural chemicals and calcium chloride used for curing concrete.

In 1929 Dow expanded outside of Michigan when a separate company was set up in Louisiana for the production of iodine. (Eventually, Dow moved its iodine operations to Long Beach, California.) In 1930 Herbert Dow passed away and left his son Willard in charge. During Willard

Dow's tenure, a continued emphasis on research spurred the creation of new processes and breakthrough products. Often the rate of development was so rapid that products were inventoried until someone could figure out uses for them. This heavy investment in research was the key to success in the chemical industry. As Willard Dow said: "The chemical industry is a changing business. A product selling in tons today may a year or two hence be a dying industry. It is our requirement that we must maintain big research staffs; we must . . . be willing to discard the old process and be equally willing to take up the new." By 1954 almost half of the chemical industry's sales were in products that did not exist ten years earlier.

During the 1930s the U.S. chemical industry was the country's fastest growing industry. In the late 1930s, and after years of research, Dow established magnesium alloy production facilities along the Texas Gulf Coast. During World War II this lightweight yet durable alloy came into great demand for the production of planes. By 1947, fifty years after the company's founding, Dow had more than $200 million in assets and annual sales of more than $130 million. There were plants in three Michigan towns, including Midland, along with plants in Canada, Texas, and California. In 1949, Willard Dow died in a plane crash and was succeeded by his brother-in-law Lee Doan, who guided the company for the next ten years. Doan worked his way up through the sales department, which he headed in 1929; became vice president in 1938; secretary in 1941; and CEO in 1949.

Dow's growth continued over the next decade primarily through overseas markets. By 1958, Dow had plants in England, India, and Australia, and ventures in Japan and Brazil were developing. After this rapid sometimes uncoordinated international expansion, Dow reached a critical juncture in the mid-1950s regarding its market focus (i.e., national or international), management control systems, and overall direction. While these issues would take time to resolve, their solutions would shape the company into the mid-1980s.

Throughout the 1960s Dow's management continued to wrestle with its strategic issues. Also during this period Lee Doan handed over the reins to his son Ted. As Dow's CEO for ten-plus years, Lee Doan had increased the company's assets from less than $300 million to $860 million, and increased sales from $200 million to $700 million. From 1962 to 1966 Dow became one of the fastest-growing U.S. companies in Europe. By 1965 the globalization of Dow's markets accounted for 25 percent of its total sales, up from 6 percent in 1952. Ted Doan realized that future profits and growth would not come from sales of bulk chemicals but from intensified research leading to more patented products. Doan also saw the need to organize Dow's 35-plus businesses into departments whereby production, research, marketing, and other functions could be better integrated. The decision to develop a matrix organization followed from this need. The organization of global research-oriented businesses worked well, and Dow grew and prospered into the 1980s.

In 1988 Dow had plants in thirty-two countries which produced over 1,800 different products. These plants and products are divided into five segments (see Appendix A):

1. Chemicals and Performance Products
2. Plastics
3. Consumer Specialties
4. Hydrocarbons
5. Unallocated

DEVELOPING DOW'S CORPORATE CULTURE

In order to effectively manage its sprawling international operations, Dow became an innovator of the matrix organizational structure. During the 1970s the matrix organization was widely heralded in the business community as an effective means to control multinational operations. However, companies soon discovered that matrix management also created unwieldy bureaucracies, conflicting priorities, and turf battles. Many companies abandoned the structure, but Dow modified and rearranged the matrix until it became integral to the company's unique corporate culture. Carl Gerstacker, Dow's Chairman of the Board during the 1970s, described the company's management approach this way: "We operate largely on the basis of group decisions and with a surprising amount of overlapping of duties and responsibilities. We are in many respects the opposite of a military organization with its carefully defined lines and bounds of authority."

In establishing its matrix organization Dow created separate product departments for chemicals, plastics, metal products, bio-products, consumer products, and packaging. Each department manager developed business teams for each group of products. As described by Don Whitehead, author of *The Dow Story:*

> These teams brought together men from marketing, research, production, and development. Linked to the business teams and reporting to them were product teams responsible for the management of certain specified products. The system also made it possible for teams to be organized for special projects and products.[2]

The matrix integrated the three basic components of the company: (1) *functional:* R&D, manufacturing, and marketing; (2) *business:* the products themselves; and (3) *geography:* the location of production facilities and markets. The organizational structure was designed to combine the flexibility and maneuverability of a small business with the strength and depth of a big company. However, once the matrix was implemented, Dow discovered it hindered efforts to establish companywide priorities. Under the decentralized matrix system, each of the three components struggled for primacy. The matrix had also created internal incentives to invest in the company's bulk chemicals business which diverted resources away from the products and markets that Dow's leadership saw as the new growth areas, namely specialty chemicals and pharmaceuticals.

To counteract this effect, Dow amended the matrix by designating small groups of senior executives whose function was to be twofold: (1) establish priorities for each product segment (ROI, market share, new product development, etc.); and (2) decide and designate one component, based on regional and market considerations, to be of primary concern to the managers in any decision-making process. The result of this change combined the benefits of decentralization attainable through matrix management with senior management control and influence over the overall direction of the company.

One example of the company's fluid organizational structure is its Technology Centers. Begun in the 1950s, their roots are grounded in a principle articulated by Herbert Dow: "If you can't do something better, why do it?" The primary mission of the centers is to seek new technologies for the continuous improvement of yield and energy efficiencies in Dow's worldwide plant operations. The centers are responsible for developing and communicating new technologies and "best practices" to all Dow facilities that use a common core technology (e.g., chemical solvents) and for the development and monitoring of performance indices for the manufacturing facilities. The indices consist of a data base spreadsheet containing from ten to fifty variables. These variables capture the costs for each plant and develop performance ratios in terms of material, maintenance costs, labor, energy efficiencies, yield efficiencies, and environmental data. (Yield efficiencies refer to the percentage of raw material that gets transformed into the final product.) The spreadsheets are published quarterly, with each plant ranked in order of how it performed in each particular category. While the centers are primarily product oriented, in recent years they have focused on industrial safety and hygiene and have played a leading role in environmental protection.

From the outset Dow has emphasized the chemical process and technological innovation. These are the hallmarks of the company's mission. As articulated by Willard Dow in the 1930s: "Our stockholders should realize that The Dow Chemical Company is not operated on the basis of a banker's opinion about a chemical process. On the contrary, our activity is controlled by the results we can show in the laboratory as well as in the financial earnings of our processes." This emphasis is reflected today in the composition of Dow's board of directors, primarily chemists and engineers rather than bankers or other financially oriented professionals. As a result of its "scientific" over fiscal emphasis, Dow's efforts in production, research, and waste reduction have reflected a commitment to implementing the best available technology, often at the expense of short-range cost considerations.

A component of Dow's corporate strategy is the long-term economic view that is incorporated into the company's decision-making process. Throughout its history Dow has made significant investments in its research with the conviction that these efforts pay off for the company in the long run. The company's adherence to this philosophy is also embodied in Dow's commitment to full-cost accounting. A system of chargebacks (known as remediation charges) helps enforce the message that today's problems should not be left to future solutions. As Jerry Martin, Director of Environmental Affairs of U.S. Operations, explains: "There has always been a strong ethic in our company that we should not do things that will incur liability to future generations. I think even in our accounting systems there's a strong philosophy at Dow that we shouldn't penalize our successors."

A further factor shaping Dow's growth and development is its leadership. Dow's corporate culture—described by employees as "the freedom to make mistakes"—has given rise to dynamic leaders at different levels of the company. The vision of these leaders, in turn, plays a significant role in influencing the company's development. Dow has successfully harnessed the power of these leaders while maintaining a relatively fluid organizational structure based on business teams and an unique style of matrix management.

EVOLUTION OF ENVIRONMENTAL POLICIES

Dow's first problems with pollution came in 1903 when odors escaping from an experimental chloroform plant prompted families living downwind of the plant to complain. These families claimed the fumes caused vomiting and nausea and killed local vegetation. In response, Herbert Dow investigated the plant and solved the problem by sealing pipes more securely. This began Dow's long and sometimes costly effort to minimize pollution.

In the 1930s Dow became the first U.S. company to incinerate organic materials rather than disposing of them in landfills. In 1948 the company built the world's largest rotary kiln incinerator at that time. These efforts took place 30 to 40 years before the emergence of a strong regulatory push to incinerate, rather than dispose of, certain hazardous chemicals. Dow's strategy in waste management was also dictated by Midland's geography, as pointed out by Jerry Martin: "We had a fairly large complex on a small river [the Tittabawassee river]. We had to do something with that waste. Necessity was the mother of invention and it led us early on to that kind of track." The company's leadership has influenced the development of Dow's environmental policy. From the mid-1960s through the 1970s Carl Gerstacker, Chairman of the Board, and Vice President of Operations, J.M. "Levi" Leathers, significantly shaped Dow's environmental policies. In 1966 Carl Gerstacker delivered a speech titled "Management's Role in Pollution Control" to the Michigan State Chamber of Commerce as part of a Water Pollution Technical Conference (see Appendix B for excerpts). In his speech Gerstacker pointed out the need to communicate to the public and to government officials and to work with regulators and the regulated industry. The quality of this speech is described by Martin: "You could give this speech today. I do incorporate a lot of it already in my speeches, and this was 22 years ago. This speech is just as perfect today as it was then. I think when I talk about foresight, there really was some farsighted management in the environmental area. I think Gerstacker is one of those guys."

One of the people inspired by Gerstacker's vision was J.M. "Levi" Leathers, then-VP of Operations at Dow. (Leathers was a legendary figure whose impact still lingers at Dow. Not only was he a fine operations manager, but "one hell of an engineer" according to a senior Dow manager. One favorite technique was to write short memos on practices he disliked. The message was terse and to the point: "KNOCK IT OFF. [signed] Levi.") In the late 1960s Dow was sued for an off-site landfill that it used for one of its chlorinated solvents plants in North Baton Rouge, Louisiana. In response to this incident Leathers pushed for more effective ways of treating wastes, whether by incineration or other methods, as opposed to putting it in the ground. As described by Martin, Leathers reasoned that "if you put the waste in that hole in the ground, you haven't solved the problem. Some day, it is going to come back and haunt somebody, and it's going to be expensive."

Leathers applied Dow's policy of full-cost accounting to waste disposal. In the near-term, Leather's decision resulted in Dow's production facilities paying 10 to 100 times more than their competitors by incinerating wastes rather than placing them in deep wells. Dow has since incorporated a cost mechanism known as a remediation recharge. If Dow can identify, relatively clearly, the product group that is responsible for the waste at an old site, the identified group must "pay the ticket" for its removal. As explained by Martin, "They are paying for some of their past sins." The system encourages proper disposal at the time the waste is created.

Both Gerstacker and Leathers typify the foresight that is integral to Dow's environmental policy development. However, there were also significant external factors that prompted Dow to take further steps in environmental protection. Although Dow continued to press ahead with its environmental policies during the 1970s, it remained isolated from the public. The managerial attitude at that time was that what Dow did "within the fence" of its facilities was not of concern to the public.

In 1966 Dow supplied raw materials to the U.S. Air Force for the manufacture of napalm. As such, the company became a target for several antiwar demonstrations. Despite the public resentment, Dow's Board of Directors decided to continue supplying the Air Force, "because," in the words of one Dow director, "we feel that so long as the United States is sending men to war, it is unthinkable that we not supply the materials they need." The anti-Dow protests during the Vietnam War made Dow managers aware of the need to develop a strategy for communicating more effectively with the public. It is an awareness that has shaped environmental communications and policy.

ENVIRONMENTAL POLICY TODAY

Substantial advances in environmental protection occurred during the 1970s as cost-effective projects in waste reduction and treatment were initiated. The late 1970s and early 1980s, however, saw a loss of momentum in continuing the pace of improvement.

In 1985 Henry Waxman, U.S. congressman and chairman of the House Subcommittee on the Environment, conducted a survey of the largest chemical companies in the United States and requested emissions data on over 200 different compounds. To respond to this survey, Dow needed to collect companywide emissions data, something it had never done before. Once Dow managers saw this data compiled companywide, they were surprised at the overall quantity of emissions and became convinced there had to be cost-effective opportunities to reduce wastes. They were also concerned that Waxman might use this data to support further regulation of the chemical industry.

While Waxman never did anything with the data, the reporting procedure marked a new era in Dow's relationship with the public. Dow found itself interacting with environmental groups that wanted proof of Dow's efforts in waste reduction and treatment. One such visit to a Dow plant in 1985, as described by Martin, sensitized management to the changing winds of public sentiment about the environment:

> We brought congressional staff people down to Louisiana just for a visit of our environmental facilities as an educational sort of thing. One was from the environmental community who really questioned us about our reduction data. The point was also made that there are people in the environmental community, especially the more radical environmental groups, (whose) objective clearly is to oppose any facility, particularly a hazardous waste facility, unless the applicant can demonstrate—I think the key is demonstrate—that they have a good waste reduction program. So you've got to have the data and the program.

Waxman's survey combined with assertions by the environmental community sent the message that emissions data were needed to communicate Dow's successes in waste reduction. Management also realized that to create internal incentives at the plant level to further reduce emissions, the data needed to be captured on an ongoing basis.

DOW'S WASTE REDUCTION PROGRAM: WRAP

Beginning in 1986, Dow established the Waste Reduction Always Pays (WRAP) program. WRAP draws together Dow's environmental policies and programs and focuses the company's commitment to environmental protection through the reduction of wastes. The goals of the program are

1. to reduce waste and emissions to the environment;
2. to provide incentives for waste reduction projects;
3. to provide recognition for those who excel in waste reduction; and
4. to reemphasize the need for continuous improvement by recognizing opportunities in waste reduction.

1. Reduction of waste and emissions to the environment. Dow's waste reduction policy involves four waste management options. In ranked order, they are

- *Elimination.* The goal is to avoid producing waste. Through research and development Dow strives to utilize production and operating processes that have the highest efficiencies.
- *Reclamation.* The next phase applies when generating waste is unavoidable. The emphasis is to recycle waste back into the production process or use it as a raw material for another process.
- *Treatment and destruction.* When reclamation cannot occur, the next phase is to treat or destroy the waste. This involves developing processes, either water treatment or incineration, for effectively eliminating waste from the environment.
- *Secure landfill.* If neither complete treatment nor destruction is possible, the remnants are placed in a secure landfill. In Dow's Michigan Division, for example, less than one percent of the wastes generated require the use of a landfill.

2. Provide incentives for waste reduction projects. Dow's leadership realizes that economic incentives are needed to cultivate a waste reduction mentality throughout the company. In 1988 the company started the WRAP Capital Projects Contest. Because of Dow's decentralized approach to managing its production facilities, each division takes a slightly different view of this program.

An "energy contest" had been in place in Louisiana since 1981. The reward was capital dollars. (Capital dollars refer to funds for new construction or remodeling. The demand for capital nearly always exceeds the available resources. Therefore, the prospect of securing additional capital dollars is a very powerful motivator at the plant level.) Each year plants submit projects demonstrating an energy savings that gives a certain return on investment (ROI). Any project that demonstrates an improvement in energy efficiency, as measured by the ROI, receives capital dollars. Only projects above a nominal cut-off can be approved. These cut-offs have ranged over the years from 30 to 100 percent.

As a precursor to the WRAP program, "yield improvement"—which refers to the maximum output from chemicals used in a given process— was added to the savings that could be captured in the return on investment (ROI). When WRAP was added to the program in 1987, it fit into the format of the energy contest, since both are aimed at the basic issue of efficiency. In fact, since WRAP was added, the contest has become more of a waste reduction/yield improvement contest than an energy contest (see box for a trend line of environmental projects). In 1988 the WRAP portion of the Louisiana Division's contest contained twenty-four of the ninety-six total projects, required $3.2 million in capital dollars, and saved over $6.7 million for an ROI of 197 percent. In 1989, 23 WRAP projects and $3.8 million in capital dollars saved Dow $10.5 million for an ROI of 267 percent.

Historical Environmental Proactive Items: Dow Chemical

Yield Improvement Programs

Energy Reduction Programs

Wastes Handled On-site as Much as Possible

Utilization of Incineration

Pollution Prevention Pays

Recharging of Environmental Expenses to Generator

Environmental Policy–Guidelines

No Liquid Hydrocarbons to Landfills

Move Away From Deep Well Injunction

Product Stewardship

Waste Reduction, Not Waste Treatment

Design, Build, and Operate Secure Landfills

Scrutiny of Outside Waste Handlers

Approval on Sale, Aquisition, or Lease of Property

Closure of Surface Impoundments

Community Awareness Emergency Response (CAER)

Continuous Improvement Process

Individual and Team Involvement

But while some positive incentives for waste reduction exist, a larger number of accounting mechanisms provide a negative incentive for the reduction of wastes. According to Dow's Corporate Director of Safety, Environmental Affairs, Security, and Loss Prevention, Robert Dostal, in many companies costs for disposing of wastes are treated as an overhead expense: "They put them [wastes] down the pipe, call in the dumpster, and send them out to their waste disposal facility. They don't necessarily get a charge-back based on the amount they sent. It's kind of a factory expense, spread so it goes to all the plants. Everybody gets [charged and] there is no incentive."

In contrast, Dow charges environmental expenses to the generator, giving the plant manager a strong incentive to minimize wastes. Under this system, managers are charged for every pound of waste generated at their plant—with no discount for volume—which requires incineration, treatment, or landfill. By charging these costs to the plants, Dow refocuses the issue of waste reduction back to the production process itself, prompting chemists and engineers to further improve upon processes. On occasion, these recharges have been set artificially high as a means to focus on a particular issue, as the Michigan Division's environmental manager at Midland describes:

> For example, a number of years ago, we had a large amount of waste drums getting burned in our incinerator. So from a cost standpoint, the way to get the attention of the managers who are generating those drums is increase the cost of disposal. Now, it only costs me $X to dispose, but we charge them three times the amount so we would get their attention. There are some things that you can do so that you can force the division, and the corporation, to a particular movement by more or less artificially setting the price on some of these services that we provide.

3. Provide recognition for those who excel in waste reduction. A key to Dow's WRAP program is recognizing employees who do a good job in waste reduction. Each year at the Louisiana Division the WRAP program publishes descriptions of all contest projects including the names of the winners and the plants they work in. More important, however, is their "Awards Presentation"—which Dow calls its version of the Academy Awards—where the Vice President of Operations presents each winner with an engraved plaque. In 1988 and 1989 Dow extended the awards presentation idea to all its U.S. divisions. In 1989, representatives from winning projects nationwide (supervisors, operators, etc.) were brought to Washington, D.C., where Dow was conducting a waste reduction seminar. The winning representatives received plaques from their congressmen. As described by Dostal, recognition works as a powerful motivator within Dow: "Some of these people had never been on a plane before. And that's where you get the emissaries going back. Boy, are they turned on."

4. Reemphasize the need for continuous improvement by recognizing opportunities in waste reduction. The Continuous Improvement Process (CIP) dates back to Herbert Dow's famous line, "If you can't do something better, why do it?" As applied to waste reduction, this translates to the company's continuously reducing its wastes to zero emissions. CIP also drives Dow's Technology Centers' efforts to constantly improve on processes.

IMPLEMENTING WRAP

Core responsibility for WRAP resides with the waste reduction coordinators in the major plant divisions across the country. At the center of these coordinators is the U.S. Area Coordinator who has no line responsibility at the division level but is responsible for overall direction of the WRAP program. The U.S. Area Coordinator is connected with Dow's executive management and acts as a conduit through which various policies in the waste reduction area are initiated.

The WRAP coordinators function similarly to the Technology Centers, with responsibility for communicating ideas and innovations in waste reduction to other divisions. WRAP coordinators also work on the WRAP capital program, such as the one at the Louisiana Division. In this respect, the WRAP coordinators are in charge of generating the bottom-up support by encouraging waste reduction ideas at the plant level. The Technology Centers also act as a conduit through which Dow's executives establish WRAP policy priorities. One of the most significant policy decisions pertained to which performance measures the centers included on their spreadsheets for monitoring plant activity. Because the selected variables would become the "scorecards" by which plants were evaluated, they would exert significant influence over how plant managers organized their priorities. The monitoring of these variables is also critical for the Continuous Improvement Process (CIP), which is a key goal in the WRAP program. There are specific Technology Centers focusing on the development of new processes for water treatment, solid waste treatment, and incineration.

The last major organizational component of Dow's WRAP program is the Waste Reduction Issue Management Team. This is the only major component of Dow's environmental programs in the Public Affairs Department. All of WRAP's other significant organizational components are linked directly into the line responsibility for facility operations.

The Waste Reduction Issue Management Team is a cross-functional group that works alongside the Technology Centers, business teams, and WRAP coordinators to encourage, measure, and recognize environmental waste reduction in Dow. This team meets quarterly to discuss current environmental issues and to develop strategies on how Dow can communicate its story about waste reduction. More important, though, is the team's efforts to *listen* to outside groups, allowing it to better understand the issue as it is perceived by others. Each time the team meets, it invites outsiders. Some of the groups that have been invited are the Sierra Club, the National Wildlife Federation, the National Committee Against Toxic Hazards, and the Environmental Protection Agency. In some respects, the team embodies the 180-degree turn that Dow has made in its public relations philosophy since the 1970s. It also reflects Carl Gerstacker's vision when he perceived a need to open channels of communication with the public.

LOOKING AHEAD

According to Dow executives, significant challenges in managing the company's response to environmental issues still exist. Internally, three questions loom in the thinking of Martin:

1. how to build upon the initial success of the WRAP program;
2. how to extend WRAP to Dow's growing international operations; and
3. how to respond to continued pressure from environmental advocacy groups on numerous other issues.

In response to the first challenge, Dow's environmental staff is considering the establishment of specific reduction goals, which further institutionalizes the Continuous Improvement Process in waste reduction. However, it will be particularly difficult to implement reduction goals with Dow's decentralized structure. The issue of waste reduction goals is part of the larger question of how WRAP fits into the company's core strategy. This is significant, considering that environmental regulatory pressures will likely produce major changes in the chemical industry's competitive environment. How Dow responds to these changes depends in part on whether the WRAP program becomes a way of life or fades from managers' attention.

The second challenge facing Dow is how to extend WRAP to its overseas plants. Given the absence of significant regulatory pressures in many foreign countries, Dow will have to work even harder to export a waste reduction mentality. The final challenge relates to how Dow shapes its role in the public policy process. Currently, Dow is taking a collaborative, long-range approach to public policy. Dow is working closely with other groups, including environmentalists, on various issues, which often leads to healthy debate. But all is not easy for Dow. As a major manufacturer of agricultural pesticides, it faces criticism from groups who claim that consumers are at increased risk of illness from exposure to foods grown with pesticides. Other groups criticize Dow's overseas marketing of pesticides and chemicals that are banned for health, safety, and environmental reasons in the United States. In response to these criticisms, Dow has developed an extensive product stewardship program and relies heavily on its Toxicology Research Laboratory where all chemicals undergo extensive testing.

Dow also faces criticism from environmentalists who challenge the effectiveness and safety of incineration disposal. In response, Dow researchers address concerns by focusing on existing and emerging technologies for incineration to further improve their units' combustion efficiency. Dow points out that it is a charter member of the Coalition for Responsible Waste Incineration. This group, formed in 1987, promotes the responsible use of high-technology incineration systems as an industrial waste management practice. Dow's environmental managers are quick to say that waste reduction is the cornerstone of their waste management program, but they also believe that by incinerating combustible hazardous wastes, instead of using land disposal, they can protect future generations. They cite organizations such as the EPA which support incineration as the best method for treatment of many wastes.

These issues underscore Dostal's belief that while the company has made significant progress through programs such as WRAP, there are many challenges to be met. Future debate will likely touch upon aspects of Dow's core business (i.e., agricultural chemicals). This will present a definite tension between choices perceived as good for the business and choices perceived as good for the environment.

In waste reduction activities, Dow's managers remain challenged to keep the company pursuing the goal of zero emissions. This must be a real goal, not an imaginary or symbolic one. Dow's leaders realize that the public will not give them credit for past accomplishments but only for the improvements they continue to make. As Jerry Martin commented:

> Waste reduction is simple, but it's not easy. I think that is important. The concepts we are talking about are not difficult concepts. The ideas we are talking about are hard ideas. You hear people who really study industry relative to waste reduction; they will tell you that the barriers are not technological or scientific, but institutional. I really believe they are right. Largely, the barriers are institutional. It's a mind-set, a management philosophy, and the institutional barriers are the ones that are really hard to overcome.

Discussion Questions

1. What are the key features of Dow's corporate culture? How do they influence the company's approach to environmental issues?
2. Mr. Gerstacker's speech in 1966 describes the Dow point of view. Which ideas are still alive in Dow's modern operations?
3. What organizational factors contribute to WRAP's success?

4. Analyze the WRAP program. What motivates a Dow plant manager, operating engineer, or truck driver to think about waste reduction? Is it the same for everyone?

5. What problems will Dow face as it applies WRAP to all of its international operations?

NOTES

1. Don Whitehead, *The Dow Story*, (New York: McGraw-Hill, 1968).

2. Ibid., p. 169.

APPENDIX A

Description of Product Segments

1. Chemicals and Performance Products. This segment consists of chemical products that serve as raw materials in manufacturing customer products or which aid in the processing of them. The industries supplied by these products range from personal care and pharmaceutical to chemical processing and pulp and paper.

2. Plastic Products. Dow is one of the largest producers in plastics. The products in this segment are used in a variety of markets from automotive and electronics to packaging and furniture.

3. Consumer Specialties. This segment consists of three main businesses: agricultural products, pharmaceutical, and consumer products. Agricultural products are used for both protection and production of crops as well as pest control. Pharmaceutical consists of prescription drugs, such as Seldane (for allergies) and Nicorette (a smoking cessation aid), and over-the-counter health products like Citrucel fiber laxative and Cepacol mouthwash. Consumer products include food-care items such as Ziploc bags and Saran Wrap, home cleaners such as Dow Bathroom cleaner and Yes detergent, and personal care items such as Perma-Soft shampoo. In July 1989, Dow announced an agreement to acquire Marion Laboratories, a pharmaceutical manufacturer.

4. Hydrocarbons. This segment involves the management of the fuels, petroleum-based raw materials, and power supplies for Dow's facilities. Dow generates all of its own power, saving up to 30 percent in costs, and is the world's largest producer of co-generated power.

5. Unallocated. This segment consists of a diverse mixture of other Dow businesses, including consolidated insurance and credit companies.

APPENDIX B

Excerpts from Speech:

Management's Role in Pollution Control

by
Carl A. Gerstacker

Dow Chemical

March 23, 1966

The message on pollution is now so imperative that we cannot afford to ignore it. The question, I believe, is no longer, as some would have you believe, "How are we going to fight this?" but "What are we going to do about it?" . . . .

The mandate to industrial management is quite clear, therefore, and it comes from the top, and it has never been more critical. Our role is simply to supply the leadership and the imagination and the drive that will spark a frontal assault on this problem.

I have been quite frankly distressed by the attitude of many of the company executives I know when the subject turns to pollution. Very often their attitude is one of "Who—Me? Pollution?" They talk about the municipalities going scot free in spite of the pollution they perpetrate, and they maintain they have done an outstanding job in pollution control. They feel they are not really contributing substantially to the problem.

My strong suspicion is that many industrial management people just have not been told the whole truth by their own people

Part of the challenge to management is to find out the truth and to act upon it

I'd like therefore to indicate five areas in which I think we in management must take the lead, and then propose a general approach. What should we in management be doing in this area?

First, it seems to me that it is the manager's job to establish the proper climate or attitude in our plants toward pollution and its control. We need to express clearly our own concern with pollution and our concern that we are taking adequate measures to control it, that we are not allowing operating errors or carelessness that permits quantities of pollutants to escape to the sewer or the river. . . .

... if we encourage such a program from the top, and reward it, then we as managers have a good start in playing the role we should be playing. . . .

Secondly, we need to do some actual checking to make sure that we have provided the proper kinds of controls in our plants. We need to familiarize ourselves with every potential contaminant in our plants whose control is essential to avoid pollution, and we need to make sure that these contaminants have been given proper consideration. . . . In some cases we will even need to devote research and development funds to the solution of these problems, and this may occasionally even be a profitable solution, if your research people happen to unearth a good use for a previously waste by-product.

In some cases you will discover that you can improve your yields and simultaneously reduce the production of waste materials, and this is profitable both ways.

In fact, on the basis of more than 30 years experience in waste control at our Midland plant, we have found that a good approach to your waste material often is not to look for a way to dispose of it but to look for a way to use it. Dispose of it as waste only as a last resort.

Third, we need to do a far better job than we have done to date in sharing our pollution control knowledge with each other. . . . We should always freely divulge our knowledge in the pollution control field, I think, so long as it has no direct bearing upon our competitive situation.

Fourth, we need to take better advantage of industry–government contacts in this area where they exist and to encourage more and better communication between industry and government in this area where they do not. . . .

We should encourage our experts in the pollution field to work with governments at all levels in the solution of problems, from the federal down to the municipal and township level. . . .

My last point concerning the managerial role is that we in industry must get off the defensive and onto the offensive, in the area of pollution. Most of the time we seem to be defending ourselves against the charges of someone who feels we have offended; and many times I'm afraid we have offended. Getting out of this posture and taking the offensive has two aspects to it—doing a good job, and telling people about it. Where we are doing a good job we should not be afraid to let people know about it.

We should encourage visits by government representatives to our plants. . . .

We need, in sum, a better public relations program than we have for industry at large in the pollution area. . . . We should make it abundantly clear that we recognize the problems and that we are in the process of doing something concrete and tangible about them.

When tax relief is needed, we should not be afraid to raise our voices and insist that we get it—and I mean this particularly in reference to tax relief measures in connection with capital investment for pollution control. . . .

What we should not do is pretend that there is no problem, or that the problem belongs to someone else.

. . . We need something to measure our performance in water quality control, something that will tell each manager whether his performance in this area is good or bad, above average or below average, whether he is improving or remaining static or falling behind.

. . . As a starter, I propose that we use what I call a Dilution Ratio Index, or DRI. Every water user takes water out, does something with it, and puts something back. This means dilution of what is put back. What we need to measure is whether what it is returned can be taken up, absorbed, diluted by the stream or body of water without impairing it for its subsequent intended uses. . . .

I do not know if the Dilution Ratio Index is the right and complete answer for all users of water, but I strongly feel that something in the nature of a DRI yardstick is badly needed. . . .

Some of my business friends have indicated to me that what they really fear in connection with pollution control is the extraordinarily heavy expense that it is going to entail over long periods of years. "Our profit margins," they tell me, "will be shot full of holes."

Our experience over the last 30 years and more in Midland indicates to us that these fears are falsely founded. We are convinced that pollution control is part of the cost of doing business, and we have always treated it that way. We firmly believe that industry can be clean and profitable at the same time, and we have amply proven this to our own satisfaction. . .

. . . Management has been challenged before and will be challenged again. I am happy that we are being challenged. That, I think, is really the basic role of management, in pollution control or in any field.

3-5

ARCO SOLAR, INC.

This case was written by Mark C. Jankus under the editorial
guidance of Alfred A. Marcus and Gordon P. Rands, both of the
Curtis L. Carlson School of Management, University of Minnesota.

In early 1988 top management at Atlantic Richfield (ARCO) had an
important decision to make concerning the future of the company's solar
energy division. The wholly owned subsidiary, ARCO Solar, Inc., was a
world leader in photovoltaic cell production (photovoltaics are semicon-
ductors that produce electricity directly from sunlight), yet in the eleven
years since ARCO had purchased the company it had never turned a
profit.[1] ARCO had instituted a restructuring plan in 1985 that called for
the company to divest itself of operations not related to its core oil, gas,
chemical, and coal businesses; yet the solar technologies being developed
by ARCO Solar seemed within a few years of profitability. ARCO was also
enjoying a reputation for good corporate citizenship for continuing to
support photovoltaic research and development for so long.

ARCO

Atlantic Richfield was originally incorporated in 1870 as the Atlantic
Refining Company. Until the 1960s it was exclusively an oil and gas business. The company was renamed when it merged with the Richfield Oil
Corporation in 1966. In 1961 ARCO expanded into the chemical and
plastics business, and by 1977 was well established in the coal business.
By 1988 ARCO was one of the largest integrated petroleum enterprises in
the industry. ARCO subsidiaries conducted oil and gas exploration, production, refining, transportation, and marketing. The chemical, plastics,
and coal operations along with the oil and gas businesses constituted the
core of ARCO's business.[2]

ARCO expanded into nonpetroleum-oriented businesses with only
limited success. In 1967 ARCO bought the Nuclear Materials &
Equipment Company, a producer of uranium-and plutonium-bearing
fuels, which it sold in 1971. Also, at one time or another, the company
had owned a newspaper, an air-conditioning company, a plant cell

research institute, and a building products operation. All were eventually sold.

The 1970s were a turbulent time for the petroleum industry. The energy crises of 1973–1974 and 1979 precipitated a national search for energy alternatives to petroleum. One of the most attractive alternatives was solar energy. The supply was not controlled by foreign countries and it was a clean source of energy. It was also abundant: sunlight striking the earth in one year contains approximately 1,000 times the energy in fossil fuels extracted during the same time period.[3] With gasoline and heating oil prices rising beyond anything the public had ever experienced, there was a great deal of enthusiasm for solar power. The enthusiasm seemed justified. Photovoltaic (PV) cells, which produce electricity directly from sunlight, were invented in 1954, and were first used to power U.S. satellites at a cost of over $1,000 per peak watt (a measure of a cell's output at maximum sunlight). By 1974 the price had dropped to $50 per peak watt; by 1977 it was $17 and was continuing to decline as the cells were improved.[4]

ARCO initiated a study of the potential of the solar energy field in 1972. By 1976, with oil apparently on the way out and solar power a promising energy source for the future, the company's studies culminated in a decision to enter the solar field. ARCO did so in 1977 with the purchase of Solar Technology International, Inc., a tiny Chatsworth, California, operation with eight employees. Solar Technology was renamed ARCO Solar, Inc.

ARCO SOLAR, INC.

Solar Technology International was founded in 1975 by an engineer, J.W. (Bill) Yerkes, with $80,000 he pulled together by mortgaging his home and obtaining loans from relatives.[5] The company produced PV panels that powered microwave repeater stations, corrosion-prevention systems in pipelines, navigational aids, irrigation pumps, electrified livestock fences, and trickle chargers for batteries on boats and recreational vehicles. When Yerkes sold the company to ARCO in 1977 for $300,000, he stayed on as ARCO Solar's first president.[6]

In 1979 the company bought a 90,000-square-foot building in Camarillo, California, and built the world's first fully automated production line for PV cells and panels. By 1980, the company was the first to produce more than a megawatt of panels in a year. Sales had more than doubled from the previous year. To interest electric utilities in photoelectric power generation, the company constructed demonstration projects where PV's potential for supplying large amounts of energy could be proven. In 1981, on the Navajo reservation in Arizona and New Mexico, the company installed a prototype power generation facility large enough to power 200 homes. The project was judged a success, and the company moved from a largely research mode into a marketing stage. An even larger demonstration project was conceived. By the end of 1982 the company had constructed a PV power facility three times larger than the biggest such plant then in existence. The $15 million, one-megawatt plant near Hesperia, California—large enough to power 400 homes—was constructed on 200 acres of Southern California high desert, an area with no strong winds to blow sand on the panels, blocking sunlight and wearing down the mechanisms.[7]

The power at Hesperia was generated by 108 "trackers," double-axis computer-controlled structures that turn to follow the sun. Each tracker had 265 1-by-4-foot 40-watt PV modules, which were in turn made of thirty-five individual single-crystal silicon cells. The trackers' ability to follow the sun boosted their power output by 40 percent over what a stationary panel could generate.[8] The electricity generated by the plant fed into the Southern California Edison grid and was purchased by the utility. The plant was constructed in six months from construction start-up to completion in December 1982, a record for a power plant. Even more impressive, the plant was completed under budget, an uncommon occurrence for a new power-generating facility.

Encouraged by the success of the Hesperia project, the company began construction of a 16–megawatt plant on the Carissa Plain, near Bakersfield, California. The 6-megawatt first phase of the project, completed in early 1984, occupied 640 acres. The project utilized several technical improvements in the PV module and tracker construction which increased each tracker's peak power output by 50 percent, reducing the number of trackers needed.[9] As in Hesperia, a utility bought the power generated by the plant at the avoided cost of generating power from its most expensive fuel, gas or oil. This rate (around 6 cents per kWh) was less than what it cost ARCO Solar to generate the power, but a 37 percent federal and state tax credit for the solar installation brought the cost down enough to justify it as a demonstration of PV's potential.[10]

Meanwhile, in 1983, ARCO Solar took the industry by surprise by announcing it would begin selling thin-film amorphous silicon products the next year, much earlier than industry analysts had thought possible. "Genesis," a one-square-foot amorphous silicon cell, was the first use of thin-film technology beyond the tiny cells used in calculators and watches. Developed by a 100-person ARCO Solar research team whose existence had been kept secret, the 5-watt module had a 6 percent conversion efficiency, a 20-year design life, and sold to distributors for about $45.[11] It generated enough electricity to maintain batteries in recreational vehicles, cars, and boats, or to power security systems or other low-power remote applications. Genesis made ARCO Solar the world leader in the race to commercialize thin-film technology.[12] The company's sales doubled again in 1984, and its international network of distributors continued to expand. By 1986 the company was selling 4,000 Genesis modules per month.[13]

ARCO Solar increasingly turned its attention to thin-film technology. The efficiencies of the thin-film cells steadily improved: By 1985 the company's researchers had a thin-film cell with a record 13.1 percent efficiency, and were predicting 20 percent efficiencies by 1990. Sales volume continued to climb due to the success of the Genesis modules. In 1986 the company entered into joint ventures with a Japanese company (Showa Shell Sekiyu K.K.) and a German firm (Siemens A.G.) to manufacture and market ARCO Solar products in the Pacific and Europe. ARCO Solar was now the largest manufacturer of PV products in the world.[14] But even though sales continued to climb the company still remained unprofitable. Research and development continued to require a large commitment (35 to 40 percent of sales revenues), and though ARCO Solar's products had improved greatly, the market for PVs, due to the oil glut, was not growing as the company had hoped.

THE PV INDUSTRY

When ARCO entered the PV industry in 1977 it was only one of a number of oil industry giants investing in the infant industry. Exxon had become involved in 1969, Shell in 1973, Mobil in 1974, and Amoco in 1979. Chevron, Union Oil of California, Occidental Petroleum, Phillips, Sohio, Gulf, Sun, and Texaco were also funding PV research. These oil companies, flush with profits from the rising price of oil, were interested in expanding into new businesses that showed promise. In the late 1970s solar energy seemed to be the energy source of the future.

As an energy source, PVs competed directly with the fossil fuels. With oil prices rising and the price of PV electricity falling, the new technology's future looked promising. Worldwide sales of PV products rose rapidly, from around $11 million in 1978 to an estimated $150 million in 1983.[15] Industry analysts forecasted a billion-dollar PV industry by 1990 and PV electricity at half the price of oil. The government's 1976 "Project Independence" goal of PV electricity at 50 cents per peak watt seemed achievable in the not-too-distant future (see Figure 3-5-1).

Figure 3-5-1

U.S. Photovoltaic Shipments, in Megawatts

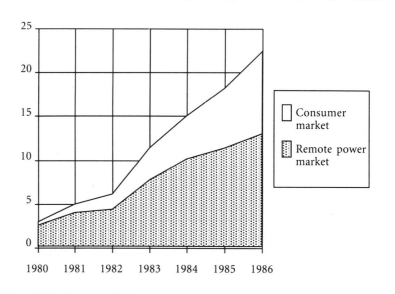

Source: U.S. Department of Energy, "National Photovoltaic Program: 1987 Program Review," April 1988.

However, things began to sour for the industry in the early 1980s. By 1982 the price of oil had begun to fall. As the nation learned to conserve energy, the demand for electricity fell below projections in many areas, and utilities, not needing new capacity, lost interest in PV demonstration projects. The oil glut that developed as the 1980s wore on made fossil fuels plentiful again and renewables like PVs appear unnecessary. The utilities that needed to expand wanted an established, uninterruptible source of power, and were unwilling to invest in an unproven technology (see Figure 3-5-2).

Another threat to PVs arose in the early 1980s: a severe cutback in the federal government's commitment to solar energy research and development. President Reagan, elected by a landslide and committed to slashing federal nonmilitary spending, cut heavily into the funding that facilitated much of the progress in PV technologies. Federal funding for solar energy (including research, business and residential tax credits, guaranteed loans for solar installations, energy conservation programs, and demonstration programs), which rose from $2 million in 1972 to $2 billion in 1978, was cut by more than half in 1982 from its 1981 level. With two exceptions, federal funding continued to drop every year for the rest of the decade.[16] In 1987 the imposition of the Gramm-Rudman-Hollings federal deficit reduction budget cuts reduced the PV research budget to the lowest level ever. The burden of financing solar energy research, of which the government had shouldered 75 percent in 1980, fell increasingly on industry alone (see Figure 3-5-3).

Besides cuts in research funding, the federal tax credits that encouraged consumers and business to invest in solar technologies expired in 1985. The 40 percent residential tax credit and 15 percent tax credit for industrial, commercial, and agricultural installations had helped the solar industry's sales to rise rapidly. While the commercial tax credits were extended in 1986 after an intensive lobbying effort by the solar

Figure 3-5-2

World Crude Oil Prices, 1977–1987

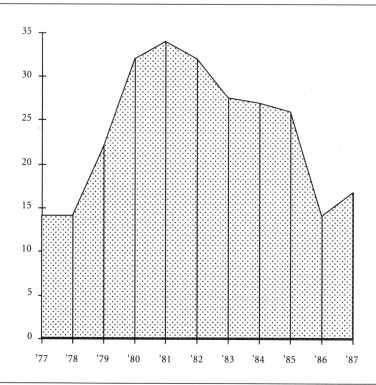

Source: Solar Energy Industries Association informational pamphlet: "Fifteen Years in Business With the Sun," 1989.

Note: This came from a promotional pamphlet put out by The Solar Energy Industries Association in 1989. The Association is headquartered in Arlington, Virginia.

Figure 3-5-3

Federal Appropriations for Photovoltaic Research and Development, 1977–1987

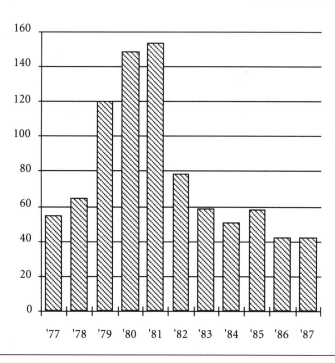

Source: Solar Energy Industries Association information pamphlet, "Fifteen Years in Business With the Sun," 1989.

energy industry, the residential credits were not renewed when they expired in 1985.[17]

By the mid-1980s the decline in crude oil prices was forcing the oil industry to slash capital spending and lay off employees. Various oil companies, particularly those forced to sell service stations and refineries, took a hard look at their portfolios, and some decided to get out of the solar energy business. Exxon's Solar Power Company ceased operations in 1983; Standard Oil wrote off the $85 million it invested in a solar energy joint partnership and quit in 1986. By 1988 ARCO and Amoco were the only major U.S. oil companies that still played a significant role in the PV industry.[18]

Foreign competition grew tougher throughout the decade. While U.S. government R&D funding fell throughout the 1980s, this was not true of some foreign governments. By 1985 the Japanese government was spending 19 percent more on PV R&D than the U.S. government. In 1988, for the first time, both the West German and Japanese governments spent more on PV research than the United States.[19] Their investments were paying off; the U.S. companies' share of the world PV market fell from 80 percent in 1981 to 60 percent in 1983 to about 50 percent in 1989.[20] In 1985, only five of the top twenty PV firms in the world were located in the United States, although ARCO Solar was number one worldwide.[21] At the same time, the market itself seemed to be stagnant. After growing rapidly in the late 1970s and early 1980s, world PV sales stalled at the $125 to $150 million level in the mid-1980s.[22] With all its promise, solar power still only accounted for 0.1 percent of the electricity generated each year.[23]

COMPETITION IN THE PV MARKET

As they had in other industries, the Japanese showed their expertise in taking an existing technology and commercializing it. In the late 1970s most attention in the PV industry was directed toward developing cheaper, more efficient single-crystal cells. These cells had the highest conversion efficiencies of any of the PV technologies, but they were also very expensive. The Japanese, however, used a new type of cell (amorphous silicon) which was much less efficient than the single-crystal cells (3 to 5 percent efficiency versus 15 to 20-plus percent efficiency) but much cheaper to produce. They used amorphous silicon cells to power small consumer electronic products like calculators. By 1985, the Japanese were selling 100 million amorphous silicon-powered calculators and other small electronic products per year. Their experience in amorphous silicon cell production gave them the early lead in PV manufacturing technology, along with economies of scale and lower production costs. In 1985 the Japanese manufacturers shipped 7 megawatts of amorphous silicon, almost all of it in consumer products, compared to 0.5 megawatts by U.S. producers.[24]

The most lucrative market for PVs, though, was utility or grid power generation. In 1987 PVs were economical in grid systems only for what is known in the utility industry as "peaking power": more costly power sources that are only used during peak load periods. The other major potential market was in providing power for areas without grid systems. Three quarters of the world's population do not have grid electricity, yet many people live in areas where sunlight is abundant and intense. Thousands of small solar power systems were already operating in these areas and the potential market seemed huge. The Department of Energy estimated that the potential market was ten to twenty times the current sales level.[25]

Most of the U.S. producers' attention was directed toward developing a cell that could generate electricity at a price competitive with fossil fuels. The price of PV electricity was falling, but whereas electricity from coal cost about 4 to 8 cents per kilowatt-hour (kWh), and oil or natural gas 5 to 10 cents per kWh, PV electricity cost about 25 to 30 cents per kWh (see Figures 3-5-4 and 3-5-5- and Table 3-5-1).[26]

By the mid-1980s "thin-film" technologies, like amorphous silicon, seemed to hold the most promise. These technologies, which used a fraction of the material required to produce single-crystal cells and less labor, were continually being refined to yield more efficient cells. By 1988 thin-film technologies had been developed to the point where they seemed to be within a few years of reaching 7 to 8 cents per kWh, which would make PVs competitive with fossil fuels and nuclear power.

Besides the emergence of thin-film technologies, there was another reason for optimism. By 1988 the search for new energy sources began to regain the momentum it had in the 1970s, although for a different reason: The threat posed by global warming was beginning to draw atten-

Figure 3-5-4

Cost of Solar Cell Per Peak Watt of Electricity Generated

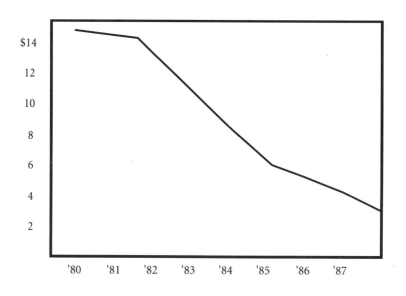

Source: Solar Energy Industries Association information pamphlet, "Fifteen Years in Business With the Sun," 1989.

Figure 3-5-5

Efficiencies of Experimental Amorphous Silicon Cells

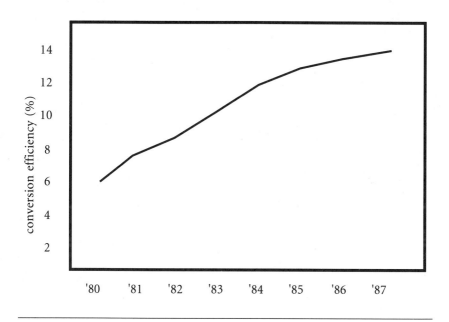

Source: U.S. Department of Energy, National Photovoltaics Program 1987 Review, April 1988.

tion. Experts warned that consumption of fossil fuels had to be reduced significantly. Also, the Three Mile Island and Chernobyl nuclear accidents severely damaged the nuclear power industry's credibility, and chances for a large role in the future of electricity generation appeared unlikely. Hydroelectric power, while clean and safe, had limited expansion potential. Solar energy's potential was once again becoming apparent.

ARCO SOLAR, INC. IN 1988

By 1988 ARCO Solar was the undisputed world leader in the PV industry, with 20 percent of the $150 million market. The company was leaner than it had been, with 350 employees, half the number it had in 1983, and the sales forecasts were optimistic; the company had a growing backlog of orders. The company's research labs had made advances in a new type of thin-film material, copper indium diselenide (CIS), which promised nondegradability and had even better efficiencies than amor-

Table 3-5-1

Estimates of PV Module Selling Prices Required to Meet Different Levelized Costs of Electricity for Central Station PV Plants[a]

Levelized Cost of Electricity (cents/kWh)	PV Module Efficiency	Required Selling Price of Modules ($/peak watt)[b]
6	10	0
6	15	0.30
6	20	0.39
9	10	0.51
9	15	0.69
9	20	0.81
12	10	0.90
12	15	1.09
12	20	1.29

[a] Based on a fixed, flat-plate PV array.

[b] This represents the price for a PV module at which a generator of electricity would be indifferent between PV-generated electricity and other sources of electricity. For example, at a levelized cost of electricity of 6 cents/kWh, an electric utility would not be interested in 10% efficient PV modules at any price. However, assuming the same levelized price of electricity, the utility would be willing to pay up to 0.30 $/peak watt for 15% efficient panels.

Source: David E. Carlson, "Low Cost Power from Thin-Film Photovoltaics," in T.B. Johansson (ed.), *Electricity: Efficient End-Use and New Generation Technologies and Their Planning Implications* (American Council for an Energy Efficient Economy: Washington, D.C., 1989).

phous silicon. The company was four to five years ahead of the competition in CIS technology, and a line of CIS cells was planned.[27]

Even though ARCO Solar was the world's leading producer of PV cells, it still had never made a profit. Its $30 million in revenue was matched every fifteen hours by its parent company.[28] Though ARCO Solar's president was confident the company could stand on its own feet within two or three years, some analysts believed that the $200 million ARCO had invested in its solar subsidiary had hurt the parent company's standing. Other criticisms began to surface in the press. Bill Yerkes, the founder and first president of the company, told the *Los Angeles Times* that "the company was screwed up two years after [ARCO] bought it. We went from making cells for $10 a watt and selling them for $15 to making cells for $32 a watt and selling them for $5."[29] Other former employees cited additional examples of instability: The company's headquarters had shifted five times, and six men had been president in twelve years (three presidents in the first three years alone). One former employee recalled how a colleague had more than a dozen different job titles during this tenure.

WHAT SHOULD ARCO DO?

Meanwhile, in 1985, ARCO had undergone a restructuring that signaled a shift in corporate strategy. Anticipating continued low oil prices, the company cut costs by $500 million, repurchased 24 percent of its outstanding common stock, and wrote off $1.5 billion for losses on the sale of assets and expenses due to personnel reductions. The Chairman of the Board retired and the CEO stepped down.

The company's new strategy was to focus on its core hydrocarbons and coal businesses. In accordance with this strategy, it seemed to make sense to sell the unprofitable solar subsidiary. On the other hand, the new CIS thin-film technology showed promise of being the basis of a line of PV cells that would be truly competitive with fossil fuels for utility-scale power generation in the next few years. Given the rising concern over global warming, an economically competitive PV cell for large-scale power generation could be a bonanza.

Finally, ARCO enjoyed a reputation as a socially responsible corporation for continuing to support its solar subsidiary when so many oil companies had dropped out of the solar energy field. Whereas in the late 1970s critics had claimed that the oil companies were buying up the solar technology in order to suppress it, Big Oil, with its deep pockets, was now generally acknowledged as being good for the PV industry. ARCO was a hero of sorts in the renewable-energy community. Should ARCO sell ARCO Solar? Top management had a difficult decision to make.

Discussion Questions

1. In making the decision about what it should do, what factors should ARCO consider?
2. What is your assessment of the potential for the products that ARCO Solar was developing?
3. Even if these products were highly promising, should ARCO decide to sell its solar holding? Why or why not?
4. In assessing whether to sell or hold on to ARCO, what role should long-term considerations relating to energy prices and supply play? What role should short-term factors play?

5. What role should "social responsibility" play in the decision that ARCO makes about its solar power holdings? Is this decision one that should be decided solely on the basis of business factors?

6. Why might a company like ARCO have trouble developing a technology like solar? From a public policy standpoint is it better that solar power development occur in large integrated energy companies like ARCO or in small firms exclusively devoted to a particular technology?

7. As a member of ARCO's Board of Directors, what would your opinion be about the future of ARCO Solar?

NOTES

1. Donald Woutat, "Atlantic Richfield Plans to Sell ARCO Solar Unit, Cites Poor Prospects for Growth," *Los Angeles Times,* February 25, 1989, p. IV–1.

2. ARCO Annual Reports, 1977–1989.

3. "Waiting for the Sunrise," *The Economist,* May 19, 1990, p. 95.

4. Solar Energy Industries Association, *Fifteen Years In Business With The Sun,* informational pamphlet, 1989.

5. Bruce A. Jacobs, "Bill Yerkes—The Sunshine King," *Industry Week,* July 8, 1985, p. 66.

6. James Bates, "Sale of ARCO Unit Casts Shadow on Future of Solar Energy Venture," *Los Angeles Times,* March 7, 1989, p. IV–1.

7. "1-MW Solar Facility Planned in California," *Electrical World,* May 1982, p. 25.

8. Don Best, "PV Power Goes On-Line in Hesperia," *Solar Age,* April 1983, p. 37.

9. "Solar Plant Is Largest," *Engineering News-Record,* April 7, 1983, p. 16.

10. Alyssa A. Lappen, "Solar Lives!" *Forbes,* August 15, 1983, p. 104.

11. Don Best, "ARCO Goes Amorphous," *Solar Age,* November 1983, p. 15.

12. Karen Berney, "Why the Outlook Is Dimming for U.S.-Made Solar Cells," *Electronics,* September 23, 1985, p. 32.

13. Bill Yerkes, "Big Oil's Future in Photovoltaics," *Solar Age,* June 1986, p. 14.

14. Don Best, "ARCO Solar Enters Joint Venture with Japanese Firm," *Solar Age,* May 1986, p. 20.

15. Kenneth R. Sheets, "Solar Power Still the Hottest Thing In Energy," *U.S. News & World Report,* May 2, 1983, p. 45.

16. Solar Energy Industries Association, *Fifteen Years in Business With the Sun.*

17. Berney, "Why the Outlook is Dimming," p. 32.

18. Matthew L. Wald, "U.S. Companies Losing Interest in Solar Energy," *New York Times,* March 7, 1989, p. 1.

19. Ibid.

20. Barbara Rosewicz, "ARCO Is Trying To Sell Solar-Panel Unit, Reversing Move Into Alternative Energy," *Wall Street Journal,* February 27, 1989, p. B–3.

21. Best, "ARCO Solar Enters Joint Venture," p. 20.

22. Lad Kuzela, "Days Are Sunny for Jim Caldwell," *Industry Week,* October 13, 1986, p. 75.

23. "Waiting for the Sunrise," p. 95.

24. Berney, "Why the Outlook is Dimming," p. 32.

25. Department of Energy, *National Photovoltaics Program: 1987 Program Review,* April 1988.

26. David E. Carlson, "Low-Cost Power From Thin-Film Photovoltaics," in T.B. Johansson (ed.), *Electricity: Efficient End-Use and New Generation Technologies, and Their Planning Implications* (Washington, D.C.: American Council for an Energy Efficient Economy, 1989).

27. Mark Crawford, "ARCO Solar Sale Raises Concerns Over Potential Technology Export," *Science,* May 26, 1989, p. 918.

28. Bates, "Sale of ARCO Unit Casts Shadow," p. IV–1.

29. Ibid.

APPENDIX A

How Photovoltaic Cells Work

A photovoltaic cell produces electricity directly from sunlight. When the sunlight strikes the surface of the semiconductor material of which the cell is made, it energizes some of the semiconductor's electrons enough to break them loose. The loose electrons are channeled through a metallic grid on the cell's surface to junctions where they are combined with electrons from other cells to form an electric current.

Different semiconductor materials' electrons are broken loose by different wavelengths of light, and some wavelengths of sunlight reach the earth's surface with more intensity than others. Consequently, much of the effort of photovoltaic research has been to find semiconductor materials that are energized by the light wavelengths that are most intense and have the potential to provide the most energy.

Single-crystal silicon cells were the first type widely used, powering satellite radios as early as 1958. These cells are energized by some of the most intense sunlight wavelengths, and have achieved conversion efficiencies (percentage of light energy converted to electricity) over 20 percent. Other, nonsilicon, single-crystal cells have achieved efficiencies over 27 percent.[1] While efficient, these single-crystal cells are expensive to produce and the crystals are difficult to grow. Much of the crystal is wasted when it is sawed into pieces for individual photovoltaic cells. Because they cost so much, their use has been limited mainly to applications where electricity is necessary and there are no other alternatives, such as in the space program.

In order to reduce production costs, researchers began to search for ways to fabricate silicon into cells that did not require the expensive and wasteful single-crystal techniques. One result of their efforts are *polycrystalline silicon cells*, which sacrifice some efficiency in return for cheaper manufacturing methods. The most efficient polycrystalline cells to date achieve better than 15 percent efficiencies. Together, single-crystal and polycrystalline cells account for two thirds of those sold.[2]

Perhaps the most promising PV technologies are the "thin-film" techniques, in which cells as large as 4 square feet—as opposed to crystalline cells which are in the neighborhood of one quarter inch in diameter—are produced by depositing a film of PV material less than one hundredth the thickness of a crystalline cell on a suitable base, or substrate. These cells are only about half as efficient as single-crystal cells, but because they can be produced for about one fourth the cost or less, they offer the greatest potential for large-scale use.

Thin-film silicon cells (called *amorphous silicon*) accounted for 37 percent of the world market for photovoltaics in 1987. One drawback to amorphous silicon cells, however, is that they typically lose about one sixth of their power output in the first few months of use. There are other thin-film materials that do not suffer from this light-induced degradation. Two of the most promising are copper indium diselenide (CIS) and cadmium telluride (CdTe). ARCO Solar, Inc. is the world leader in CIS technology. The company has developed a 4-square-foot CIS cell with a 9 percent conversion efficiency, demonstrating that large-scale applications of thin-film technology are feasible.

A Texas company, Photon Energy, Inc., has developed an inexpensive, simple process for applying CdTe to panels as large as ARCO's, achieving 7 percent efficiency. The company has managed better than 12 percent efficiencies in the laboratory and expects to do even better in the near future.

Besides improving conversion efficiencies by developing new photovoltaic compounds, researchers have been breaking efficiency records by "stacking" cells. These "mechanically stacked multijunction" (MSMJ) cells are actually two cells pasted together. The top cell extracts the energy from one part of the light spectrum, and the lower cell uses the energy from a different part. A MSMJ cell composed of a single-crystal gallium arsenide cell and a single-crystal silicon cell achieved a better than 30 percent efficiency last year, and researchers believe that a three-layer cell with a 38 percent efficiency is possible.[3] Efficiency improvements via stacking of more economical thin-film cells are also being investigated.

The continuing improvements in conversion efficiencies are especially remarkable considering that as recently as 1982, theoretical physicists believed that the maximum achievable efficiency of a solar cell was 22 percent. The highest efficiency achieved at that point was 16 percent. Now, theoreticians estimate that 38 to 40 percent is the limit, although the physics of thin-film technology is not completely understood.

Other Sun-Powered Energy Sources

Photovoltaics are not the only way of utilizing the sun's energy.[4] In fact, PVs are not even the major producer of electricity from sunlight. That distinction belongs to solar thermal technologies. Solar thermal systems work by using the heating rays of the sun to warm air, water, or oil for space heating or thermal power generation. Luz International of Los Angeles is the world's largest producer of solar thermal electric plants. The company's seven plants in California's Mojave Desert produce 90 percent of all solar-generated power in the world. Company officials estimate that solar thermal plants occupying just one percent of the Mojave could supply all of Southern California Edison's peak power requirements. Solar thermal facilities, which on sunny days can achieve conversion efficiencies twice that of some PVs, generate power at a cost equal to late-generation nuclear plants, and the cost is dropping.

Biomass technologies focus on developing quick-growing plants that can be burned to extract the solar energy the plants store. A promising biomass technique involves growing certain types of algae in shallow ponds located in the desert. The algae produce an oil which can be extracted and used as fuel.

Ninety percent of the wind-generated electricity in the United States is produced by wind turbines located in three mountain passes in California. These three passes have been credited with having 80 percent of the world's usable wind supply, although experts estimate that under the right conditions wind power could generate up to 5 percent of the nation's electricity. The California turbines accounted for one percent of California's electrical production in 1989. Production of new wind-powered facilities has been sluggish since tax credits for such construction ended in 1985, and also because at current prices wind power is not quite competitive with fossil fuels.

Hydro power, which is the cheapest power source, is the largest generator of electricity among the renewables. However, its potential for further expansion is limited, since all the most convenient rivers have already been dammed. Altogether, renewables (hydro, wind, solar, biomass, and geothermal) account for about 9 percent of the electric power generated in the United States.

$\sim$

NOTES TO APPENDIX A:

1 Neelkanth G. Dhere, "Present Status of the Development of Thin-Film Solar Cells, *Vacuum*, Vol. 39, Nos. 7–8, p. 743.

2 "Waiting for the Sunrise," *The Economist*, May 19, 1990, p. 95.

3. Dana Gardner, "Solar Cells Reach Efficiency Highs," *Design News*, April 24, 1989, p. 38.

4. Information in this section is adapted from James R. Chiles, "Tomorrow's Energy Today," *Audubon*, January 1990, p. 58.

3-6

ASHLAND OIL TANK COLLAPSE

This case was written by Deborah Crimmins under the editorial guidance of Professors James E. Post and Susan Samuelson, as a basis for class discussions. © 1989, Public Affairs Research Program, Boston University, 621 Commonwealth Avenue, Boston, MA 02215.

Shortly after 5:00 p.m. on Saturday, January 2, 1988, the operator at Ashland Oil's Floreffe terminal heard a thunder-like sound and turned to see a 4-million-gallon oil tank collapse. A 30-foot wave of diesel oil erupted from the tank, burst over the containment dike, and surged toward Pennsylvania's route 837 and the Monongahela River. In the days following the tank's collapse, Ashland responded to constant media attention, informed the public about the situation, and coordinated cleanup efforts with federal, state, and local officials.

ASHLAND OIL

Ashland Refining Company was founded in Kentucky in 1924. In 1936 Ashland consolidated with Swiss Oil Corporation and incorporated as the Ashland Oil and Refining Company. Ashland was primarily a regional refiner and marketer of oil until Orin E. Atkin's tenure as Chairman and CEO. According to *Business Week*, "A voracious dealmaker, he [Atkin] took charge in 1965 and transformed Ashland from a regional refiner with $448 million in sales to a $9.5 billion powerhouse by the time he was ousted in 1981."[1] During this period Ashland acquired a number of oil and chemical companies.

Along with growth, Atkin brought controversy. In 1973 he was fined $1,000 for an illegal contribution to the Committee to Re-elect the President [Nixon]. In 1975 the Securities and Exchange Commission (SEC) charged Ashland with illegal campaign contributions of nearly $800,000 between 1967 and 1973. Still later, SEC charged that Ashland had made $4 million in questionable overseas payments. Because 22 percent of its crude oil was imported from Iran, Ashland was hard hit during the 1979 oil crisis. Allegations were made that Ashland paid millions of dollars to preserve oil supplies from Abu Dhabi and Oman during this period. Ashland was also in a dispute with the National Iranian Oil Company over $283 million worth of oil the company received just before the embargo.

In May 1981 Ashland announced Atkin was retiring to pursue personal business interests, and John R. Hall was named Chairman and CEO. Hall joined Ashland in 1957, was named President of Ashland Chemical in 1971, and Executive Vice President of Ashland Oil in 1981. Hall was characterized as "unflamboyant, matter-of-fact, but knows where he wants to go."[2] He strengthened the core-refining business by investing in the Catlettsburg refinery, closing some operations, and slashing inventories. In 1984 Ashland sold a number of unrelated operations, including insurance and pollution control businesses.

Hall had dealt with a number of crises since 1981. These included charges by the SEC that Ashland made $28.7 million in illegal payments to foreign officials, a lawsuit by former employees who claimed they were fired for refusing to cover up those payments, and the arrest of former CEO Atkin for selling documents to the Iranians. Hall also guided Ashland through a takeover attempt. In March 1986 the Belzberg family of Canada revealed they owned 9.2 percent, or 2.6 million shares of Ashland's stock. They offered $1.8 billion for the company. One day after this bid, Kentucky's legislature passed an antitakeover law intended to prevent outsiders from "wrest[ing] control of the corporation from a board deeply committed to the well-being of Kentucky."[3] Since 1981 Ashland contributed $10 million to Kentucky's educational institutions. Ashland settled with the Belzbergs by buying their shares for $134 million. Shortly afterward, Ashland's board authorized the repurchase of up to 27 percent of the company's outstanding shares and established an employee stock ownership plan.

In 1988 Ashland Oil was the largest of the "independent" oil companies. Unlike major national and international companies that integrate into every facet of the petroleum industry, independents traditionally focus on one segment of the business. Ashland concentrated on refining and marketing and ranked sixtieth in the Fortune 500 for fiscal 1987, fifteenth among oil companies in sales, and twelfth in profits.

In 1988 Ashland consisted of seven groups: Petroleum, Superamerica, Valvoline, Chemical, Engineering and Construction, Exploration, and Coal. The largest group, Ashland Petroleum, ranked thirteenth in U.S. oil refining capacity with 346,500 barrels per day out of the total U.S. capacity of 15,067,800 barrels per day. Ashland's three refineries, located in Catlettsburg, Kentucky, St. Paul Park, Minnesota, and Canton, Ohio, operated at 93 percent of capacity during fiscal 1988. Ashland main-

tained twenty-three terminals in nine states, including fifteen river terminals, and owned the largest private tank barge fleet on inland waterways.

Ashland's other groups included: Superamerica, which operated 500
retail station–store combinations in seventeen states and 1,500 gasoline
outlets; Valvoline, which marketed the third ranked branded motor oil
and operated 175 oil change outlets; Ashland Chemical, which was the
largest distributor of thermoplastic resins and a petrochemical marketer;
Engineering and Construction, which owned reserves of 2.4 million barrels of domestic crude, 212 billion cubic feet of natural gas, and foreign
reserves of 45 million barrels; and a 46 percent ownership of Ashland
Coal and 50 percent of Arch Mineral, both of which mined in four states.

ASHLAND'S SAFETY AND ENVIRONMENTAL RECORD

After the tank's collapse, Ashland's environmental record came under
scrutiny. J. Dan Lacy, Ashland's Vice President of Corporate
Communications, reported that the company had six small spills over the
five years before the collapse, with the largest fine being $2,000. Richard
Golob of World Information Systems commented, "On oil pollution,
Ashland has no major black marks, no major accidents until now. It has
had oil tank storage spills in the past, but any company involved in storing oil has too."[4]

In July 1986 Ashland agreed to pay a $762,500 penalty for water pol-
lution at its Catlettsburg refinery that spanned over six years. The company attributed these problems to equipment malfunctions and weather
conditions. However, the EPA's Roger O. Pfaff said Ashland had a raft of
pollution problems including failure to obtain permits and meet emissions limits.[5] Ashland's 1988 Annual Report stated plans to spend an
additional $30 million in air and water quality controls in 1989. Ashland
had spent $25 million during 1988 on air and water controls.

Safety incidents included an August 1984 explosion at a Freedom,
Pennsylvania, facility, which killed three workers and resulted in OSHA
violations. An August 1982 explosion at the Canton, Ohio, refinery
caused that facility to close for thirty days.

RESPONSE TO THE SPILL

Immediately after the collapse the operator on duty radioed the barge to
stop pumping and notified the terminal manager, the National Response
Center, and the Coast Guard. An initial check revealed no oil in the nearby Monongahela River. The Coast Guard, the first federal agency on the

scene, discovered oil in the river later that evening. After assessing the magnitude of the problem—approximately 750,000 gallons had escaped the containment dike and were flowing into the river through storm sewers—the Coast Guard commander requested assistance from National Strike Force, closed the Monongahela to river traffic, and directed boom placement in the river. An initial cleanup plan was formulated during a meeting of the Coast Guard and Ashland. Roger Shrum, Ashland's Oil Media Relations manager, traveled to the scene within hours of the spill.

The firm hired by Ashland to clean up the oil spill arrived at 7 a.m. on Sunday, January 3, followed by the EPA and the Coast Guard Strike Force. However, cold temperatures (approximately 26° F), rapid currents, a system of locks and dams, and equipment designed for ocean spills (as opposed to river spills) hampered cleanup efforts. The oil slick flowed north with the Monongahela River into the Ohio River. Glen Cannon, Pittsburgh's Public Safety Director, stated, "The problem is that this is so massive. It's bank to bank from here to Elizabeth [near Floreffe]."[6] Pennsylvania's governor Robert Casey declared a state of emergency on Monday, January 4, and mobilized the National Guard to help with water distribution.

Back at corporate headquarters, Chairman Hall and President Charles J. Luellen talked with staff both on- and off-site. They felt Ashland's emergency management team was handling the situation adequately. Lacy remarked, "He [Hall] didn't want to make an official appearance until he could provide some answers." Hall called Governor Casey late that evening: "I told him we intended to clear up the mess as fast as we could."[7]

On January 4 Ashland headquarters uncovered several disturbing details. The collapsed tank was reconstructed from 40-year-old steel, a proper permit had not been obtained for construction, and hydrostatic testing had not been performed on the tank. Also, the possibility of major water shortages for 750,000 people became apparent. Lacy noted, "That changed the situation completely. It was no longer a situation in which we could simply do everything to clean up the river. All of a sudden people were involved very directly and they needed answers." Ashland lawyers advised Hall to refrain from making a public statement because of liability considerations, but Hall decided, "Our company had inconvenienced the lives of a lot of people and I felt it was only right to apologize."[8] To reassure investors and the public, Ashland announced the company held $400 million in insurance with a $2.5 million deductible through OIL Insurance, an oil industry mutual insurance company in Bermuda. The Bermudian company, with forty-nine members and $1 billion in assets, provided property, well control, and third-party pollution liability coverage.

On Tuesday, January 5, Hall flew to Pittsburgh, visited the spill site, and held a news conference. At the conference Hall stated:

> First, I want to thank everyone who participated in the cleanup activity. Many people have worked long hours—under difficult, cold, windy conditions—including voluntary organizations, government employees, and Ashland Oil employees.
>
> On behalf of Ashland Oil, its officers and directors, I want to apologize to the people of the Pittsburgh area for the inconvenience they have experienced as a result of this incident. The company is working with all appropriate government agencies in an effort to clean up the damage as rapidly as possible.

Hall acknowledged the tank was reconstructed from 40-year-old steel, admitted no written permit was obtained, and said hydrostatic testing had not been performed. He announced the hiring of Battelle Memorial Institute of Columbus, Ohio, to conduct an independent investigation into the collapse.

Meanwhile, at the scene, Ashland, the EPA, the Coast Guard, and a number of state, local, and private agencies continued to work on two fronts: the cleanup of the river and the terminal, and the water shortage problem. The Coast Guard Strike Force had been brought in at Ashland's expense, and approximately 130 contracted employees worked on the cleanup of thirty-eight river miles on the Monongahela and the Ohio. They used 20,000 feet of boom and recovered about 204,000 gallons of oil from the river and 2.95 million from the terminal. Despite these efforts, short-term environmental damage included the death of 10,000 fish and 2,000 birds. The cold weather minimized some effects because animals were hibernating or had migrated, but it hindered the cleanup. A Coast Guard spokesman stated, "Cold is helping only in that it is congealing the oil. It makes it easier to contain. The basic problem is that it is miserable to work in this stuff."[9]

Ashland's efforts to minimize water shortages included providing boats for water testing and planes for flyovers of the spill. They also placed booms around water intake valves, bought carbon feeder for a number of water plants, and provided water barges and trucks. A total of sixteen water facilities were affected, but only the Robinson Township Authority could not maintain service. The Robinson Township Authority had 17,000 customers without water for up to five days and 200 customers waterless for a week. They were able to reopen intake valves eight days after the spill.

Ashland made advance payment against expenses to a number of local organizations that participated in the cleanup. These included checks of

$210,000 to Allegheny County and $165,000 to Western Pennsylvania Water Company. Allegheny County Commission Chairman Thomas Foerster stated, "I can't recall, at any time in my government service, that I've found a company that was involved in something like this—that has been totally up front with us, cooperative . . ."[10] Ashland also gave a $250,000 grant to the University of Pittsburgh's Center for Hazardous Materials Research to assess the ecological and environmental impact of the spill. Ashland authorized long-range environmental impact studies by Battelle Memorial Institute. On January 14 Ashland opened a Pittsburgh office under the direction of Corporate Vice President Phillip Block. This office coordinated with government agencies on the remaining clean-up and oversaw claims processing. By September 1988 Ashland had paid $15 million in cleanup costs and claims. Most of this was covered by insurance.

REGULATIONS AND STANDARDS FOR OIL STORAGE AND SPILLS

There were a number of federal, state, and local regulations applicable to oil storage and spills. The Clean Water Act (CWA) specified strict and absolute liability for oil spills. The CWA authorized the federal government to remove a spill unless the owner or operator had properly undertaken its removal. Spills had to be reported to the National Response Center. In addition, the CWA required a Spill Prevention Control and Countermeasures (SPCC) plan for any facility that stored more than 660 gallons of oil in an aboveground tank or had more than 1,320 gallons of combined storage. The site-specific SPCC plan had to identify potential equipment failures and contingency plans in case a spill reached water. Furthermore, the plan had to be certified by a registered professional engineer and kept at the facility where the EPA could review it. Penalties for noncompliance could range up to $5,000 per day. After the collapse the EPA found inconsistencies on tank volumes and containment areas in Ashland's plan as well as lack of a site-specific contingency plan for spills.

In practice, there had been limited inspections of the estimated 650,000 facilities subject to SPCC regulations. The Floreffe terminal had not been inspected within the previous five years. EPA Region III had performed approximately 100 inspections per year. Nationally, inspections decreased from 3,412 in 1976 to 1,109 in 1987, while spills increased in the same period from 1,478 to 3,103. Of the inspections performed, about 60 percent of the plans were found to be deficient.

U.S. representative from Pennsylvania Doug Walgren criticized these regulations at the hearing before the Committee on Merchant Marine and Fisheries on May 26, 1988:

> The greatest dismay was to find out that there really was so little federal regulation that we could have relied on to assure public safety in these circumstances. . . . The EPA spill containment regulations are broad and vague, and they essentially, at least until this point, have left the industry in the role of setting its own standards, and then policing its own response to those standards, and conducting whatever inspections are conducted.

A number of bills for new regulations were proposed in both the House of Representatives and the Senate, but none were passed.

The Occupational Safety and Health Administration (OSHA) also regulated oil storage, specifying that tanks should be no less than 3 feet apart, and foundations and supports had to be fire resistant for two hours. The containment dikes were required to hold the contents of the largest tank and were restricted to an average height of 6 feet. Testing of tanks and compliance with American Petroleum Institute (API), Underwriter's Laboratory, or American Society of Mechanical Engineers standards were also required.

There were no federal construction standards for aboveground tanks in 1988. However, the Hazardous and Solid Waste Amendments of 1984 and the Superfund Amendments and Reauthorization Act of 1986 established a trust fund and regulations for underground storage tanks. The EPA had established an Office of Underground Storage Tanks and proposed requirements for underground tanks design, installation, and release detection requirements.

Another piece of federal legislation applying to oil spills was the Refuse Act of 1899. This prohibited discharging refuse into navigable waters without permission of the Army Corps of Engineers. In addition, the U.S. Coast Guard regulated transportation facilities that transfer oil in bulk.

At the state level, the Pennsylvania Clean Streams Law did not require a permit for oil tanks but it did require a Preparedness, Prevention, and Contingency (PPC) plan for tanks over 50,000 gallons. The PPC plan included information about dikes, ability for cleanup, and a plan for notifying local emergency response officials. The Ashland PPC was prepared in 1970; the Department of Environmental Resources (DER) found it inadequate and out of date after the spill. The DER did not conduct routine reviews of tanks, but estimated that out of the 6,500 tanks in this category in Pennsylvania, about ten to twelve leaks were reported each year.

In Pennsylvania, the state fire marshal's office issued construction permits for oil tanks except in Allegheny (where Floreffe was located) and Philadelphia counties. The Allegheny County fire code based its construction standards on the API standard 650. The code required notification of hydrostatic testing, so the fire marshal could choose to attend. Companies could be subject to fines of $200 for noncompliance. With a primary emphasis on fire prevention, the fire marshal's office did not employ engineers qualified to inspect tank construction.

The American Petroleum Institute, an industry association founded in 1919, issued a number of voluntary but generally recognized standards. These standards were frequently incorporated in fire code standards. The API-650 outlines standards for materials, design fabrication, erection, testing, and inspection of welded-steel oil storage tanks.

RECONSTRUCTION OF TANK

The Pennsylvania Tank Collapse Task Force (TCTF), appointed by Governor Casey, investigated the reconstruction of the tank. They concluded, "Ashland, its employees, and some contractors displayed a pervasive pattern of negligence and ignorance in selecting, assigning, constructing, supervising, and inspecting the reconstruction project."[11]

The project originated in 1985 when personnel at the Floreffe terminal decided tank 1338 required repair or replacement. At the same time, Allied Oil, an Ashland subsidiary, sold its Whiskey Island, Ohio, terminal. The terms of the December 16, 1985, sale authorized Ashland to remove any of Allied Oil's tanks. The Floreffe staff evaluated the costs of repairing tank 1338, moving Allied Oil's tank WI–16 (48 feet in diameter and 120 feet high holding 96,000 barrels), or moving a smaller tank (55,000 barrels) from Birmingport, Alabama. Constructing a new tank was not considered. An inspector examined WI–16 and found it structurally sound except for the floor. He also recommended dismantling by cutting through the old welds. Floreffe staff decided to move WI–16 because this option was cheaper per barrel stored than the other two options.

After the Floreffe project engineer was assigned, he solicited verbal bids on the project from Ashland's qualified vendor list. The sole criterion for qualification was insurability. He accepted the lowest bid of $174,391 submitted by Skinner Tank Company. The contract with Skinner Tank stated that the tank would be constructed under the API-650 standard. However, starting with the dismantling, the TCTF found many deviations from good construction practices: Skinner Tank cut down the tank to the right of the old welds instead of through the center, removed the insulation by driving over the steel plates with a small bull-dozer, allowed a crane to fall on some of the plates, and may not have taken proper care with the transportation of the steel. The TCTF also found Ashland did not take an active role in overseeing the project.

Back at Floreffe, the project engineer talked with the Allegheny County fire marshal's office and sent them information on the project. Later, after checking on the permit application, he assumed verbal approval was given to begin construction without a written permit. After the collapse, Fire Marshal Martin Jacobs claimed his office had not approved construction. However, in October 1988, after the task force report was issued, a memo from Chief Inspector Charles Kelly was found stating he had inspected the Floreffe terminal and had given verbal approval.

During the reconstruction at Floreffe—which the TCTF also found only loosely monitored by Ashland personnel—the Skinner Tank crew did not follow any written welding or construction procedures. After the tank was completed, Skinner Tank performed a diesel penetration test; diesel oil was sprayed on the welds and the tank was checked for penetration. This test was not required by API-650 and it was unclear whether the whole tank or just sections were tested. Radiographs of the welds were required by API-650 and were performed. The project engineer calculated that 40 welds should be tested while the TCTF later calculated that the standard required 119 radiographs. In addition, when the contractor who performed the radiographs reported that twenty-two of the thirty-nine welds examined were substandard, no action was taken by the Ashland project engineer. Finally, a hydrostatic test—complete filling of the tank with water—was rejected by the Floreffe Manager of Facilities as taking too much time. The manager also incorrectly believed the oil penetration test, not the hydrostatic test, was required by API-650. The tank was put into service in August 1987 with an initial load of 800,000 gallons of oil.

The TCTF concluded:

> At each step along the way, Ashland as an entity failed to take any active role in controlling its contractors or establish any procedures which might lead to a quality job. It was a passive consumer of the worst kind—apathetic as to potential problems, ignorant of actual events, unwilling to take any engaged role. Its employees were both institutionally and often personally unable to respond any other way. Both the details and big picture equally escaped Ashland's attention. Compared against the applicable standards, its industry peers, or even common sense, Ashland's conduct and procedures can only be

considered grossly negligent. The structural collapse at Floreffe can be directly traced to the supervisory bankruptcy at Ashland.[12]

The Task Force's enforcement recommendations included pursuing civil action against Ashland, having the Attorney General consider criminal prosecution, and noting that Skinner Tank Company was also liable for civil prosecution.

Hall commented, "We clearly had a problem in the terminal department, which we've moved to correct. That doesn't say the rest of the company has a problem."[13] Ashland was disappointed with the tone of the report and felt that seeking maximum civil penalties was counterproductive since Ashland had made every effort possible to clean up the spill.

CAUSE OF THE TANK FAILURE

There were a number of reasons why an oil storage tank could fail—tensile or strength failure, fatigue, or compression. In May 1988 Battelle determined that the tank collapsed because of brittle failure. This type of failure was related to the toughness rather than the strength of the material, and required three basic conditions—a notch or flaw, low toughness, and stress. The flaw was found to have been caused years before by a cutting torch. The tank's steel, which was over forty years old, was found to have adequate strength for the application, but it lost its toughness at temperatures below 80° to 100° F as determined by a Charpy V-Notch test. The stress of filling the tank to capacity in cold weather brought all three requirements of brittle fracture together. At the Whiskey terminal, the tank had held a heavier type of oil, but it had been insulated and heated.

SENATE HEARING

On February 4th, 1988, the U.S. Senate Subcommittee on Environmental Protection held a hearing to examine federal, state, and company response to the spill. Current and proposed regulations as well as similar incidents were discussed. Hall, testifying on Ashland's role in the cleanup, summed up his remarks:

> In closing, let me say that Ashland Oil has operated in the Ohio River valley for more than 60 years without an incident of this type, and we are proud of that record. We are embarrassed by this incident, but we are proud of the valiant efforts that our employees

have made in containing the spill and in helping to keep the water supplies going.

We hope you will agree that Ashland has handled this unfortunate incident in a responsible fashion. And let me assure you that we intend to continue to do so.

After Hall's statement, Senator Baucus commented: "It's not often, in fact it's rare, that a major company like Ashland would come before this committee with such candor in such an apparent effort to try to find the causes of the problem and try to find the solution. I think all of us commend you very much."

Senator Heinz of Pennsylvania spoke about a new bill that would regulate aboveground storage tanks more closely. Other senators felt that current regulations could be modified and pointed to the lack of resources available to the EPA and the Coast Guard for enforcement and cleanup. In evaluating the response to the spill, the issue of whether the EPA should have declared the spill a "federal spill" was considered. In his written statement, Mark McClellan, Deputy Secretary of the Pennsylvania Department of Environmental Resources, stated:

> We found to our dismay that the procedures within which the federal officials operated hampered their ability to take action without extensive and delaying consultation with each other and with the responsible party. Specifically, because federal officials did not as we requested declare this a "federal spill" they had to receive authorization from Ashland Oil for every response action. Inability to reach the appropriate Ashland officials at the very early stages delayed response action that may have minimized the spill's impact.

James Seif, Regional Administrator of EPA Region III, gave a different perspective on this issue in his testimony:

> The fact is that it is not a federal spill except that they all are in terms of the regulatory jurisdiction: it's Ashland's spill. The spiller must clean it up. Appropriately enough, when the spiller doesn't, or can't, or won't, then a federal fund should be activated. In fact, I was confronted with a willing and apparently able responsible party who was working very hard, and I think in retrospect, effectively, to do the job.

Richard Golob, of the *Oil Spill Intelligence Report,* testified about other similar spills. The Floreffe spill was the largest since a well in Ranger, Texas, blew in November 1985, spilling 6.3 million gallons. He also cited nine major spills between 1978 and 1988 attributable to structural failures.

LEGAL AFTERMATH

In July 1988 Ashland entered into a consent decree with the EPA. The terms included Ashland paying $680,000 in costs, cleaning up the soil and groundwater, monitoring future discharges, creating a new SPCC plan, hydrostatically testing the remaining tanks, and undertaking an environmental compliance audit. Ashland was also fined $31,800 by OSHA: $30,000 for failing to repair the defective welds; $1,000 for an inadequate dike; and $800 for failing to establish a written safety plan. In addition, Pennsylvania's Governor Casey instructed state environmental officials to seek maximum civil penalties against Ashland.

In September Ashland was indicted on two misdemeanor charges of violating the Refuse Act and the Clean Water Act. These were the most stringent charges possible. An Ashland press release stated, "The company is disappointed that criminal actions will be pursued in light of Ashland's efforts to mitigate the spill's impact and the fact that the company quickly accepted responsibility for the incident."[14] In Pittsburgh, U.S. Attorney J. Alan Johnson stated, "The criminal law is directed toward the conduct that brought it [the spill] about, not what happened afterward."[15] In February 1989 Ashland pleaded no contest to these charges and in March was fined $2.25 million. This was the largest fine for a fuel spill in the United States. Federal District Judge Gustave Diamond commented, ". . . It was something more than simple negligence that the company was guilty of." Ashland called the fine "excessive" and considered whether or not to appeal.[16] Ashland also faced twenty class action civil lawsuits for damages as a result of the spill.

CHANGES AT ASHLAND

At the May 26, 1988, hearing before the U.S. House of Representatives' Committee on Merchant Marine and Fisheries, Phillip Block, Vice President of Ashland Oil, testified about changes since the spill:

> Four employees from the engineering department and the trucks and terminals operating group subsequently were reassigned. Ashland has stated that all future tank construction will be in full compliance with the material, welding, and testing specifications of API-650.
>
> As a result of the collapse of the Floreffe tank, a review of Ashland's tank facilities was undertaken to determine their physical condition. While the review is not yet completed, 146 facilities with more than 1,000 tanks have been inspected to date. Where appropriate, remedial actions indicated by the review have been under-

taken or scheduled for the near future. Organizational and procedural changes to strengthen environmental compliance efforts are
under review, and several changes already have been made.

Ashland had closed the Floreffe terminal after the spill and reopened
it in stages. Three additional tanks with storage capability of 272,000 barrels were built at the site with new steel in compliance with applicable
industry standards.

J. Dan Lacy wrote about the less tangible effects on Ashland of the
tank collapse:

> The public's reaction to the decision to be open and to accept
> responsibility indicates that cooperating with officials and doing
> what it takes to make the situation right is a prudent course to fol-
> low in the management of a crisis. In fact, by quickly taking respon-
> sibility—by being a good corporate citizen—Ashland actually
> earned public trust rather than lost it.[17]

Discussion Questions

1. Evaluate Hall's role in the cleanup process. What was his objective? Could it have been better implemented? Is this a good
   strategy? Why?
2. Assume the role of the press, politicians, employees, affected
   communities, and shareholders. Assess Hall's actions and statements. Identify potential positive and negative impacts of Hall's
   actions.
3. Why was it important for Ashland to control the cleanup process? Identify the advantages and disadvantages of having
   Ashland manage the cleanup process. Would these consequences have changed if the spill was declared a "federal spill"?
4. Review the steps Ashland took to reduce future spills. Is this an
   effective strategy? Why? What other actions would you recommend?
5. What role did the EPA and the state's fire marshall have in the
   Ashland disaster? How active and extensive should industry be
   in self-regulation?
6. Were the penalties leveled against Ashland just? What message
   does this send to industry? Should Ashland's proactive cleanup
   role have been considered in determining penalties? Why?

$\sim$

NOTES

1. Zachary Schiller, "Ashland Just Can't Seem to Leave Its Checkered Past Behind," *Business Week*, October 31, 1988, p. 2.
2. Seth H. Lubove, "Ashland Chief Seen Able to Handle Crisis by Belzbergs' Takeover Proposal," *Wall Street Journal*, March 31, 1986, p. 34.
3. Seth H. Lubove, "Kentucky Aid for Ashland Marks Power of Firm and Fears of Outside Ownership," *Wall Street Journal*, April 1, 1986, p. 64.
4. Don Hopey and Matthew Brelis, "Jefferson Spill 1st Major 'Black Mark' against Ashland Oil's Safety Record," *Pittsburgh Press*, January 10, 1988, p. 1.
5. Schiller, "Ashland Just Can't Seem to Leave Its Checkered Past Behind," p. 124.
6. "Collapse of Diesel Tank Pollutes Drinking Water Near Pittsburgh," *New York Times*, January 4, 1988, p. A15.
7. Clare Ansberry, "Oil Spill in the Midwest Provides Case Study in Crisis Management," *Wall Street Journal*, January 8, 1988, p. 21.
8. Ibid.
9. Philip Shabecoff, "Tools' Mismatch to Task Hampering Oil Cleanup," *New York Times*, January 6, 1988, p. A19.
10. J. Dan Lacy, "How Ashland Oil Made the Best of an Unfortunate Situation," *AMC Journal*, August 1988, p. 8.
11. Tank Collapse Task Force, *Report into the Collapse of Tank 1338*, June 22, 1988, p. iii.
12. Ibid., p. 79.
13. Schiller, "Ashland Just Can't Seem to Leave Its Checkered Past Behind," p. 124.
14. Ruth Marcus, "Ashland Oil Is Indicted in Pennsylvania Oil Spill," *Washington Post*, September 16, 1988, p. A4.
15. Ibid.
16. "$2.25 Million Fine in '88 Spill," *New York Times*, March 10, 1989, p. A16.
17. Lacy, "How Ashland Oil Made the Best of an Unfortunate Situation," p. 10.

3-7

DU PONT FREON®
PRODUCTS DIVISION

This case was written by Forest Reinhardt, Ph.D. candidate in Business Economics, Harvard University, under the supervision of Professor Richard H. K. Vietor, Harvard Business School, as the basis for class discussion, rather than to illustrate either effective or ineffective handling of an administrative situation. © 1989 by the National Wildlife Federation.

"Evidence of Ozone Depletion Found Over Big Urban Areas; Pattern Widens; Severity Surprises Experts" ran a front-page headline in The *Washington Post* on March 16, 1988. The day before, atmospheric scientists from an interagency governmental research team, headed by the National Aeronautics and Space Administration (NASA), released new information linking chlorofluorocarbons (CFCs) to the destruction of stratospheric ozone. The scientists reported that ozone depletion was more severe and widespread than anticipated. Furthermore, there was now hard evidence that CFCs contributed to ozone depletion over Antarctica. Since stratospheric ozone shielded the earth from ultraviolet radiation, the depletion of the ozone layer allowed increased levels of radiation to reach the earth's surface. This was likely to cause increases in skin cancer rates and damage to crops and fisheries.

Invented in the 1930s, CFCs were widely used in a variety of industries because they were chemically stable, low in toxicity, and non-flammable. CFCs were the leading heat transfer agent in refrigeration equipment and air-conditioning systems for buildings and vehicles. They were used in the manufacture of various kinds of foam, including building insulation. And they were used as solvents and cleaning agents in semiconductor manufacturing and other businesses. In Europe and Japan CFCs were widely used as propellants in aerosol containers, although this practice was banned in the United States.

While no substitutes existed for many of these commercial uses, concern for stratospheric ozone led, in September 1987, to an international accord under which CFC production was to be held at its 1986 level and production cut in half by 1999 (see Table 3-7-1). But the newest scientific evidence cast doubt on whether even these reductions would protect the ozone layer.

For Joe Glas, who ran the Freon® Products Division of E.I. Du Pont de Nemours and Company, these new findings posed an extraordinary challenge. As the world's largest manufacturer of CFCs, Du Pont earned $600 million in revenues from this business in 1987. In the early 1980s Du Pont led CFC producers and users in opposing CFC regulation, citing the uncertainty of the science. Recently, though, Du Pont took the opposite tack and pushed industry to support the international regulatory accord.

Despite its reversal in position, Du Pont was severely criticized in the press and in Congress for not doing more. A New York University physician, testifying at a House of Representatives hearing on ozone depletion, described a "near epidemic" increase in skin cancer rates. Senate hearings on the issue were scheduled for March 30, and Du Pont officials would have to testify. Glas needed to decide whether the Freon® Products Division should do nothing and let the regulatory process run its course, take an active role in support of or in opposition to further controls, or take some unilateral action such as cutting back its own CFC production.

THE CFC BUSINESS

CFCs were a class of chemical compounds containing carbon, fluorine, and chlorine. There were two main classes of CFCs: chlorofluoromethanes and chlorofluoroethanes. The Du Pont Company, which had invented most CFCs, marketed them under the trademark "Freon."

Chlorofluoromethanes consisted of two commercially important variations: CFC-11 and CFC-12. In the United States CFC-11 was used primarily as a blowing agent for foams. End-products range from the soft foams used in mattresses, furniture, and car seats (about 20 percent of blown foam applications), to foams used in food packaging and as insulation in refrigerators (about 20 percent) to the rigid foams used as insulation in the construction of new buildings (60 percent). CFC-11 was also used in the United States in special, unregulated aerosols. CFC-12 was used primarily as the coolant in refrigeration systems, including home refrigerators and air conditioners for buildings, cars, and trucks. Its secondary uses included foam blowing. In Europe and Japan CFC-11 and -12 were widely used as aerosol propellants. The chlorofluoroethanes consisted of CFC-113, -114, and -115. CFC-113 accounted for more than 95 percent of the total use of chlorofluoroethanes. They were used primarily as solvents in the electronics and defense industries to clean high-value electronic components like printed circuit boards. In the United States this use accounted for about half of CFC-113 demand; other applications included metal degreasing, dry cleaning, and cleaning medical implants and guidance systems (see Table 3-7-2).

A similar class of compounds, HCFCs, was composed of carbon, chlorine, fluorine, and hydrogen. Although not strictly CFCs, HCFCs were sometimes lumped into the same category. The most important HCFC was HCFC-22. About a third of HCFC-22 production was used as raw material in the manufacture of Teflon and other polymers. Significant end-uses of HCFC-22 included air conditioning for buildings (but not for vehicles) and commercial refrigeration equipment. A third class of compounds, called Halons, shared many of the same properties of CFCs and HCFCs, including the propensity to deplete stratospheric ozone. However, production of Halons was small relative to that of CFCs. They were mainly used in commercial and military fire protection systems.

CFCs and Ozone Depletion

CFCs were widely used because of their distinctive properties. CFCs did not react readily with other materials during the manufacture of final products or while those products (like refrigerators) were being used. Their stability also meant that, once released to the atmosphere, CFCs would not react with other effluent to form smog. Further, CFCs were nontoxic to humans. CFCs could be immediately released to the atmosphere upon use (if, for example, they were used as solvents and then allowed to evaporate), or they might remain locked into a final product (a rigid foam, for example, or a refrigerator) for several years after manufacture. But sooner or later all CFCs created were released into the environment.

Because of their stability, what happened to CFCs after their release was a matter of little concern. In 1972 an industry consortium formed to study the environmental fate of CFCs. Then in 1974 Mario Molina and Sherry Rowland, two chemists at the University of California at Irvine, postulated that CFCs could be responsible for widespread destruction of stratospheric ozone. According to their theory, CFCs tended to migrate slowly to the stratosphere, the upper level of the atmosphere between 15 and 30 miles above the earth's surface. There they were broken into their constituent elements by ultraviolet radiation from the sun. The released chlorine atoms of CFCs then acted as a catalyst in a series of reactions that convert ozone (O_3) into oxygen (O_2). Because the chlorine acted as a catalyst rather than a reagent, a single chlorine atom could destroy large

Table 3-7-1

Total World & U.S. Production of CFCs

		Millions of Pounds					Share of Total			
		11	12	113	total		11	12	113	total
1970	World	537	660	102	1299		41%	51%	8%	100%
	U. S.				n/a					n/a
1975	World	654	821	150	1625		40	51	9	100
	U. S.				n/a					n/a
1980	World	642	819	272	1733		37	47	16	100
	U. S.	158	295	126						
1985	World	688	809	545	2042		34	40	27	100
	U. S.	176	302	161						
1987	World	745	898	650	2293		32	39	28	100
	U. S.	223	368	189						

Note: In 1985 and 1987, U. S. firms also produced 9 million pounds of CFC-114 and 10 million pounds of CFC-115

n/a not available.

Sources: Du Pont estimates and testimony of Elwood Blanchard, Executive Vice President, E. I. Du Pont de Nemours and Company, before the Senate Environment and Public Works Committee, March 30, 1988.

Table 3-7-2

Consumption of CFCs and Halons
(In millions of pounds)

	Aerosols	Foam Blowing	Refrigeration	Solvent	Other	Total
U. S.						
CFC-ll	10	151	15	0	0	175
CFC-12	16	48	189	0	48	301
CFC-113	0	0	0	151	0	151
CFC-114	0	7	2	0	0	9
CFC-115	0	0	10	0	0	10
Halon 1211	0	0	0	0	6	6
Halon 1301	0	0	0	0	8	8
Total	26	206	215	151	62	660
World Totals						
CFC-ll	257	439	67	0	48	810
CFC-12	342	132	479	0	48	1001
CFC-113	0	0	0	389	0	389
CFC-114	0	23	7	0	0	30
CFC-115	0	0	19	0	0	19
Halon 1211	0	0	0	0	15	15
Halon 1301	0	0	0	0	15	15
Total	599	594	571	389	127	2280
% of Total	26.2	26.0	25.0	17.1	5.5	100%

Note: Numbers are not consistent with production estimates in other tables.

Source: EPA, Regulatory Impact Analysis Protection of Stratospheric Ozone, Chapter Four, Washington, D.C., December 1987.

numbers of ozone molecules. And because CFCs persisted for long periods before breaking down to form free chlorine, the effects of today's use of CFCs would not be felt for decades or even centuries.

As an artificial pollutant in the lower atmosphere, ozone was one of the most unhealthy constituents of smog. Societies spent billions of dollars trying to control its levels. However, in the upper atmosphere, ozone blocked out some of the sun's ultraviolet radiation and prevented it from reaching the earth's surface. Therefore, stratospheric ozone depletion allowed higher levels of ultraviolet radiation to reach the earth. Higher rates of skin cancer in humans, as well as damage to crops and fisheries, were likely to result. A one percent decrease in stratospheric ozone concentrations could result in a two percent increase in the amount of ultraviolet radiation reaching the earth's surface. In turn, a one percent increase in cumulative exposure to ultraviolet radiation was expected to result in a two percent increase in the incidence of skin cancer (see Figure 3-7-1).

The ozone depletion mechanism postulated by Rowland and Molina was only a theory. Empirical verification was unavailable in 1974, and could not be expected for years because of the difficulties in measuring actual levels of stratospheric ozone. Some 300 million tons of ozone were created and destroyed each day in a dynamic stratospheric equilibrium. For natural reasons, ozone levels in the stratosphere vary widely over the course of each day, each year, and each multiyear sunspot cycle. Further, even if a trend toward lower ozone concentrations could be detected, it would be difficult to be sure that CFCs were responsible.

To simulate the chemical and physical processes that determined ozone levels in the stratosphere, computer models were built by government agencies, academic institutions, and industry groups. These models used data on estimated chlorine-ozone reaction rates, the persistence of chlorine in the stratosphere, the effects of other stratospheric contaminants, and global meteorological patterns as inputs to assess the effects of various levels of CFC loadings. The goal was to confirm modeling results by the empirical data.

The problem of matching observations to models was significant. Ozone concentrations were affected not only by CFCs but by a host of other natural and man-made gases, including carbon dioxide, oxides of nitrogen, and methane. This difficulty was compounded by the "one dimensional" nature of the models. Actual ozone concentrations over time were different not only at different altitudes but at different latitudes. Since the models predicted only averages across all latitudes, they were difficult to verify using empirical data. In response, scientists tried to develop "two-dimensional" models that would predict ozone concentrations at different

Figure 3-7-1

Some Physical and Chemical Processes Influencing the Ozone Layer and Climate

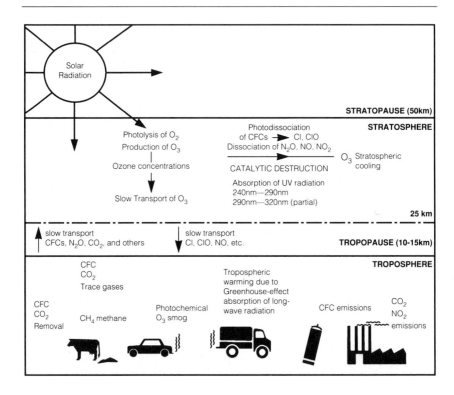

Major Ozone Modifying Substances Released by Human Activities

Chemical	Source
CFC-11 ($CFCl_3$) $\Big\}$ CFC-12 (CF_2Cl_2)	Used in aerosol propellants, refrigeration, foam blowing and solvents
CFC-22 ($CHClF_2$)	Refrigeration
CFC-113 ($C_2Cl_3F_3$)	Solvents
Methyl Chloroform (CH_3CCl_3)	Solvent
Carbon Tetrachloride (CCl_4)	CFC production and grain fumigation
Halon 1301 ($CBrF_3$) $\Big\}$ Halon 1211 (CF_2ClBr)	Fire extinguishant
Nitrus Oxides (NO_2)	By-product of industrial activity
Carbon Dioxides (CO_2)	By-product of fossil fuel combustion
Methane (CH_4)	By-product of agricultural, industrial, and mining activities

Source: World Resources Institute, "The Sky Is the Limit: Strategies for Protecting the Ozone Layer" (Washington, D.C., November 1986).

latitudes and altitudes over time, but two-dimensional models were more difficult to create, more expensive to run, and even more sensitive to scientific uncertainty. (Because both kinds of models also had a temporal element, the "one-dimensional" models were actually two-dimensional and the "two-dimensional" models were really three-dimensional. In counting the dimensions of a model, however, the temporal dimension was ignored.)

Almost as soon as the news of Rowland and Molina's work reached the press, American consumers began switching to nonaerosol packaging for common household products like deodorant. The U.S. Environmental Protection Agency (EPA) considered it prudent to ban certain "nonessential" uses of CFCs. The ban took effect in 1978; its main impact was to stop the use of CFCs as an aerosol propellant, except for essential medical and military uses. In 1973 the United States consumed about half of all CFCs manufactured worldwide, and aerosol uses accounted for about half of this consumption. Manufacturers of products that used aerosol containers switched to other propellants, including carbon dioxide, propane, and butane. U.S. sales of CFCs peaked in 1973.

With the exception of Canada, Norway, and Sweden, other governments did not impose bans on aerosol uses of CFCs. The European Economic Community promulgated voluntary, nonbinding guidelines for CFC aerosol uses in 1980, and this led to gradual reductions in these uses over time, not enough, however, to offset western European and Japanese trends toward increasing CFC use. CFC use grew apace in the developing world. In the United States, consumption of CFCs fell by 50 percent when aerosols were banned, but climbed slowly back toward its mid-1970s level as demand in the nonaerosol sectors grew. Shortly before the 1980 presidential election the EPA announced it was investigating the need for further restrictions on CFCs. Following the Reagan victory, with "regulatory relief" an important item on the new administration's domestic agenda, the EPA's investigation was curtailed, although never formally terminated.

During the early 1980s refinements of the computer models led many scientists to believe that Rowland and Molina had overstated the ozone depletion problem. These scientists claimed that depletion from CFCs was likely to be less than the 1974 predictions. In 1979 the National Academy of Sciences (NAS) predicted that continued growth in CFC use would lead to a loss of 16.5 percent of the stratospheric ozone by the time a new equilibrium was reached (perhaps 100 years later). In 1982 the NAS reduced its estimate to a depletion level of 5 to 9 percent. Two years later the estimate fell again to between 2 and 4 percent. At the same time actual monitoring of stratospheric ozone levels produced no hard evidence that any depletion was occurring. Finally, CFC production during this period was flat because of restrictions on aerosols and the worldwide recession in the early 1980s.

Then, in 1985, with CFC production again on the rise as the world economy recovered, British scientists working in Antarctica reported a dramatic decrease in springtime stratospheric ozone concentrations above that continent. The presence of this "hole" in the ozone layer called into question a whole generation of scientific models. The new findings hinted that model results had been too optimistic, and raised the possibility that ozone depletion might be occurring more rapidly than even Molina and Rowland predicted.

Reactions to this new information varied widely. The Natural Resources Defense Council and other environmental groups called for a worldwide production ban. Congress held hearings, and The *New Yorker* published an article highly critical of the CFC industry and especially Du Pont. Interior Secretary Donald Hodel drew some ridicule for suggesting that ozone depletion problems could be mitigated through the use of suntan lotion and sunglasses. Government and industry scientists hurried to update their models, while diplomats held meetings to bring about an international consensus on the ozone problem. A report by NASA and the United Nations World Meteorological Organization said that, based on new model calculations, it might be possible to allow CFC production to increase by 1.5 percent per year without any deleterious effects on the ozone. However, in the prevailing political climate, controls tighter than a cap on the growth rate were inevitable. In Montreal in September 1987 virtually all of the world's industrial nations pledged to cap production of CFC-11, -12, -113, -114, and -115 in their respective countries at its 1986 levels by 1989. Total production levels were to be cut back to 30 percent of 1986 levels by 1994 and to 50 percent of 1986 levels by 1999. Halon production was to be capped in 1993. The Montreal Protocol allowed certain exemptions for developing countries. It also provided for amendment should the scientific conclusions about the effects of CFCs change (see Table 3-7-3).

The Protocol was to take effect when countries responsible for two thirds of global CFC production had ratified it. Individual countries could decide how to allocate CFC production among producers, subject to an overall ceiling for each country expressed in terms of ozone depletion potential. (Different CFCs have different potencies as depleters of ozone; the Protocol accounted for this. For instance, one pound of CFC-11 was thought to have the same potential to deplete ozone as 1.25 pounds of CFC-113.)

Even before the treaty was negotiated, a suit by the Natural Resources Defense Council forced the EPA to resume its investigation into further CFC regulatory controls. After the Protocol, the EPA proposed mandatory cutbacks of production on the same schedule as the international protocol.

According to the EPA, failure to make such cutbacks could lead to an increase of about 150 million cases of nonmelanoma skin cancer among current and future U.S. populations born before 2075, and an increase of about 3 million cases of premature deaths from skin cancer among these populations. The EPA also predicted large increases in cases of cataracts (a debilitating eye condition) as a result of increased exposure to ultraviolet radiation. Damage to crops and aquatic organisms, including several commercially important fish species, was also predicted. According to the EPA, CFCs also played a small role in the trend toward global warming. Finally, the EPA concluded that while the costs of mandatory substitution would be significant, the costs of doing nothing were substantially greater (see Figure 3-7-2).

In December 1987 the EPA proposed its regulations for implementing the Protocol, which set limits on the amount of CFCs each firm could sell in the U.S. market. The limit for each firm was based on the firm's 1986 production, weighted according to the ozone depletion potential of each compound. Under that limit, firms could choose how much of each CFC to produce; a firm with permits to make 1,000 tons of CFC-11 could instead produce 1,250 tons of CFC-113 (or 250 tons of CFC-11, 250 tons of CFC-12, and 625 tons of CFC-113). Firms could also transfer production and sales rights among themselves to take advantage of scale economies in production. In the absence of regulation, CFC use was expected to grow at about the level of GNP in the industrialized world, and somewhat faster in developing countries. Capping production, much less cutting production, could lead to substantial price increases, particularly in the short run when users had not yet switched to other substances or otherwise curtailed their consumption of CFCs (see Tables 3-7-4 and 3-7-5).

The EPA expressed concern about the large "windfall profit" that could accrue to CFC producers as regulatory shortages drove prices upward. These profits might be as high as $600 million per year for the first few years after the Protocol took effect, with a discounted value of $9 billion over the period 1990–2010. The EPA considered a fee or tax to capture these profits for the U.S. Treasury instead of allowing them to fall to CFC producers; however, the EPA's statutory authority to do so was unclear.

Table 3-7-3
Production Capacity for CFCs and HCFC-22, United States, Europe, and Japan: 1985

	Plants	Capacity[a]
United States		
Du Pont	5	706
Allied-Signal	4	364
Pennwalt	1	143
Essex	1	99
Kaiser	1	77
Europe		
ATOCHEM (France)	2	375
ICI (UK)	1	276
Hoechst (Germany)	1	194
Montefluos (Italy)	2	190
Du Pont (Netherlands)	1	110
All Other (7)	9	317
Japan		
Daikin Kogyo	2	143
Asahi Glass	1	132
Du Pont–Mitsui[b]	1	66
All Other (2)	2	37

[a]Figures are in millions of pounds per year annual capacity as of 1985; they include CFCs -11,-12, -113,-114,-115, and HCFC-22.

[b]Du Pont and Mitsui each own a half of the plant.

Source: Maria Geigel, "CEH Product Review: Fluorocarbons," Chemical Economics Handbook, SRI International, 1985.

Table 3-7-4
Average Production Cost Data for CFCs: 1985
(In cents per pound)

	CFC–ll	CFC–12	CFC–113
List Price	60	71	92
Discount	16	6	5
Selling price	44	65	87
Costs of production			
Raw materials	26.7	39.4	33.5
Freight	4.4	6.5	6.1
Labor	2.8	4.1	4.8
Depreciation	4.4	6.5	8.7
Overhead	4.4	6.5	8.7
Research	0.7	1.1	1.7
Total	43.4	64.1	63.5
Earnings (pretax)	0.6	0.9	23.5

Source: Casewriter estimates.

Figure 3-7-2

Global Ozone Depletion for Alternative Control Options Cases

(a)

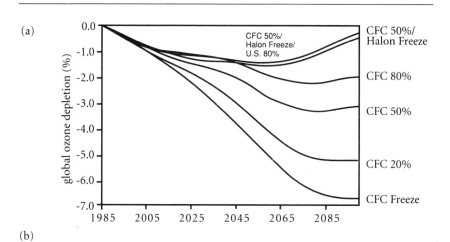

(b)

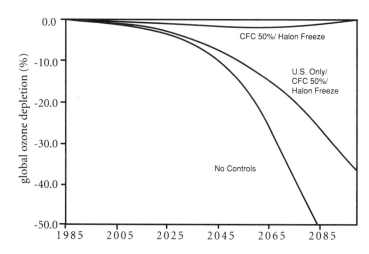

Source: EPA Regulatory Impact Analysis.

Note: The charts show projected changes on stratospheric ozone over time under various reductions of CFC production. For example, "CFC 50%" shows the ozone levels the EPA expected if CFC production were cut by 50%.

Table 3-7-5

Economic Implications of Potential CFC Restrictions

Effect of Protocol on CFC Usage
(weighted CFC usage of covered compounds)

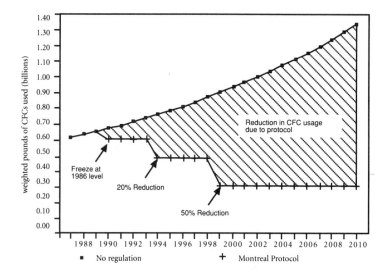

CFC–11 Price Under Protocol
(optimistic assumption case)

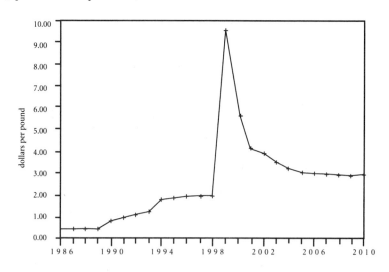

Source: Report by Putnam, Hayes, and Bartlett, Inc. for the Alliance for Responsible CFC Policy, December 2, 1987.

DU PONT'S BUSINESS STRATEGY

E.I. Du Pont de Nemours and Company was founded in the early 1800s as an explosives manufacturer. One hundred years later, Du Pont was the world's first firm to adopt the divisional structure which became standard for large corporations; it also developed modern management techniques for analyzing and controlling decision making in a large, decentralized operation. By 1987 Du Pont ranked ninth in the Fortune 500, with over $30 billion in revenues. Its products ranged from gasoline, plastics, and pesticides to sophisticated biomedical equipment (see Table 3-7-6).

In addition to modern management, Du Pont's name was synonymous with the harnessing of science for commercial ends. Nylon and Teflon were invented in the firm's laboratories in 1938. Later, Orlon and Dacron fabrics, Lycra spandex fiber, Tyvek packaging materials, and Kevlar for bulletproof vests were developed by Du Pont chemists. The influence of science on the company extended beyond the product line, pervading the corporate culture. Du Pont managers routinely spoke of the company as being "science-driven" and were unimpressed with companies that could not be described this way. Du Pont did not ignore the marketplace, as its $30 billion in sales attested. But its middle managers saw themselves fundamentally as scientific problem solvers with the tools to serve an increasingly technological society.

Joe Glas embodied this scientific culture. An Iowa native, Glas earned a Ph.D. in chemical engineering from the University of Illinois and joined Du Pont in 1964 as a research engineer. After holding nine positions in five states, Glas became the director of the Freon® Products Division in 1985. At important meetings Glas listened not only to his business managers but to Ph.D. chemists Mack McFarland, who was hired to appraise and develop ozone science, and Joe Steed, who headed the team responsible for the division's scientific, governmental relations and public affairs policies. Du Pont's organizational structure is illustrated in Figure 3-7-3. The Freon® Products Division, with 1,200 employees involved in the production and sales of CFCs, was a microcosm of the Du Pont scientific and managerial culture. It was a self-contained profit center with its own production, marketing, and R&D staffs. Virtually all its revenue came from the sale of CFC-11, -12, -113, -114, and -115 and HCFC-22.

Du Pont enjoyed international patent protection on CFCs through the late 1940s. Just as the patents expired, demand for CFCs skyrocketed as building and vehicular air-conditioning and household aerosols became common. Du Pont did not begin manufacturing CFCs in Europe and Japan until after indigenous firms had become entrenched. Still, by virtue

Table 3-7-6
Du Pont Sales, Income, and Assets, By Business Segment: 1987

	AIC	Biomed	Coal	Fibers	ICP	OilProd	OilMktg	Polymer	Consol
Sales	4554	1273	1828	5352	3347	3132	9336	3946	30468
ATOI	463	48	157	624	182	100	177	349	2100
Assets	2889	1417	2629	3502	2649	5080	4066	2874	28209
Investments (gross)	323	127	127	501	279	932	213	444	3035
ATOI/Sales	10.2%	3.8%	8.6%	11.7%	5.4	3.2%	1.9%	8.8%	6.9%
Sales/Assets 1.080%	1.576	0.898	0.695%	1.528%	1.263	0.617	2.296	1.373%	1.080%
ATOI/Assets	16.0%	3.4%	6.0%	17.8%	6.9%	2.0%	4.4%	12.1%	7.4%
Inv't/Assets	11.2%	9.0%	4.8%	14.3%	10.5%	18.3%	5.2%	15.4%	10.8%
% Sales growth	15.8	10.2	18.8	10.4	14.6	10.7	13.7	3.4	12.2
% ATOI growth	92.1	-45.5	20.8	15.1	7.7	N M	-57.2	31.2	17.3
% Asset growth	-2.2	18.4	-2.6	14.4	8.6	-1.7	4.1	5.5	16.8
% Inv't growth	4.2	33.7	-6.6	13.1	6.1	19.3	-8.6	11.3	10.9
% of DP Sales	14.9	4.2	6.01	17.6	11.0	10.3	30.6	13.0	100.0
% of DP ATOI	22.0	2.3	7.5	29.7	8.7	4.8	8.4	16.6	100.0

Note: All data are from Du Pont annual reports. ATOI means 'after-tax operating income.' It is the standard internal Du Pont measure of operating profits. It includes provisions for income tax but not a charge for capital costs. Sales figures include intersegment sales which are subtracted when calculating consolidated sales. Consolidated data on assets and investments include corporate assets and investments and thus, exceed the business segment totals. AIC is Agricultural and Industrial Chemicals; Biomed is Biomedical Products; ICP is Industrial and Consumer Products; OilProd is Petroleum Exploration and Production; OilMktg is Petroleum Refining, Marketing and Transportation; and Polymer is Polymer Products. Consol means consolidated. NM means not meaningful. The Freon® Products Division is part of the Agricultural and Industrial Chemicals Segment.

of its early scientific leadership in CFCs, it was by far the world's largest producer, and the only firm with a significant worldwide presence.

Figure 3-7-3

DuPont Organizational Chart
(excerpt)

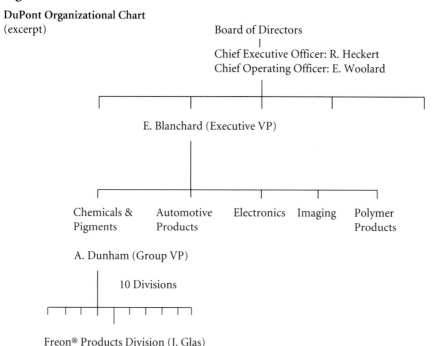

Board of Directors

Chief Executive Officer: R. Heckert
Chief Operating Officer: E. Woolard

E. Blanchard (Executive VP)

Chemicals &   Automotive   Electronics   Imaging   Polymer
Pigments   Products   Products

A. Dunham (Group VP)

10 Divisions

Freon® Products Division (J. Glas)

MANUFACTURING AND MARKETING

Du Pont maintained the largest CFC manufacturing facilities in the world. In 1987 it operated eleven plants, including six in Europe, Japan, and Latin America and five in the United States. The company made CFC-11 and -12 in New Jersey and California, HCFC-22 in Kentucky and Michigan, and CFC-113 in Texas. The Freon® Products Division accounted for 2 percent of Du Pont revenues in 1987 (the figures for the preceding years were 2.2 percent, 1.7 percent, and 1.8 percent), about 2 percent of corporate assets, and about 0.9 percent of Du Pont's employees.

Profitability in the CFC business resembled that of other oligopolistic organic chemicals businesses, at least until Rowland and Molina ignited concern about effects on the ozone. The drastic decline in aerosol demand left all U.S. producers with substantial overcapacity in CFC-11 and -12. Du Pont lost a third of its CFC business. The losses were even heavier for the smaller U.S. producers that did not make HCFC-22 or CFC-113 nor have significant international operations.

Du Pont, Allied, and Pennwalt each closed plants producing CFC-11 and -12 after the aerosol ban; only one of six producers left the market. Real list prices fell by about 20 percent during the late 1970s; actual prices, which reflected discounts given by manufacturers, fell even further. After-tax operating income for the Freon® Division was only 1.6 percent of sales between 1974 and 1979, and by 1984 recovered only slightly, to about 3 percent. Efforts by Du Pont to lead CFC-11 and -12 prices upward met with failure. Small producers cut prices to achieve higher capacity utilization and thereby offset Du Pont's scale economies. As a result, Du Pont's capacity utilization was the most cyclical in the industry.

CFC-11 and -12 varied widely in their ultimate value to different customers. For example, CFCs accounted for 20 percent of the raw material costs of blown foams. By contrast, a refrigerator costing $800 might contain half a pound of CFCs (at 60 cents per pound), and a $6,000 air-conditioning system might contain no more than $10 worth of CFCs. Makers of CFC-11 and -12, however, allowed their customers to capture essentially all of the CFC surplus through their failure to rationalize after the aerosol ban. In an attempt to escape from this price war, Du Pont sold hundreds of blends of CFCs, each tailored to a specific application. It also aggressively marketed its auxiliary services. It worked with consumers on new applications, offered training and education programs, and tried to provide better service than its competitors. As a result, Du Pont commanded a slight price premium over other producers. However, despite all these efforts, CFC-11 and -12 remained commodities, and companies fundamentally competed on price.

In the early 1980s, when Du Pont management concluded that costs were too high and that the CFC business was "not earning its keep," it slashed costs. At an expense of some $75 million, Du Pont extended the scope of its backward integration into chlorocarbon production. Total annual capital expenditures peaked in 1984 at $68 million. Ironically, the chloroform capacity was never used as Du Pont's suppliers scrambled to accommodate the company, offering to sell it chlorocarbons at a lower price than Du Pont could offer itself. Although the $75 million investment was written off, Du Pont's operating profits improved somewhat as a result of its improved raw materials cost position, averaging 4 percent during the period between 1984 and 1987 even after accounting for the write-off. Since 1984 the Freon® Division's annual capital expenditures declined at a rate of about 30 percent a year through 1987. Du Pont continued efforts to cut costs following the mixed success of backward integration. Most cost cutting centered on incremental improvement of yields and on continuing reductions in operating and maintenance costs. By 1987 Du Pont managers felt their efforts enabled them to become the nation's lowest-cost CFC producer.

The picture was brighter for CFC-113. Du Pont and Allied were the only U.S. producers. Many CFC-113 users were quite price insensitive; the cost of CFC-113 to clean a printed circuit board was trivial compared to the price of the board itself. CFC-113 buyers were more willing than CFC-11 and -12 consumers to regard the chemical as part of a broadly defined service that included troubleshooting and training. With weak currencies in the early 1980s, some Japanese and European firms tried to invade the U.S. CFC-113 market, but Japanese manufacturers were capacity constrained so that only British and French imports were significant. Pretax operating profits for Du Pont and Allied in CFC-113 were thought to exceed 20 percent of sales. During the Montreal Protocol negotiations and after the Protocol was passed, Du Pont shunned a short-term profit maximization strategy. Rather, Du Pont's strategy tempered the Protocol's regulatory effects so as not to drive price-sensitive customers out of the market. "If we raise price to the market clearing price, we may drive some of the low-value consumers out of business," said one Du Pont official. "Then they won't be around when we introduce substitutes. We might instead want to maximize the number of current customers so we can switch them to other products later." "We now see the ozone/regulatory situation as a marketing opportunity for substitutes," another manager said. "If we can show them [customers] we have a leadership position in alternatives, then they see that as a contribution to their current business." Some other CFC makers, however, managed their businesses for maximum short-run cash flow, knowing the usefulness of their plants was limited.

SUBSTITUTE DEVELOPMENT

Du Pont and other manufacturers worked to synthesize less stable HCFCs (and substances containing no chlorine) that would not reach the stratospheric ozone layer. Du Pont invested more heavily in developing such chemicals than any of its competitors. This investment varied as scientific concern over ozone depletion waxed, waned, and then exploded again. In the late 1970s during the initial furor over ozone depletion Du Pont spent $3 to $4 million per year in attempts to identify substitutes. Between 1981 and 1985 Du Pont spent practically nothing on substitute development because it doubted further regulatory restrictions on CFCs were forthcoming and because the substitutes were uniformly more expensive. "There was obviously no interest in the marketplace to go to alternatives at three times the price [of existing compounds]," said one Du Pont manager. In 1986 research on substitutes jumped to $5 million, and doubled again the following year; in 1988 Du Pont planned to spend more than $30 million.

Testing potential substitutes for toxicity, as required by the EPA before products can be brought to market, is time-consuming and expensive. For a standard two-year toxicity study in which laboratory animals inhale high concentrations of the chemical and are checked for tumors and other problems, 100,000 pounds of chemical might be required at a cost of perhaps $20 per pound. The manufacture of chemicals for testing was typically contracted out to specialty chemical firms. Costs were even higher than the projected prices of the substitutes, because the amounts required were small and no firm had significant experience in making the new chemicals.

In 1987 Du Pont estimated that the alternative HCFCs, if they passed the toxicity and odor tests, might be produced at full commercial scale at costs two to five times higher than existing CFCs; raw material costs would be higher, and the new chemical processes used to make the substitutes were more complicated. Old CFC plants could not easily be retrofitted to produce the new compounds. Further, the new manufacturing processes were sufficiently different that yields were expected to be low for the first several years. In addition to new products, manufacturers were interested in expanding the use of HCFC-22. HCFC-22 was not regulated under the Montreal Protocol or by the EPA because it was less stable than other CFCs and was thought not to reach the stratosphere. As of late 1987 the status of substitute development in each of the major CFC applications was as follows: for foam blowing, HCFC-22 could be substituted for CFC-11 and -12 in some applications. Some chlorocarbons could also be used for foam blowing and were widely available, but many were thought to be carcinogenic, and some were ozone precursors (i.e., they led to higher ozone levels in the lower atmosphere, and contributed to the health problems caused by smog).

Du Pont was ahead of its competitors in developing other chemicals that could be used in foam blowing. Attempts focused on two substances, HCFC-141b and HCFC-123. These were chemically similar to CFCs but reacted faster upon release to the environment and did not reach the stratosphere. No viable large-scale manufacturing process had been devised, however. In the case of HCFC-123, the Freon® Division was still searching for an effective catalyst for production. The substances were estimated to cost from 1.5 to four times as much to produce as CFC-11.

In some solvent markets served by CFCs, chlorocarbons could be sub-stituted, but they presented the same problems in this application as in foam blowing. Furthermore, chlorocarbons did not meet the technical specifications of the electronics manufacturers, and no substitutes for this use had yet been identified. Chlorocarbons could not be used in air-conditioning systems. HCFC-22 was a possible substitute, but its application to automobile air-conditioning was problematic. The automobile industry estimated it would take a billion dollars in research and from five to seven years to redesign mobile (vehicular) air-conditioning systems to use HCFC-22 rather than CFC-12. Du Pont was testing a possible substitute, HFC-134a, which was likely to cost three to five times as much as CFC-12. It contained no chlorine and hence would not affect stratospheric ozone. However, production difficulties centered on the lack of a catalyst and on the need for multistep manufacturing processes. In the refrigeration mar-ket, no substitutes for CFCs were commercially available in 1988, although Du Pont was optimistic that HFC-134a could serve this market as well.

Finally, numerous substitutes existed for the remaining aerosol appli-cations of CFCs. In 1978 most U.S. makers of aerosol packaging switched to simple compounds like propane and butane rather than more-expen-sive propellants made by Du Pont. Because of the short time between the aerosol ban's promulgation and its effective date, aerosol producers had little time to test other products (propane and butane were flammable, an undesirable characteristic for a propellant). Du Pont hoped the longer lead times of the Montreal Protocol would allow European and Japanese aerosol producers to try Du Pont's more sophisticated, less flammable, but more expensive substitutes.

DU PONT'S POLITICAL STRATEGY

Du Pont subscribed to a companywide "Safety, Health and Environmental Quality Policy," which read in part, the company "will comply with all applicable laws and regulations" and "will determine that each product can be made, used, handled, and disposed of safely and consistent with appropriate safety, health, and environmental quality criteria." Adopted in 1971 at a time when Earth Day and new pollution control legislation focused public attention on industrial pollution, the environmental parts of the policy formalized what Du Pont managers saw as an ethos of cor-porate responsibility. In the Freon® Products Division, this policy was paraphrased, "If we can't make it safely, we won't make it at all." In prac-tice, the policy meant that Du Pont would comply with government regu-lations or with its own standards, whichever were more strict.

In 1974, when ozone depletion first came to light, Du Pont felt the science was too weak to justify the widespread regulation of demonstrably useful chemicals. At the same time, Du Pont publicly promised to change its position if the scientific case against CFCs solidified. In advertisements in newspapers and magazines, Du Pont's chairman Irving Shapiro said that "should reputable evidence show that some fluorocarbons cause a health hazard through depletion of the ozone layer, we are prepared to stop production of these compounds." Dr. Raymond McCarthy, a Du Pont scientist, testified in Congress to the same effect: "If credible scientific data . . . show that any chlorofluorocarbons cannot be used without a threat to health, Du Pont will stop production of these compounds."

Beginning in 1972, Du Pont invested in basic ozone science. Under the auspices of the Chemical Manufacturers Association, Du Pont and other CFC makers formed the Fluorocarbon Program Panel to pool funds for science and oversee industry research on ozone depletion. Total Du Pont expenditures on atmospheric science, aimed at a better understanding of the ozone depletion problem rather than at any immediate commercial advantage, averaged $1 million per year through the ensuing decade. After aerosols were banned in the United States, Du Pont and other U.S. CFC manufacturers continued to sell CFCs for use as aerosols in non-U.S. markets. These sales were not precluded by U.S. or foreign regulation, and the company felt that science did not warrant the elimination of aerosol uses. Thus, continued sales were seen as consistent with Du Pont's environmental policy. But as one manager put it, "We don't actually chase that kind of business very hard."

In 1980, when EPA threatened further restrictions, Du Pont was instrumental in forming the Alliance for Responsible CFC Policy. This trade association, which was unusual in that it included both CFC producers and consumers, lobbied Congress and the EPA for what it deemed a measured response to the ozone issue. In 1980 the Alliance orchestrated a flood of 2,000 letters to the EPA opposing further regulation. Alliance literature placed great emphasis on the essential nature of CFC uses— electronics manufacture, energy conservation, and air conditioning— and on the high cost and relative unattractiveness of substitutes. One Du Pont executive estimated that Du Pont spent several million dollars per year on research for alternatives, responses to EPA proposals, contributions to the Alliance, and other expenditures related to CFC policy.

From 1980 to 1986 Du Pont led industry opposition against further CFC controls. Du Pont felt that if more regulatory action were taken it should be international. U.S. industry had suffered from its government's unilateral restrictions on aerosols. While ozone depletion was on the back burner both at the EPA and internationally, the basic science underwritten by Du Pont bore fruit when the firm developed the first credible two-dimensional model of stratospheric ozone. By mid-1986 the two-dimensional scientific models of ozone depletion showed that significant sustained increases in CFC emissions were likely to decrease ozone. These new model results, combined with the disturbing new evidence of the Antarctic "hole," were sufficiently worrisome that Du Pont changed its position. According to a press release written by Steed's ozone policy team, "It would be prudent to limit worldwide emissions of CFCs while science continues to work to provide better guidance to policy makers." Because Du Pont felt that only international action would be effective, the company supported "the development and adoption of a protocol under the United Nations Vienna Convention for the Protection of the Ozone Layer to limit worldwide CFC emissions." Du Pont worried that further unilateral action by the United States would provide an excuse for other nations to delay regulating their producers, as had occurred with the aerosol ban.

Other Alliance members at first resisted this change in policy. Most thought that restrictions on the rate of growth of CFC production, not on the actual levels of production, would be sufficient. However, as scientific and public concern over ozone depletion continued to mount, the Alliance acknowledged the need for production caps. The Alliance, like Du Pont, was emphatic in its support for international action. It supported an international accord partly out of fear of the competitive disadvantages that could arise if the United States acted alone, and partly because some members felt that once the issue reached the international negotiating table, the Europeans and Japanese would reject any measures stronger than a production cap. By the time the Montreal Protocol was enacted, however, it went far beyond the cap that most observers anticipated, with reductions in total output scheduled for the 1990s. Nonetheless, Du Pont and the Alliance supported its ratification. Du Pont's reading of the available science at the time was that the Protocol's measures would protect the ozone layer with a significant safety factor.

THE IDES OF MARCH

In late February 1988 three senators from the Environment and Public Works Committee wrote to Du Pont CEO Richard Heckert reminding him of Du Pont's promise to stop production should reputable evidence show that fluorocarbons cause a health hazard. The senators suggested the time had come. "We request and urge," they wrote, "that within the next twelve months, the Du Pont Corporation cease all further production and sale of chlorofluorocarbons 11, 12, 113, 114, and 115," unilaterally if necessary.

Heckert restated Du Pont's position on the ozone issue. "Du Pont stands by its commitment," he wrote in a letter drafted by the Freon® Division staff, but "at the moment, scientific evidence does not point to the need for dramatic CFC emission reductions." The Freon® Division did not want to buckle under pressure if that pressure had no scientific basis, so the letter it wrote for Heckert emphasized the continuing uncertainty of the science. The letter pointed out that there was no certain linkage between CFCs and ozone depletion, that recent empirical studies had shown decreases in ultraviolet radiation at the earth's surface, and that the health effects of ozone depletion were also uncertain. Because of the importance of many CFC uses, the senators' proposal for a unilateral Du Pont cutback was "both unwarranted and counterproductive." CFC markets needed time to develop and adapt to improved substitutes. To interfere with a smooth transition through drastic production cutbacks would be "irresponsible," Heckert wrote. Ten days after Heckert sent his letter, the United States became the first major nation to ratify the Montreal Protocol. The Senate voted 83 to 0 in favor of ratification.

The next day, March 15, scientists on the interagency Ozone Trends Panel headed by NASA issued the Executive Summary of their report. While couched in careful language, the report described a fundamental change in the scientific understanding of the CFC-ozone connection. First, there was hard empirical evidence of reductions in stratospheric ozone concentrations, not just over Antarctica but over temperate, populated regions as well (see Figure 3-7-4). The model had predicted a 0.5 percent decline in ozone at these latitudes, but the measured depletion was 2.5 percent. Second, the causal link between CFCs and ozone depletion over Antarctica was finally established: The spatial patterns of ozone depletion strongly indicated that CFCs were responsible for the ozone "hole." Third, ozone levels over Antarctica were lower not just during the Antarctic spring, but year-round. Fourth, while previous model results suggested that the Protocol would result in little net depletion of ozone, improved two-dimensional models forecasted continuing ozone decreases even if the Protocol were implemented. The model results were doubtful, mainly because the mechanisms responsible for the Antarctic "hole" might not affect the ozone of temperate latitudes in exactly the same way. At least one panel member, though, called the new evidence the long-awaited "smoking gun." Further, stratospheric chlorine from CFCs would continue to increase if no further measures than the Protocol were taken (see Figure 3-7-5). Only a nearly complete phase-out of CFCs appeared to offer any margin of safety for the ozone layer, according to this evidence.

Figure 3-7-4

Observed Changes in Ozone at Temperate Latitudes, 1969–1986

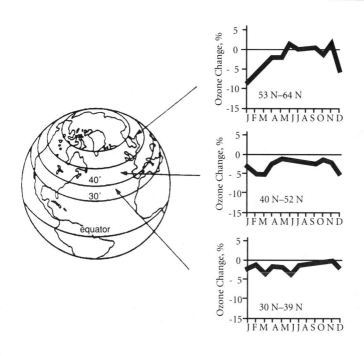

Source: NASA, March 1988.

Steed and McFarland attended the Ozone Trends Panel press conference on March 15 and conferred with other team members. McFarland, a member of the panel, had been prohibited from revealing data from the panel's investigation prior to the public release. As the only industry representative on the panel, however, he read the entire draft report, not only the Executive Summary. The two men phoned Glas and other Du Pont executives in Wilmington with an assessment that the findings were accurate. This appeared to mean that several of the statements Heckert had made to the Senate about ozone science had been overtaken by events.

Glas heard national coverage of the report on the evening of March 15. He summoned Steed and McFarland to his office early the next morning. They presented the more detailed analysis they had prepared after

Figure 3-7-5

Effect of CFC Reduction Rates
(Chlorine from CFCs)

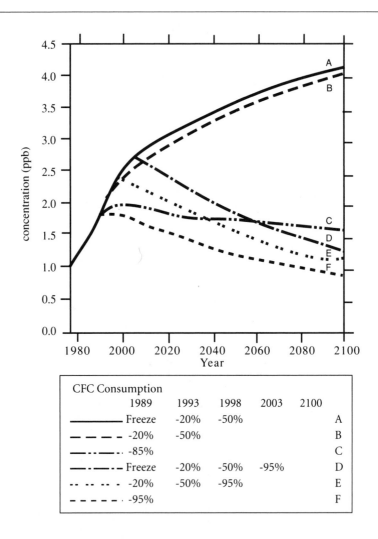

CFC Consumption						
	1989	1993	1998	2003	2100	
———— Freeze	-20%	-50%				A
— — — -20%	-50%					B
—··—··- -85%						C
—·——·- Freeze	-20%	-50%	-95%			D
·· ·· ·· - -20%	-50%	-95%				E
— — — — · -95%						F

Source: Du Pont, "Fluorocarbon/Ozone Update," July 1988.

arriving home the night before, including the plot shown in Figure 3-7-4. Glas needed to decide whether Du Pont should now change its strategy— and he needed to decide quickly. Heckert had called and wanted to know *that day* what the Freon® Products Division intended to do.

Discussion Questions

1. What choices does Joe Glas have at the end of the case? Which option would you choose? Why?
2. What are the likely effects of the Montreal Protocol on the market for chlorofluorocarbons? What are the likely effects on the political environment? Distinguish between the domestic and international settings.
3. What will happen if some nations do not adopt the Montreal Protocol? Will Du Pont's business strategy be jeopardized? What can companies such as Du Pont do under those circumstances?
4. What ethical considerations should Du Pont's management weigh in deciding how to respond?

EPILOGUE

On Wednesday, March 16, 1988, Joe Glas decided to recommend to Heckert and the Du Pont Board of Directors that the company stop manufacturing the CFCs regulated under the Protocol. Because of difficulties in developing substitutes and obtaining regulatory approval to produce them, the exit would be phased over a ten-year period. But Du Pont planned to stop manufacturing CFCs -11, -12, -113, -114, and -115 and Halons by 1999, when the Montreal Protocol would require a cutback to 50 percent of 1986 levels. The same day Glas and Joe Steed took the recommendation to Glas's boss, Archie Dunham, who ran the Chemicals and Pigments Department of which the Freon® Division was a part. Dunham concurred in the recommendation. Glas and Steed then took the recommendation to Elwood Blanchard, a Du Pont executive vice president, who also concurred. The next day Glas was out of town honoring a long-standing commitment with a major customer. In his absence Steed and McFarland presented the recommendation to the company's Executive Committee, which consisted of the inside directors of the corporation. The committee agreed with the decision. McFarland was a research scientist and Steed had no direct business responsibility. No business manager from the Freon® Division was in the room when the Executive Committee made its decision. Dwight Bedsole, who oversaw all of the division's U.S. manufacturing and marketing, commented later, "Not one time that week did anyone discuss what effect this decision could have on the financial end of the business."

Glas and his staff worked through the weekend on a plan for communicating the decision to employees, competitors, and customers, as well as the press, government agencies, Congress, and environmental groups. They also began planning the transition from a division that made regulated CFCs to a division that would make substances that were not yet commercial and in some cases hardly invented. Du Pont received widespread accolades for its announcement of a complete phase-out of regulated CFCs. Yet some observers noted that the company had not announced a firm timetable. Others speculated that Du Pont was out to dominate the substitute markets. Du Pont's competitors either kept silent or commented they were still reviewing the science and were not sure that such drastic action was warranted.